Philippians
and Philemon

Philippians
and Philemon

JAMES W.
THOMPSON
and
BRUCE W.
LONGENECKER

Baker Academic

a division of Baker Publishing Group
Grand Rapids, Michigan

Published by Baker Academic
a division of Baker Publishing Group
P.O. Box 6287, Grand Rapids, MI 49516-6287
www.bakeracademic.com

Printed in the United States of America

Library of Congress Cataloging-in-Publication Data
Names: Thompson, James, 1942– author. | Longenecker, Bruce W., author.
Title: Philippians and Philemon / James W. Thompson and Bruce W. Longenecker.
Other titles: Philemon
Description: Grand Rapids : Baker Academic, 2016. | Series: Paideia: commentaries on the New Testament | Includes bibliographical references and index.
Identifiers: LCCN 2016006548 | ISBN 9780801033391 (pbk.)
Subjects: LCSH: Bible. Philippians—Commentaries. | Bible. Philemon—Commentaries.
Classification: LCC BS2705.53 .T46 2016 | DDC 227/.607—dc23
LC record available at http://lccn.loc.gov/2016006548

16   17   18   19   20   21   22   7   6   5   4   3   2   1

Contents

Figures and Tables

Figures

Tables

Foreword

Paideia: Commentaries on the New Testament is a series that sets out to comment on the final form of the New Testament text in a way that pays due attention both to the cultural, literary, and theological settings in which the text took form and to the interests of the contemporary readers to whom the commentaries are addressed. This series is aimed squarely at students—including MA students in religious and theological studies programs, seminarians, and upper-division undergraduates—who have theological interests in the biblical text. Thus, the didactic aim of the series is to enable students to understand each book of the New Testament as a literary whole rooted in a particular ancient setting and related to its context within the New Testament.

The name "Paideia" (Greek for "education") reflects (1) the instructional aim of the series—giving contemporary students a basic grounding in academic New Testament studies by guiding their engagement with New Testament texts; (2) the fact that the New Testament texts as literary unities are shaped by the educational categories and ideas (rhetorical, narratological, etc.) of their ancient writers and readers; and (3) the pedagogical aims of the texts themselves—their central aim being not simply to impart information but to form the theological convictions and moral habits of their readers.

Each commentary deals with the text in terms of larger rhetorical units; these are not verse-by-verse commentaries. This series thus stands within the stream of recent commentaries that attend to the final form of the text. Such reader-centered literary approaches are inherently more accessible to liberal arts students without extensive linguistic and historical-critical preparation than older exegetical approaches, but within the reader-centered world the sanest practitioners have paid careful attention to the extratext of the original readers, including not only these readers' knowledge of the geography, history, and other contextual elements reflected in the text but also their ability to respond correctly to the literary and rhetorical conventions used in the text. Paideia commentaries pay deliberate attention to this extratextual repertoire in order to highlight the ways in which the text is designed to persuade and move its readers. Each rhetorical unit is explored from three angles: (1) introductory matters; (2) tracing the train of thought or narrative or rhetorical flow of the argument; and (3) theological issues raised by the text that are of interest to the contemporary Christian. Thus, the primary focus remains on the text and not its historical context or its interpretation in the secondary literature.

Our authors represent a variety of confessional points of view: Protestant, Catholic, and Orthodox. What they share, beyond being New Testament scholars of national and international repute, is a commitment to reading the biblical text as theological documents within their ancient contexts. Working within the broad parameters described here, each author brings his or her own considerable exegetical talents and deep theological commitments to the task of laying bare the interpretation of Scripture for the faith and practice of God's people everywhere.

Mikeal C. Parsons
Charles H. Talbert
Bruce W. Longenecker

Abbreviations

General

BCE	before the Common Era	NT	New Testament
CE	Common Era	OT	Old Testament
chap(s).	chapter(s)	trans.	translated by, translation (in)
Eng.	English Bible verse numbering	v(v).	verse(s)
esp.	especially	×	when preceded by a numeral, designates how often an item occurs
lit.	literally		

Bible Texts and Versions

ASV	American Standard Version	NET	New English Translation
ESV	English Standard Version	NIV	New International Version
KJV	King James Version	NRSV	New Revised Standard Version
LXX	Septuagint, Greek Old Testament	RSV	Revised Standard Version
NEB	New English Bible		

Papyri and Inscriptions

CIL	*Corpus Inscriptionum Latinarum*. Berlin: G. Reimer, 1862–.		Dittenberger. 2 vols. Leipzig: Hirzel, 1903–5.
IG	*Inscriptiones Graecae: Editio minor*. Berlin: de Gruyter, 1924–.	Pap. Heid.	Veröffentlichungen aus der Heidelberger Papyrussammlung.
OGIS	*Orientis Graeci Inscriptionum Selectae*. Edited by Wilhelm	P.Enteux	Ἐντεύξεις: Requêtes et plaintes adressées au Roi d'Egypte au

IIIe siècle avant J. C. Edited by
O. Guéraud. Cairo, 1931–32.

P.Oxy.   The Oxyrynchus Papyri.
Edited by B. P. Grenfell, A. S.
Hunt, et al. 75 vols. London:
Egypt Exploration Society,
1898–2010.

SIG   *Sylloge Inscriptionum Grae-
carum.* Edited by Wilhelm
Dittenberger. 3rd ed. 4 vols.
Leipzig: Hirzel, 1915–24.

Ancient Corpora

OLD TESTAMENT
Gen.	Genesis
Exod.	Exodus
Lev.	Leviticus
Num.	Numbers
Deut.	Deuteronomy
Josh.	Joshua
Judg.	Judges
Ruth	Ruth
1–2 Sam.	1–2 Samuel
1–2 Kings	1–2 Kings
1–2 Chron.	1–2 Chronicles
Ezra	Ezra
Neh.	Nehemiah
Esther	Esther
Job	Job
Ps(s).	Psalm(s)
Prov.	Proverbs
Eccles.	Ecclesiastes
Song	Song of Songs
Isa.	Isaiah
Jer.	Jeremiah
Lam.	Lamentations
Ezek.	Ezekiel
Dan.	Daniel
Hosea	Hosea
Joel	Joel
Amos	Amos
Obad.	Obadiah
Jon.	Jonah
Mic.	Micah
Nah.	Nahum
Hab.	Habakkuk
Zeph.	Zephaniah
Hag.	Haggai
Zech.	Zechariah
Mal.	Malachi

DEUTEROCANONICAL BOOKS
Jdt.	Judith
1–4 Macc.	1–4 Maccabees
Sir.	Sirach/Ecclesiasticus
Tob.	Tobit
Wis.	Wisdom of Solomon

NEW TESTAMENT
Matt.	Matthew
Mark	Mark
Luke	Luke
John	John
Acts	Acts
Rom.	Romans
1–2 Cor.	1–2 Corinthians
Gal.	Galatians
Eph.	Ephesians
Phil.	Philippians
Col.	Colossians
1–2 Thess.	1–2 Thessalonians
1–2 Tim.	1–2 Timothy
Titus	Titus
Philem.	Philemon
Heb.	Hebrews
James	James
1–2 Pet.	1–2 Peter
1–3 John	1–3 John
Jude	Jude
Rev.	Revelation

OLD TESTAMENT PSEUDEPIGRAPHA

| 1 En. | 1 Enoch |
| Jos. Asen. | Joseph and Aseneth |

DEAD SEA SCROLLS

| 1QM | War Scroll |

RABBINIC WORKS

| m. 'Abot | Mishnah 'Abot |

APOSTOLIC FATHERS

1 Clem.	1 Clement
Did.	Didache
Ign. Eph.	Ignatius, To the Ephesians
Ign. Pol.	Ignatius, To Polycarp
Ign. Rom.	Ignatius, To the Romans
Ign. Smyrn.	Ignatius, To the Smyrnaeans
Pol. Phil.	Polycarp, To the Philippians

Ancient Authors

AESCHYLUS

| Ag. | Agamemnon |
| Pers. | Persae |

ANONYMOUS

| Auct. Her. | Auctor/Rhetorica ad Herennium |

ARISTOTLE

Eth. nic.	Ethica nicomachea
Pol.	Politica
Rhet.	Rhetorica

CICERO

Amic.	De Amicitia
De or.	De oratore
Deiot.	Pro rege Deiotare
Flac.	Pro Flacco
Inv.	De inventione rhetorica
Lig.	Pro Ligario
Marcell.	Pro Marcello
Off.	De officiis
Rab. Perd.	Pro C. Rabirio Perduellionis Reo
Tusc.	Tusculanae disputationes

DIO CHRYSOSTOM

| Or. | Orationes |

DIOGENES LAERTIUS

| Vit. | Vitae philosophorum |

EPICTETUS

| Diatr. | Diatribai (Dissertationes) |

EURIPIDES

| Alc. | Alcestis |
| Bacch. | Bacchae |

HOMER

| Od. | Odyssey |

HORACE

| Carm. | Carmina |

ISOCRATES

| Archid. | Archidamus |

JOHN CHRYSOSTOM

| Hom. Phil. | Homilies on Philippians |

JOSEPHUS

Ant.	Jewish Antiquities
J.W.	Jewish War
Life	The Life

OVID

| Met. | Metamorphoses |

PHILO

Agr.	De agricultura
Conf.	De confusion linguarum
Decal.	De decalogo
Flacc.	In Flaccum
Fug.	De fuga et inventione
Jos.	De Iosepho

Legat.	*Legatio ad Gaium*		*Caes.*	*Caesar*
Mut. Nom.	*De mutatione nominum*		*Is. Os.*	*Isis and Osiris*
Opif.	*De opificio mundi*			
Praem.	*De praemiis et poenis*		**POLYBIUS**	
Prob.	*Quod omnis probus liber sit*		*Hist.*	*Historia*
Spec. Leg.	*De specialibus legibus*			
Virt.	*De virtutibus*		**QUINTILIAN**	
			Inst. or.	*Institutio oratoria*
PLATO				
Apol.	*Apologia*		**SENECA**	
Leg.	*Leges*		*Ben.*	*De beneficiis*
Phaed.	*Phaedo*		*Ep.*	*Epistulae morales*
Resp.	*Respublica*			
			TERTULLIAN	
PLUTARCH			*Apol.*	*Apologeticus*
Amat.	*Amatorius*		**XENOPHON**	
Amic. mult.	*De amicorum multitudine*		*Apol.*	*Apologia*

Reference Works

BDAG W. Bauer, F. W. Danker, W. F. Arndt, and F. W. Gingrich. *A Greek-English Lexicon of New Testament and Other Early Christian Literature*. 3rd ed. Chicago: University of Chicago Press, 2000.

BDF F. Blass, A. Debrunner, and R. W. Funk. *A Greek Grammar of the New Testament and Other Early Christian Literature*. Chicago: University of Chicago Press, 1961.

EDNT Horst Balz and Gerhard Schneider, eds. *Exegetical Dictionary of the New Testament*. 3 vols. Grand Rapids: Eerdmans, 1990–93.

IDBSup Keith Crim, ed. *Interpreter's Dictionary of the Bible: Supplementary Volume*. Nashville: Abingdon, 1976.

LCL Loeb Classical Library

LSJ H. G. Liddell, R. Scott, H. S. Jones, and R. McKenzie. *A Greek-English Lexicon*. 9th ed. with rev. supplement. Oxford: Oxford University Press, 1996.

MM James Hope Moulton and George Milligan. *The Vocabulary of the Greek Testament Illustrated by the Papyri and Other Non-literary Sources*. London: Hodder & Stoughton, 1949.

TDNT Gerhard Kittel and Gerhard Friedrich, eds. *Theological Dictionary of the New Testament*. Translated by Geoffrey W. Bromiley. 10 vols. Grand Rapids: Eerdmans, 1964–76.

TLNT Ceslas Spicq. *Theological Lexicon of the New Testament*. Translated and edited by James D. Ernest. 3 vols. Peabody, MA: Hendrickson, 1994.

Philippians

James W. Thompson

Introduction to Philippians

The impact of Paul's letter to the Philippians on the Christian tradition is disproportionate to its modest size. With the letter's high concentration of autobiographical reflection covering Paul's life from infancy (3:4–6) to his approaching death (1:21–26), it shapes the popular view of the apostle. It describes in graphic detail the radical change in his life (3:7–11) and offers more introspection (1:21–26; 4:10–13) than any other letter. Here one meets the one who was joyful in chains (1:12–18), content in the midst of humiliating circumstances (4:10–13), and confident in facing death (1:21–26). With his radical change of values (3:1–11), he has served as the paradigm of conversion.

As the letter of one who faced a possible death sentence, Philippians provided the words that would subsequently be echoed by the martyrs. Ignatius, on his way to martyrdom in Rome, seeks to attain Christ (*Rom.* 5.3; cf. Phil. 3:8) and die in him (*Rom.* 6.1; 7.2; cf. Phil. 1:21), knowing that he can do all things through Christ who strengthens him (*Smyrn.* 4.2; cf. Phil. 4:13). Similarly, the *Martyrdom of Polycarp* alludes to Philippians in describing Polycarp's willingness to die in imitation of Christ (1.2; Bockmuehl 1995, 70).

Passages from Philippians have shaped Christian reflection and piety. Paul's desire to depart and be with Christ (1:23) was expressed in Thomas à Kempis's *Imitation of Christ* (1.12) and has been echoed in many hymns that speak of going to heaven when we die (Bockmuehl 1995, 74). No passage in the NT has received more scrutiny than 2:6–11, commonly identified as the Philippian hymn. Both the phrase "form of God" (2:6) and the claim that Christ "emptied himself" (2:7) played a role in the christological controversies of the first four centuries and have been the subjects of continuing analysis since then. The affirmation that "our citizenship is in heaven" (3:20) influenced Augustine's concept of the *City of God* and has influenced the popular understanding of heaven as the true homeland of believers (Bockmuehl 1995, 85).

Among the undisputed letters of Paul, Philippians and Philemon are the only ones written from prison. Many other letters from prison come later as witnesses to the consequences of confessing Jesus as Lord and challenging existing ideologies. From Dietrich Bonhoeffer's *Letters and Papers from Prison* to Martin Luther King's "Letter from Birmingham Jail," letters from prison speak of matters of ultimate importance. The fact that they are written from prison gives them an urgency they might not otherwise have (cf. Grieb 2007, 261). Paul's repeated references to his chains (1:7, 13–14, 17) indicate the gravity of the situation in which he and the Philippians are partners.

Philippi and the Origin of the Philippian Church

When Paul arrived in Philippi, the city was a Roman enclave in the Greek world. As he approached the city from the port city of Neapolis along the Via Egnatia, he would have seen milestones inscribed in Latin. As he entered the city, he would have seen Roman temples and Latin inscriptions everywhere. If he had gone to the theater, he would have seen performances in Latin. While the majority of the people spoke Greek, the elite of the city spoke Latin and were citizens of Rome (Hecking 2009, 23–24). Indeed, inscriptions erected by private citizens proudly proclaimed that the donor was a Roman citizen, a member of the tribe of Voltinia (Pilhofer 2009, 13). Romans owned most of the land and dominated local institutions (cf. Tellbe 2001, 212). Thus Philippi was unlike any other city visited by Paul, who could have imagined that he had left

Figure 1. Map of Macedonia

the cities shaped by Greek culture and entered the Roman world as he began his ministry there.

Before the Romans settled in Philippi, the city had been an insignificant village. Philip II of Macedon first gave it prominence when he annexed it into his kingdom in 356 BCE, gave it his name, and fortified it with new walls (Koukouli-Chrysantaki 1998, 6). When the Romans arrived, the city was still a small town (cf. Strabo 7, frg. 41) populated primarily by Thracians and Greeks-Macedonians (Koch 2006, 144; cf. Bormann 1995, 19). Roman influence began in 168 BCE, when Philippi became a Roman colony, and continued in 146 BCE, when it was incorporated into the Roman province of Macedonia. Major Roman influence began only after the battle of Philippi in 42 BCE, in which the victors, Mark Antony and Octavian, defeated the assassins of Julius Caesar, Cassius, and Brutus. This victory prepared the way for the creation of the Roman Empire and the establishment of Philippi as a Roman colony (Bakirtzis and Koester 1998, 8). A group of Antony's veterans, including members of his praetorian guard, settled in the city (Tellbe 2001, 213; cf. Cassius Dio 51.4.5–6). After the battle of Actium in 31 BCE, in which Octavian defeated Mark Antony and Cleopatra, Octavian established a military post in the city, filled it with army veterans and other Roman citizens, and gave it the *ius Italicum*, signifying that the city was on Roman soil (Tellbe 2001, 212). With its strategic location on the Via Egnatia connecting Rome and Byzantium, Philippi grew from a small town into a political and economic center within the Roman Empire (Bormann 1995, 26–27).

The religious profile of Philippi reflects the diversity of the inhabitants. Numerous inscriptions attest to the presence of the indigenous cult of the Thracian horseman (Pilhofer 2009, 15). Deities of Anatolia, Syria, and Egypt are also attested in the inscriptions at Philippi. However, no evidence has been found for the presence of Jews in the city. Philippi was dominated by Roman religions, of which the imperial cult was the most prominent (Tellbe 2001,

Figure 2. The *Via Egnatia*

Figure 3. The Roman Forum

214). Lukas Bormann (1995, 42–44) lists fourteen inscriptions describing the priests and priestesses of the imperial cult. Temples created for the worship of the emperor and his family were the most sacred structures in Philippi (Hellerman 2005, 86). Indeed, the cult of the emperor, while existing alongside other religions, marginalized their respective cults or integrated them into the imperial cult (cf. Bormann 1995, 65).

While Roman religion tolerated other religions, it accepted no conflict of loyalties. Beginning with the reign of Augustus, all inhabitants of the Roman Empire, including the adherents of foreign cults, were expected to acknowledge the Roman gods by participating in the rituals of the imperial cult (Tellbe 2001, 84). Since Roman religion was not a matter of private beliefs, the entire population was expected to participate in the festivals, public meals, and celebrations associated with the imperial cult (cf. Cassius Dio 51.20) and to take an oath of loyalty to the caesar (Bormann 1995, 50). The involvement of the whole population in the festivals reinforced the cohesion and the social hierarchy of Roman rule. While Jews were tolerated by the Romans, they were the frequent objects of derision by the Roman elite. Cicero, for example, said of the Jews, "The demands of their religion were incompatible with the majesty of our Empire, the dignity of our name, and the institutions of our ancestors" (*Flac.* 69, cited in Tellbe 2001, 236). Even associations were required to demonstrate their loyalty to the state (cf. Bormann 1995, 221–22). Since no city was more Roman than Philippi (Koch 2006, 145), Paul's conflict with the established order was inevitable.

Consistent with his practice of preaching in strategic cities, Paul also preached in Philippi (Acts 16:11–40). Luke's narrative indicates the distinctiveness of this Roman setting for the establishment of the church. While Paul visits other Roman colonies (e.g., Antioch of Pisidia, Iconium, and Lystra), only in Philippi does Luke indicate that the city is a colony, describing it as "the first city of Macedonia, a colony" (Acts 16:12). In contrast to the narrative of Paul's visit to other cities (cf. 13:5, 14, 43; 14:1; 17:1, 17; 18:4, 7, 19), Luke does not mention his preaching in synagogues, which probably reflects Luke's knowledge of the absence of Jews in the city. Luke indicates that Paul entered the city and remained some days (Acts 16:12) before he went outside the city, expecting to find a place of prayer (*proseuchē*) outside the gate (Acts 16:13). This information may also suggest a knowledge that only Roman cults were permitted within the city walls. Although *proseuchē* can be synonymous with "synagogue" in some instances, Luke is probably suggesting that the *proseuchē* is an informal meeting place, apparently in the open air (BDAG 879). That Luke mentions only women listeners also suggests an informal gathering (Acts 16:13). The only convert named is Lydia, who, along with her household, was baptized (16:15). Lydia is not Jewish but "one who worships God" (16:14), a term used frequently for gentiles who attended synagogue services (cf. Acts 13:43, 50; 17:4, 17; 18:7). That Paul's first convert is a godfearing woman is consistent with Luke's focus on the conversion of godfearers (cf. 13:43; 17:4; 18:7). The establishment of the church among godfearing women anticipates both the prominence of women (cf. Phil. 4:2–3) and the exclusively gentile composition of the Philippian church.

According to the common pattern in the narrative of Paul's preaching in Acts, his preaching in each city is followed by the conversion of some from the synagogue and by the hostility of others. Because of the hostility from the synagogue, Paul must leave town prematurely (cf. Acts 13:48–52; 14:1–6, 19–21; 17:1–9, 10–13; 18:1–6; 19:8–10). In Philippi, however, the antagonists are not Jews but the Roman populace. Indeed, the conflict with Roman power dominates the narrative. While Luke first describes the conflict as the result of the financial loss by the masters of a slave girl whom Paul healed from a spirit of divination (Acts 16:19), the charges brought by the masters to the magistrates and the crowds indicate that the larger issue was the conflict with Rome. The charges are twofold. First, the masters charge that "these men are Jews who are throwing our city into confusion" (16:20b), thus accusing Paul and his companions of being politically subversive and a threat to the *pax Romana* (Tellbe 2001, 234). Second, they charge that Paul and Silas "proclaim customs [*ethē*] that are unlawful for us Romans to accept" (16:21). By healing a girl with a Pythian spirit—that is, one who was inspired by the Roman god Apollo—Paul challenged the god with whom Augustus identified himself (Tellbe 2001, 237). The "customs" that Paul and Silas introduce involve an entire way of life based on the good news (*euangelion*) of the crucified Savior who is now Lord. Inasmuch as Roman ideology claimed that the power of Caesar is the good news and that Caesar is Lord, the accusers bring a political charge against Paul and Silas. The conflict resulted in one of many imprisonments suffered by Paul (cf. 2 Cor. 6:5; 11:23). As a result of the earthquake that occurred while Paul and Silas were in prison, a second gentile household—that of the unnamed jailer—was also baptized (Acts 16:33). At the end of the narrative, Paul's Roman citizenship is mentioned for the first time (Acts 16:37–40). In describing the conflict that occurred in the city, Luke accurately depicts the essential Roman character of Philippi, the gentile composition of the church, and the conflict between the new movement and Rome.

While Paul does not refer to these events in the letters, Luke's narrative is consistent with Paul's memory of the situation in Philippi. According to Acts 17:1–9, Paul went from Philippi to Thessalonica, where some also believed, while others responded with hostility. In 1 Thessalonians, Paul recalls these events, reminding the readers that he had preached to them only after he had "suffered previously and been treated disgracefully" in Philippi (1 Thess. 2:2).

Although Luke reports the conversion of the households of Lydia and the jailer, he does not mention the establishment of the church. However, Paul left behind an established community with whom he shared a continuing relationship. The Philippians sent Paul financial support more than once (Phil. 4:16; cf. 1:5; 4:15; cf. 2 Cor. 11:7–9), and they participated in the collection for the saints in Jerusalem (2 Cor. 8:1–6; cf. Rom. 15:26). Paul's statement that he had "robbed other churches" in order to serve the Corinthians and that the Macedonians had ministered to his needs (2 Cor. 11:8–9) is probably a reference to the support from the Philippians. When news of Paul's imprisonment reached them, they sent gifts to Paul that were delivered by their minister, Epaphroditus (Phil. 2:25–29; 4:18), who almost died in the process.

The names of Lydia and the jailer never appear again, but four names of the Philippian members appear in the letter. Epaphroditus (2:25–30), Euodia, and Syntyche (4:2) are Greek names, apparently of servile origin. Clement (4:3) is a common Roman name. Neither elite Roman citizens nor Jews appear to be members of the Philippian church. These names probably offer a window into the composition of the Philippian church, suggesting that the community is composed primarily of freed slaves.

Occasion and Literary Integrity

Philippians, like the other Pauline letters, is a continuation of an earlier communication and a substitute for Paul's presence. Any attempt to determine the

Figure 4. The Crenides River, the apparent location of Lydia's baptism

immediate occasion for this stage in Paul's conversation with the Philippians requires the resolution of a prior question that has puzzled scholars since the seventeenth century. Interpreters have attempted to explain the change of tone between 3:1 ("rejoice in the Lord") and 3:2 ("look out for the dogs, look out for the evil workers, look out for the mutilators"). Is Philippians a single letter written on one occasion or a composite of two or more letters written at different occasions? In the twentieth century a near-consensus emerged, especially among German scholars, that Philippians is a composite of two or three letters written on different occasions. Interpreters have observed the following:

- The section 1:1–3:1 has the common structure of a complete Pauline letter, including the salutation (1:1–2), thanksgiving (1:3–11), disclosure formula describing recent events (1:12–26), paraenetic instructions (1:27–2:18), a travel report (2:19–30), and "finally" followed by "rejoice in the Lord" (3:1), a common feature at the end of Paul's letters (cf. 2 Cor. 13:11).
- Only in 1:1–3:1 does Paul mention his imprisonment.
- In 3:2–21 Paul warns against false teachers, who are not mentioned in 1:1–3:1. The polemical tone of 3:2 is a sharp break from the more irenic tone of 1:1–3:1. Thus interpreters have maintained that 3:2–21 is part of

9

a separate letter and that it has both a different occasion and purpose. It is a polemical response to false teaching in Philippi.

- Scholars have also noticed that the note of thanks in 4:10–20 is anomalous at the end of a letter. As a thank you note, it comes at an unexpected place. The passage is a self-contained unit without reference to the rest of the letter.

As a result of this analysis, interpreters have argued that Philippians is a composite of two or three letters. Some (e.g., Gnilka 1968, 10–13) combine 4:10–20 with 1:1–3:1, maintaining that Philippians is composed of two letters. The more common view is that Philippians incorporates all or part of three letters, written in the following sequence. Letter A (4:10–20), a brief thank-you note, was sent first, shortly after Paul received the gift brought by Epaphroditus (see 4:18). Letter B (1:1–3:1) was sent from prison to reassure and console the Philippians (cf. Standhartinger 2006a, 417–35). Letter C (3:2–21) was sent after Paul learned more about the situation in Philippi. Among those who maintain that Philippians is a composite letter, disagreement exists over the placement of 4:1–9 and the concluding greetings in 4:21–23 (cf. Bormann 1995, 110–15; Garland 1985, 155). Thus a composite letter presupposes more than one occasion.

Because false teachers are mentioned only in 3:2–21, this section has been the focus of attempts to reconstruct the identity of the opponents and the occasion either for this unit or for the entire letter. The "dogs, the evil workers, and the mutilators" (3:2) are one group. The reference to the mutilators (*katatomē*) as paronomasia on *peritomē* (circumcision) suggests that the opponents are identical to those Paul combats in Galatians. At the end of the chapter (3:18–19), Paul warns against enemies of the cross of Christ "whose god is the belly." Some exegetes argue that Paul, in his statement "not that I have been made perfect" (3:12), engages in a polemic against those who claim to have reached perfection. These scattered references have suggested to some interpreters that Paul is fighting on two fronts (against Judaizers in 3:2–11 and against libertines in 3:18–19) or against one group, which they describe by synthesizing the evidence. Walter Schmithals (1957, 315) argues that the opponents are Jewish Christian Gnostics who both insist on circumcision and claim to have reached perfection (cf. Koester 1961–62, 331–32). Neither solution, however, is satisfactory. No evidence exists for the Jewish Christian Gnostics proposed by Schmithals. Furthermore, chapter 3 engages in no polemic against these false teachers but is primarily Paul's autobiographical reflection and call for imitation (3:17). The opponents are negative examples that provide the background for recognizing Paul as the positive example. While the false teachers may be a potential threat to the church, Paul gives no indication that they are a present threat to the community.

While theories about the composite nature of Philippians and the polemical nature of chapter 3 have been widely accepted, scholars in the past generation have demonstrated the unity of the letter. Loveday Alexander (1989, 92–94) maintains that Philippians contains the basic topics found in ancient family letters, including the salutation (1:1–2), reassurances from the sender, report of recent events (1:12–26), prayer for the recipients (1:3–11), and final greetings (4:21–23). She argues that family letters did not contain the linear argument that is expected from a speech or essay. Recent studies have identified Philippians as a letter of friendship, observing that the language of friendship appears in every section of the letter. David Garland (1985, 158) demonstrated numerous thematic and verbal connections between chapters 2 and 3. Chapter 2 portrays the downward spiral of Jesus's descent from his status "in the form of God" to his death on the cross (2:6–8), while chapter 3 depicts Paul's downward spiral from the benefits he once had to his being "conformed" to the death of Christ (3:10).

Other thematic links indicate the unity of Philippians. Garland (1985) has observed the close parallel between the instruction in 1:27–30 and 4:2–3. One may also observe the close verbal links between the thanksgiving in 1:3–11 and the final thank-you note in 4:10–20. These verbal links indicate that Philippians is a singular communication from Paul to the Philippians. Consequently, the letter has a single occasion and purpose (Reed 1997, 416–18).

The immediate occasion for the letter is Paul's imprisonment (1:7, 13–14, 17), to which he refers as "the things that have happened to me" (1:12; cf. 2:23). Paul has been imprisoned many times (2 Cor. 6:5; 11:23), but now he anticipates a trial in which he will give a defense (1:7), recognizing that this imprisonment may result in a death sentence (1:21–26). His conflict with Roman power is evident in his reference to the praetorian guard (1:13) and to Caesar's household (4:22). He does not mention either the place or the conditions of his imprisonment because his focus is on the future of the church he has established. He refers to his imprisonment only with the word *desmos* (lit. "shackles"), but he does not indicate whether the term is intended literally or metaphorically. Shackles were common in ancient prisons, where the prisoners were bound at the feet, hands, and neck (Standhartinger 2013, 147; Wansink 1996, 46–49). Unlike others who write from prison, he does not mention the torture, the darkness, the hygienic conditions, the hunger, or the oppressive heat that accompanied imprisonment (cf. Standhartinger 2013, 148–52). That Paul receives visitors, sends messengers, and writes letters may suggest that his imprisonment corresponds to the house arrest described in Acts 28:23–25.

While tradition has consistently maintained that Philippians is written from Rome during the imprisonment described in Acts 28, interpreters in the past century have disputed the Roman provenance of the letter, observing that the multiple communications suggested in 2:19–30 and the distance between Rome and Philippi require an extended period of time. Observing that Paul was in prison many times, interpreters have suggested that Philippians was written either during the Caesarean imprisonment (see Acts 23:33–26:32) or from

Ephesus. Because of the proximity between Ephesus and Philippi and Paul's extended stay in Ephesus, many scholars conclude that Philippians was written from Ephesus. However, the traditional view that the letter was written from Rome is the most likely. Neither Acts nor Paul refers to an Ephesian imprisonment. The extended imprisonment described at the end of Acts coheres with the situation in Philippians. The references to the "praetorian guard" (1:13) and to "Caesar's household" (4:22) most likely suggest that Paul is in Rome (Schnelle 1998, 131–32; Cassidy 2001, 126). The references to an impending trial that could result in a death sentence make Rome the most likely place of writing. Paul probably wrote around 62 CE.

The occasion for Philippians is not only Paul's imprisonment but also the events in Philippi that endanger the church. His assurance to the community that his imprisonment will "rather result in the advance of the gospel" (1:12) suggests that the Philippians are anxious (cf. 4:6) about the future of the gospel as well as their own future. The exhortation not to be intimidated by the adversaries (1:28) suggests that the Philippians are also confronted by Roman power and the charges of sedition. Indeed, Paul indicates that the Philippians suffer (1:28), are partners in tribulation (4:14), and are engaged in the same struggle with him (1:30). The consistent theme of suffering (e.g., 1:28–30; 2:8; 3:10; 4:14–15) suggests that the church is faced with adversaries from the local populace. The original charges that Paul undermines the unity of Roman society were probably also directed at the local community (Portefaix 1988, 188–90).

Two major themes of Philippians give a further indication of the issues facing the Philippian church. Paul's references to suffering and death offer a window into the questions that the Philippians are asking. He repeatedly mentions his imprisonment (1:7, 13–14, 17), suffering (1:30; 3:10; 4:14), and readiness for death (1:18–26; 2:17). He offers the example of Jesus as one who died on a cross (2:8) and recalls that Epaphroditus nearly died (2:25–30). While he desires to share in the sufferings of Christ, he warns of those who are enemies of the cross of Christ (3:18–19). The worship of one who died on a cross and the participation in his sufferings are contrary to the values of the Roman society. Conversion to one who died on a cross would have been a sign of disloyalty to the government, and it would have resulted in severe economic and social consequences for believers, including their exclusion from trade guilds, the rupture of social relations, and divorce by the unbelieving spouse (cf. Oakes 2001, 63–70). Paul addresses this theme by interpreting their suffering as the prelude to their ultimate glory, not as a misfortune. He intends to give them a new *phronēsis*—a disposition and attitude—that is different from that of the surrounding culture.

The second consistent theme is the unity of the community (1:27–2:5; 2:12–14; 4:2–3). Many interpreters maintain that the apparent quarrel between Euodia and Syntyche is the occasion for Paul's appeal to the community "to have the same mind-set" (4:2). However, the presence of adversaries is enough to provide the background to Paul's repeated insistence on unity. Believers were probably divided over the proper response to their marginalization. While some were steadfast in faith while being labeled enemies of the Roman order, others were probably tempted to accommodate to the power of Rome.

Philippians, Epistolography, and Rhetoric

Philippians, like the other Pauline letters, is a substitute for Paul's presence. Paul adapts the common conventions of letter writing that have been attested in the ancient papyri, including the identification of the author and recipient (1:1), greeting (1:2), disclosure formula (1:12, "I want you to know"; cf. Rom. 1:13; 2 Cor. 1:8; 1 Thess. 4:13), a request introduced by *parakalō* ("I appeal," 4:2), and final greetings (4:21–23). As in his other letters, Paul has a thanksgiving (1:3–11), autobiographical reflections (1:12–26; 3:2–21), an announcement of an impending visit (2:19–30; cf. Rom. 15:22–29; 1 Cor. 4:14–21; 16:5–9; 2 Cor. 13:1–10; Philem. 22), and ethical exhortations (1:27–2:18; 4:1–9). Neither the adaptation of the outer frame from ancient letter forms nor the itemizing of the common topics that Philippians shares with other letters, however, explains the distinctive character of the letter. Consequently, interpreters have attempted to gain a more precise understanding of the genre of Philippians in order to determine its central focus.

Scholars in the last generation have observed the importance of letter writing in antiquity and the classification of types of letters by epistolary theorists as a clue to the distinctive character of Philippians. Of the twenty-one types of letters identified by Demetrius, the friendly letter has significant parallels to Philippians, as Loveday Alexander (1999) has shown. Like the friendly letter, Philippians contains the theme of presence-absence (cf. 1:27; 2:12), a longing to be reunited with the recipient (cf. 4:1), and an expression of concern for the other (cf. 1:7).

Numerous phrases echo ancient discussions of friendship. Friends are "of one soul" (cf. Phil. 1:27), think the same thing (cf. Phil. 2:2), and engage in the sharing of gifts (cf. 4:10–20). Friends also present themselves as moral exemplars and write to encourage the formation of those who are less experienced. The classic examples are the letters of Seneca to Lucilius, which contain the personal example and moral advice of the older man to the younger man. In Philippians, Paul presents himself as an example to the readers (see 1:12–26; 3:2–21; 4:10–20) and gives moral advice (1:27–2:18; 4:1–9). Thus several scholars (e.g., Stowers 1991, 107; White 1990, 206–7) have identified these parallels and described Philippians as a hortatory letter of friendship (Fitzgerald 1992, 320; Stowers 1991, 107). John Fitzgerald (1996, 157) concludes that the purpose of the letter is to elevate the Philippians' understanding of friendship.

An Example of a Letter of Friendship

"Even though I have been separated from you for a long time, I suffer this in body only. For I can never forget you or the impeccable way we were raised together from childhood up. Knowing that I myself am genuinely concerned about your affairs, and that I have worked unstintingly for what is most advantageous for you, I have assumed that you, too, have the same opinion of me, and will refuse me in nothing. You will do well, therefore, to give close attention to the members of my household lest they need anything, to assist them in whatever they might need, and to write us about whatever you should choose." (Pseudo-Demetrius, *Epistolary Types*, Malherbe 1988, 33)

Loveday Alexander notes the numerous parallels between Philippians and ancient family letters. In comparing Philippians to a letter of Apolinaris to his mother, she notes that the latter has, in addition to the introductory and concluding formulae, a prayer for the recipient, a message of assurance from the traveler that all is well ("I want you to know that I got to Rome all right"), and a request for information about the recipient. The purpose of the letter is to strengthen familial bonds. She sees a similar purpose in Philippians (Alexander 1989, 87–101).

Unlike ancient letters, however, Philippians is not private correspondence, but oral communication dictated to an amanuensis and read to an assembled congregation. The letter never uses the terms *philia* (friendship) or *philos* (friend), and the readers are composed of an assembly of men and women (and presumably children), not the aristocratic participants in the letters of friendship. Because of the oral nature of Paul's letters, scholars have employed the categories from ancient rhetorical theorists to understand the argument of Philippians. Ancient handbooks delineated rhetoric as the study of invention, arrangement, style, memory, and delivery. They classified speeches according to the setting in which they were delivered: (a) forensic oratory for the law court argued over events of the past; (b) deliberative oratory, intended for the democratic assembly, argued about the future course of action; and (c) epideictic oratory, the speech of praise or blame, was intended for festive occasions. Among the categories of ancient rhetoric, interpreters have given special attention to the invention and arrangement of Paul's letters, demonstrating that they present persuasive arguments that can be analyzed with rhetorical categories.

Philippians, like Paul's other letters, does not fit precisely into either the ancient epistle or oration. Paul's letters are intended to be heard by a community in a setting that is not comparable to those of the ancient letter or speech. He speaks with authority, gives commands, and employs arguments that were unknown to ancient rhetorical theorists. Nevertheless, one can observe in Philippians features that can be explained on the basis of ancient rhetoric. As letters intended to shape the future course of action, most of Paul's letters have points of similarity to the deliberative speech. While the salutation and the greetings have the closest parallel to ancient letters, the body of Paul's letters reflects a rhetorical strategy that can be analyzed with the categories of ancient rhetoric. One can observe the development of Philippians as a coherent argument that corresponds largely to the arrangement that ancient rhetorical theorists (e.g., Aristotle, Cicero, Quintilian) commended.

Exordium (1:1–11). The handbooks indicate that the purpose of the *exordium* is to introduce the topic and make the audience favorably disposed, thus preparing the hearer for the message that follows (cf. Aristotle, *Rhet.* 3.14.6). Philippians 1:3–11, like the other thanksgivings in Paul's letters, performs that function. Paul makes the audience favorably disposed by recalling his prayers for them (1:3–6, 9–11) and by describing his concern for his listeners (1:7–8). He describes their partnership in God's grace (1:7) and expresses confidence in their future (1:6, 9–11; cf. Quintilian, *Inst. or.* 4.1, 34, 419).

Paul introduces the topics for discussion in 1:3–11. In 1:4 he mentions his joy, introducing a major theme of the book (see 1:18; 2:18; 3:1; 4:4). In 1:7 he uses the phrase *touto phronein* ("think this"), introducing the letter's pervasive use of the word *phronein* (cf. 2:5; 3:15; 4:10). In his thankfulness for their partnership (*koinōnia*, 1:5; cf. *synkoinōnoi*, 1:7), he introduces a major theme of the book (cf. 2:1; 3:10). Their partnership involves both financial support and participation in suffering (4:14–15). In 1:7 he mentions his imprisonment for the first time, anticipating further references in 1:13–14, 17. In his confidence that God will bring them to completion (1:6), he anticipates 2:12–13. His prayer that they abound in love (1:9) and choose the better things (1:10) points forward to the moral instruction in the remainder of the letter.

Narratio (1:12–26). In the *narratio*, the speaker describes and interprets recent events (Cicero, *Inv.* 1.19.27). The *narratio* provides the occasion for the speaker to offer an insight into his own character. According to Aristotle, the *diēgesis* (Latin *narratio*) must be able to reflect the ethos of the speaker (*Rhet.* 3.16.8). Quintilian declares that one should gain faith and trust, which derive from the personal reputation of the speaker (*Inst. or.* 4.2.25). Paul's letters frequently proceed from the thanksgiving to autobiographical reflection and a rehearsal of recent events (cf. 1 Cor. 1:10–17; 2 Cor. 1:8–2:13; Gal. 1:10–21; 1 Thess. 2:1–12). Prior to making a request, Paul presents his own ethos as an example for the readers. Paul's thanksgiving is followed by news about himself and an interpretation of the news of his imprisonment (1:12–26). He informs the Philippians of recent events and presents himself as a model of one who can rejoice in the midst of suffering before he makes a request to the readers. Thus this section functions as the *narratio* (Greek *diēgesis*), which recalls and interprets recent events. As one who faces hostility and imprisonment, he exhibits the confident outlook that he expects of his listeners in their own difficult situation. His *narratio* prepares the way for the instructions to the Philippians to face adversity with a mind-set similar to that of himself. More than any other letter, Philippians uses the first-person singular and the call for imitation (cf. 3:17; 4:9).

Propositio (1:27–30). The *propositio* states the thesis of the argument and outlines the case to be argued. Paul's letters frequently contain a thesis statement that is the basis for the argument. In 1:27–30 Paul turns from his own affairs to his primary interest: the formation of the community. In the imperative "Live out your citizenship worthily of the Lord" (1:27), he anticipates the later claim that our citizenship is in heaven (3:20). The exhortation to maintain harmony in the face of adversity is the central argument of the letter (1:27; cf. 2:1–4, 14–15; 4:2–3). The foci of unity and suffering will dominate the remainder of the letter.

Probatio (2:1–4:1). The *probatio* is the basic argument of the speech. After stating his thesis (1:27–30), Paul argues the case in 2:1–4:1, demonstrating how the community can live in harmony in the midst of adversity. In the first argument, he appeals not to Scripture but to the community's story, indicating that the community can be of one mind if it recalls the mind it has in Christ. Paul's desire is to develop a common *phronēsis*, or moral reasoning, that is contrary to the dominant *phronēsis* in the society. He argues both from example and from the new *phronēsis* that comes with the story of Christ.

a. 2:1–11. In 2:1–11 Paul elaborates on the imperative in 1:27 (2:1–4) and argues the case by recalling the story of Christ. This is both an argument from example and a narratival description of the reversal of values that is required to maintain unity.

b. 2:12–18. The imperatives in 2:12–18 continue an elaboration on the *propositio* in 1:27–30 and describe the implications of the story of Christ in 2:1–11 for communal behavior. Paul establishes the moral reasoning (*phronēsis*) that he encourages, calling for readers to work out their own salvation by conforming to the story in 2:6–11.

c. 2:19–30. While the future travels of Timothy and Epaphroditus recall the travelogue in Paul's other letters (cf. Rom. 15:22–29; 1 Cor. 16:5–9; Philem. 22), Paul's focus here is on these two coworkers as the embodiment of the values he commends. This is an argument from example, one of the commonplace proofs in ancient rhetoric.

d. 3:1–4:1. Interpreters have frequently examined chapter 3 to determine the nature of the opposition Paul faces. While the opponents are mentioned only in 3:2, 18–19, in the remainder of the chapter Paul presents himself as an example to emulate (3:17). Paul mentions opponents in contexts where they function as the alternative to the appropriate conduct (see 2:20–21). He is less interested in real opponents than he is in drawing a sharp contrast between hypothetical opponents and the appropriate mind-set (see 3:15). The primary function of the opponents is as a negative model (Wick 1994, 92). They are the antitype of those who have the mind of Christ (Wick 1994, 92). They are not prepared to humble themselves and conform their lives to the cross.

Peroratio (4:2–23). The function of the *peroratio* is to recapitulate the argument. The final chapter of Philippians recapitulates the major themes of the letter; thus it functions as the *peroratio* of the letter. The appeal to Euodia and Syntyche to think the same thing (4:2) recalls the earlier appeal to the whole community to think the same thing (2:2). The memory that Euodia and Syntyche "struggled together" (4:3) recalls Paul's earlier instruction for the whole community to "struggle together" (1:27). The exhortation to "rejoice in the Lord" (4:4) recapitulates a constant thread from the earlier parts of the letter (2:18; 3:1). The exhortation not to be anxious (4:6) reiterates the earlier encouragement not to be intimidated by the adversaries (1:28).

Philippians 4:10–20 is neither a letter fragment nor merely a thank-you note but a recapitulation of a major theme of the letter and intended to strengthen the relationship between Paul and the Philippians (cf. Snyman 2007, 175). Paul is oblique in expressing gratitude because he has a larger rhetorical purpose. His self-presentation in 4:11–13 concludes a series of autobiographical reflections (1:12–26; 3:2–21), adding pathos to the argument. Interpreters have observed the significant links between the *exordium* (1:3–11) and 4:10–20.

"I rejoiced in the Lord" (4:10)	"with joy" (1:4; cf. 1:18; 2:18; 3:1)
"To think about me" (4:10, *hyper emou phronein*)	"to think about you" (1:7, *phronein hyper pantōn hymōn*)
Partners (*synkoinōnoi*) in affliction (4:14)	partners (*synkoinōnoi*) in grace (1:7)
You partnered (*ekoinōnēsen*, 4:15)	partnership (*koinōnia*, 1:5)

While the form of the concluding comments in 4:21–23 conform to the customary end of a letter, they also serve a rhetorical purpose. The greetings to "all the saints" (4:21) form an *inclusio* with the opening salutation "to all the saints in Christ Jesus" (1:1) and Paul's thanksgiving "for all of you" (1:4), reaffirming the emphasis on the unity of the community (Snyman 2007, 181). Greetings from "those who are in Caesar's household" (4:22) reassures a community suffering under Roman power that the gospel has even reached into the heart of the Roman Empire. Thus their struggle is not in vain.

The Purpose of Philippians

The ultimate purpose of Philippians, and indeed of Paul's entire ministry, is to ensure that the community he established will be blameless at the day of

An Outline of Philippians

Exordium: **Thanksgiving and prayer for moral formation (1:1–11)**

Opening greetings: Establishing a relationship (1:1–2)

The thanksgiving: Between past and future (1:3–11)

Partnership in the past (1:3–6)

Affections and partnership (1:7–8)

Petition for the future (1:9–11)

Narratio: **The present and future advance of the gospel (1:12–26)**

The advance of the gospel in the present (1:12–18a)

The advance of the gospel in the future (1:18b–26)

Paul's imprisonment and ultimate salvation (1:18b–20)

Living and dying (1:21–24)

Paul's continuing presence and the joy of faith (1:25–26)

Propositio: **Citizens united in an alternative commonwealth (1:27–30)**

Probatio: **Examples of faithful living (2:1–4:1)**

The ultimate example (2:1–11)

A reversal of values (2:1–4)

The mind of Christ (2:5–11)

Following the example of Christ (2:12–18)

God at work (2:12–13)

A blameless and pure community (2:14–16)

Poured out as a libation (2:17–18)

The examples of Timothy and Epaphroditus (2:19–30)

The example of Timothy (2:19–24)

The example of Epaphroditus (2:25–30)

The example of Paul (3:1–4:1)

Rejoice in the Lord (3:1)

Paul's conversion and change of values (3:2–11)

The true circumcision (3:2–3)

Paul's gains and losses (3:4–7)

Paul's participation in the sufferings of Christ (3:8–11)

From the present to the future (3:12–21)

Pressing on to perfection (3:12–14)

Acquiring a new mind-set (3:15–16)

Good and bad examples (3:17–21)

Concluding the argument: Stand firm (4:1)

Peroratio: **Summarizing the case (4:2–23)**

Concluding instructions: United in moral behavior (4:2–9)

The "same mind" for Euodia and Syntyche (4:2–3)

Final ethical advice (4:4–9)

The "thankless thanks" (4:10–20)

Final greetings: A community in God's grace (4:21–23)

Christ (2:16–17; cf. 1:10; 1 Cor. 1:8). The Philippian church faces major obstacles, however, before it can reach that goal. Indeed, according to all normal calculations, a community that probably includes fewer than fifty people and faces the derision and hostility of a proud Roman city has little chance of survival. Paul writes to reassure the Philippians that apparent obstacles can be the occasion for the advance of the gospel (1:12) and that the future belongs, not to Roman power, but to the people of God (see 1:28; 3:20–21). His task is to offer an alternative way of seeing reality and a set of values—a communal *phronēsis*—that will produce the habits and conduct that will result in their moral formation before the day of Christ.

Paul's first task is to reaffirm the communal identity that will be the foundation for their way of life. While the majority population regards them with disdain and hostility, Paul reminds them who they are (Kraftchik 2008, 241). Only they among the residents of Philippi are "the saints" who are "in Christ" (1:1). Unlike others, only they are the true "circumcision," the people who "worship in the Spirit and boast in God" (3:3), as Paul's emphatic "we" indicates (3:3). That is, they have an identity within Israel, the ancient people of God. In contrast to the "many" who are enemies of the cross, their "citizenship is in heaven" (3:20). While the citizens of Philippi honor Caesar as Lord and Savior, this community acknowledges the ultimate Lord and Savior. As these contrasts indicate, while this community interacts daily with the larger society, it has a clear identity that separates them from the larger society. Despite their apparent insignificance, they shine as lights in the world (2:15).

Communal identity requires a shared narrative that unites the people, placing them within a larger story (Miller 2010, 13–14). While Paul places the community within Israel's story of the God who will ultimately triumph over all other powers (3:20–21), the centerpiece of the community's narrative is the one who emptied himself (2:7), died on a cross (2:8), and was ultimately exalted (2:9–11). This story, embodied in the lives of exemplars who also have sacrificed themselves for the sake of others (2:19–30; 3:2–21), has become the community's story. It is a sharp alternative to the narrative of the larger society.

The believers also participate in the narrative of their own existence, for they now exist in the middle between the time when God began a good work in them and the time when God's work among them will be complete (1:6). Paul's prayer for their moral formation (1:9–11) and his exhortations establish a communal ethos and urge them to participate in God's work of bringing them to completion.

Their narrative provides their *phronēsis*, the moral reasoning that is the foundation for their habits and conduct. The community will overcome the obstacles that face them only when they are united by the story that shapes their imagination and values.

The *phronēsis* is the foundation for the moral formation that he encourages among his readers. The focus of the letter's *propositio* is on the proper conduct of those who belong to an alternative commonwealth. Thus the ultimate purpose of Philippians is to inculcate the behavior for which Paul prays (1:9–11), a community composed of people with varied backgrounds who "think the same thing" (2:2) and shine like stars among the residents of Philippi (2:15).

PART 1

Philippians 1:1–11

*Exordium: Thanksgiving
and Prayer for Moral Formation*

Introductory Matters

Consistent with the common template for ancient letters, Paul begins this correspondence (1:1–2) with the identification of the author and readers and a greeting that he adapts to fit his relationship with his readers. As in other letters, Paul also identifies Timothy as co-sender (cf. 2 Cor. 1:1; Col. 1:1; 1 Thess. 1:1 [with Silvanus]; cf. 1 Cor. 1:1, "Paul and Sosthenes"). References to a co-sender are rare among ancient Greek letters. The precise role of the co-sender is uncertain, for Paul speaks in the first-person singular throughout Philippians and commends Timothy as his messenger to them (2:19–23). Paul probably chooses to include the names of co-senders who have a relationship to the readers. Timothy was with Paul at the founding of the church and at the time of writing of the letter. Timothy plays the role of emissary elsewhere and was capable of explaining Paul's ways (1 Cor. 4:17). Along with Silvanus, he shares in the proclamation of the gospel (2 Cor. 1:19). Thus Paul probably mentions Timothy because of the latter's special relationship to the church at Philippi.

Like other ancient letter writers, Paul employs a descriptive title. Whereas he gives his apostolic credentials elsewhere (Rom. 1:1; 1 Cor. 1:1; 2 Cor. 1:1; Gal. 1:1; cf. Eph. 1:1; Col. 1:1), he does not mention his apostleship in Philippians, 1 Thessalonians, or Philemon. The absence of the apostolic credentials probably reflects his undisputed role as founder and mentor to the church. Only in Philippians does he describe himself and Timothy as "slaves [*douloi*] of Christ Jesus," although in Romans (1:1) he describes himself both as slave and apostle. The image would have been graphic in households where slaves (*douloi*) and masters (*kyrioi*) lived together. Jesus Christ is the *kyrios* (Phil. 1:2; 2:11; 4:5), and Paul is the *doulos*. While the word would have negative resonance with upper-class readers, it would also have connoted one who is commissioned by another. Paul would have known the LXX descriptions of God's messengers. Moses (LXX 2 Kings 18:12; Ps. 104:26 [105:26 Eng.]; Mal. 3:24 [4:4 Eng.]), David (2 Sam. 7:5; Ps. 88:4, 21 [89:3, 20 Eng.]), Abraham (Ps. 104:42 [105:42 Eng.]), Jacob (Isa. 48:20; Jer. 26:27 [46:27 Eng.]), and the prophets (Amos 3:7; Jer. 25:4) were *douloi* of God. *Doulos* appears also in salutations of three of the catholic letters (James 1:1; 2 Pet. 1:1; Jude 1). The very way the word *doulos* occurs in these texts reveals its function as a recognized title of legitimacy (D. Martin 1990, 54). To be the slave of an important leader carried authority (D. Martin 1990, 55). While *doulos* is an honored title in the Septuagint, for the gentile Philippians it would have been understood as a common slave (Ascough 2003, 123).

Unlike most ancient letters, Philippians is no private correspondence but is addressed to "all the saints [*hagioi*] in Christ Jesus who are in Philippi with the overseers and servants" (1:1). Paul addresses his readers throughout the letter in the second-person plural, signifying the corporate identity of the hearers. He does not speak of the *ekklēsia* of the Philippians, as he does in other letters (1 Cor. 1:2; 2 Cor. 1:1; Gal. 1:2), but of "all of the saints" (cf. 1 Cor. 1:2, "to the church of God in Corinth, sanctified in Christ, called to be saints"). *Hagioi*, like the other designations for the community, identifies the gentile community with Israel. In some instances Paul addresses his letters to the "saints" (*hagioi*) rather than to the *ekklēsia* (Rom. 1:7; Phil. 1:1; Col. 1:2), while in other instances he employs forms of both words (1 Cor. 1:2; 2 Cor. 1:1). "Holy ones" (*hagioi*) is apparently a synonym for *ekklēsia* and a significant aspect of the election tradition. Paul describes the gentile readers in Romans and 1 Corinthians as "called to be saints" (Rom. 1:7; 1 Cor. 1:2; cf. Thompson 2014, 38–40). This common designation is drawn from Lev. 19:2, "you shall be holy as I am holy." Although the Philippians are a gentile church, they find their identity as being "holy ones," the people who have been separated from the surrounding culture. This is common, especially in the introduction of the letters (cf. Rom. 1:7; 1 Cor. 1:2; 2 Cor. 1:1; Eph. 1:1; Col. 1:2).

As the holy ones "in Christ Jesus," the believers are "in Christ" (cf. 1:29; 2:1, 5, 19, 24; 3:1, 3, 9, 14; 4:1, 4, 10, 13, 19, 21) and "in the Lord"—one of the most frequent designations for the church. Believers are "in Christ" because they have been baptized "into Christ" (Rom. 6:3; Gal. 3:27; cf. 1 Cor. 12:13) and "with Christ" (Rom. 6:4). Thus Christ is the sphere in which they live and the foundation for their existence as a community.

Only in Philippians does Paul add to the usual salutation the phrase "with the overseers and servants" (*syn episkopois kai diakonois*), terms that in later ecclesiastical usage became "bishops and deacons" in English translations. Among the undisputed letters of Paul, the *episkopoi* and *diakonoi* appear together only here (cf. 1 Tim. 3:1–10), although both terms appear separately in numerous places in the NT (*episkopoi* in Acts 20:28; 1 Tim. 3:2; Titus 1:7; *diakonos* in Rom. 16:1; 1 Cor. 3:5; 1 Tim. 3:8, 12). Some later manuscripts and John Chrysostom (*Hom. Phil.* 1.1) render the passage "to the fellow overseers" (*synepiskopoi*). Although some interpreters (John Chrysostom, *Hom. Phil.* 1.1–2; Hawthorne 2004, 11; Collange 1979, 41) have maintained that Paul refers to only one group ("overseers who serve"), both the grammar of the passage and subsequent developments in the early church (cf. 1 Tim. 3:1–15; cf. Pol. *Phil.* 5.2; 6.1; 11.1; *Did.* 15.1) suggest that Paul refers to two groups (Selby 2012, 83). He does not mention their roles, and he does not address them again in the letter.

The office of *episkopos* was well known in the OT and Mediterranean world. In the OT it is used for roles that involve oversight of the people (e.g., Num. 31:14; Judg. 9:28; 2 Kings 11:15). In the civic life of the ancient city, the *episkopos* (lit. "overseer") supervised projects such as the construction of public buildings or the administration of local markets (Cotter 1993, 102). Voluntary associations used this terminology for their leaders. *Episkopos* is used in an inscription from Thera that refers to financial officers of an association (*IG* XII/3 329; Dibelius 1937, 60). The evidence for the use of *episkopos* in associations is clear, but the specific function attached to it is ambiguous, as officials seem to have held different job descriptions in different associations (Ascough 2003, 81; Reumann 1996, 90). The Philippians probably used terms for leaders from a world they knew—of government, guilds, societies, and the household.

Scholars debate the extent to which local leadership developed among the churches. In the later correspondence, the *episkopoi* and *diakonoi* were office holders who met the requisite qualifications. In Titus (1:5–7), the *episkopos* is equivalent to the *presbyteros* (elder). Ignatius argues that the church needs a singular *episkopos* (*Magn.* 6.1). We may assume that the *episkopoi* had some kind of supervisory role in the community, while the *diakonoi* had a serving role.

Paul adapts the common Hellenistic greeting *chairein* to "grace [*charis*] to you and peace [*eirēnē*] from God our Father and the Lord Jesus Christ" (Phil. 1:3), a phrase that appears regularly in his letters; only 1 Thessalonians lacks "from" God the Father (1:1) in the greeting. In addition to altering the traditional *chairein* (greetings) to *charis* (grace), Paul has added peace (*eirēnē*), which appears in Jewish letters (Hebrew *shalom*; e.g., Ezra 4:17–22; 5:7–17). To ensure that his readers know the source of grace and peace, he adds "from God our Father and the Lord Jesus Christ." Thus Paul incorporates both Greek and Jewish greetings into his letters, placing a Christian stamp on the traditional form. It is uncertain whether Paul is echoing an existing liturgical expression or has created this form himself (Adams 2010, 48).

With the exception of 2 Corinthians and Galatians, Paul's undisputed letters begin with a thanksgiving, introduced by either the singular "I give thanks" (*eucharistō*, Rom. 1:8; 1 Cor. 1:4; Phil. 1:3) or the plural "we give thanks" (*eucharistoumen*, Col. 1:3; 1 Thess. 1:2; cf. 1 Thess. 2:13; 2 Thess. 1:3, "we must give thanks"), which forms the main clause of the sentence. Although the thanksgivings contain considerable variety in content and length, one may identify components that are present in multiple letters. Paul gives thanks (a) "to God" (*tō theō*), (b) for the recipients ("for all of you," Rom. 1:8; 1 Cor. 1:4, "for you" [plural]; cf. Phil. 1:3; 1 Thess. 1:2), (c) frequently referring to his memory (*mneia*, Rom. 1:9; 1 Thess. 1:2; Philem. 4) of them, and (d) often mentioning the constancy of his prayers for them (*pantote*, "always," Rom. 1:10; 1 Cor. 1:4; Phil. 1:4; Col. 1:3; 1 Thess. 1:2, Philem. 4). In most instances the main clause is modified by "because" (*hoti*), expressing the reason for the thanksgiving (Rom. 1:8; 1 Cor. 1:5), and one or more participial phrases (Phil. 1:4, 6; Col. 1:4; 1 Thess. 1:2–5; Philem. 5). The thanksgivings also have telic clauses expressing purpose or result ("so that" [*hōste*]: 1 Cor. 1:7; 1 Thess. 1:7; cf. 2 Thess. 1:4; "in order that" [*hopōs*]: Philem. 6) and a phrase introduced by "just as" (*kathōs*, 1 Cor. 1:6; Phil. 1:7; Col. 1:6; 1 Thess. 1:5; cf. 2 Cor. 1:5). An eschatological climax (1 Cor. 1:8; Phil. 1:9–11; 1 Thess. 1:2–10) also appears frequently. Consistent with the concern of the letters for ethical formation, Paul expresses gratitude for the ethical transformation and faith of the hearers (cf. Rom. 1:8; 1 Cor. 1:4–9; 1 Thess. 1:3–5; Philem. 4–7). These features suggest that Paul is adapting a basic template in each of his letters.

Paul Schubert first identified this basic template in 1939, maintaining that a common denominator exists for the introductory thanksgivings and that the basic backbone for them is present in Philemon, Paul's shortest letter (1939, 12). He argued that this form was a common literary convention in the Hellenistic Age (1939, 180), which the apostle adapted for his purposes. Following Schubert, interpreters have maintained that the basic template, like the introductory greetings, is a common literary convention among Greek-speaking people in the Hellenistic Age. More recent studies have shown, however, that it was never a set phrase among ancient letters (Arzt 1994, 37), although it appeared occasionally. A constant feature of the letters was the wish for the good health of the recipients (*formula valetudinis*), to which a thanksgiving was sometimes attached. While some of the motifs common in Paul's letters (e.g., the reports of the writer's prayers, the motif of remembrance) are also common in ancient letters, the introductory phrase "I [we] give thanks" is rare.

The content of the introductory thanksgivings in Paul's letters differs significantly from those in ancient letters, which usually express gratitude for recent good news, including rescue from danger or recovery from a disease (Arzt-Grabner 2010b, 157–58; Pao 2010, 106). Paul's letters express gratitude not only for recent news but also for the spiritual progress of the recipients, focusing on what God has done in the past and will do in the future. While the thanksgiving appears occasionally in ancient letters, Paul's thanksgivings are distinctive insofar as they express gratitude to God for the church. They are also distinctive because of their length. In Philippians and 1 Thessalonians, for example, the thanksgivings comprise a major portion of the letter.

> **Philippians 1:1–11 in the Rhetorical Flow**
>
> ▶ *Exordium*: **Thanksgiving and prayer for moral formation (1:1–11)**
>
> Opening greetings: Establishing a relationship (1:1–2)
>
> The thanksgiving: Between past and future (1:3–11)
>
> Partnership in the past (1:3–6)
>
> Affections and partnership (1:7–8)
>
> Petition for the future (1:9–11)

While the special circumstances in Galatians may account for the absence of the thanksgiving, 2 Corinthians has an introductory blessing rather than a thanksgiving, which also appears in Ephesians and 1 Peter. The blessing form, consisting of "blessed is . . ." followed by an extended periodic sentence, has a long history in Jewish liturgy and hymnody. It has many of the same characteristics as the thanksgiving, including one or more dependent clauses praising God, a causal statement ("because God has . . ."), and an eschatological climax (2 Cor. 1:7). Like the introductory thanksgiving, it has an elevated style and is a form of praise. James M. Robinson argues persuasively that both the thanksgiving and blessing formulas echo the Jewish liturgy, which Paul has appropriated for his communities. The expression "I give thanks" is common in the hymns (*Hodayoth*) at Qumran (Robinson 1964, 194). He indicates that both *eucharistō* and *eulogētos* are variant forms of the Hebrew "blessed" (*berakah*).

Paul's introductory thanksgiving probably echoes his own preaching. As Schubert indicates, Paul's adaptation of the ancient form includes the specific concerns of the letter. In Phil. 1:3–11, he includes features both from ancient letters (e.g., the appeal to memory) and from the liturgy that was rooted in the synagogue.

Tracing the Train of Thought

Opening Greetings: Establishing a Relationship (1:1–2)

1:1–2. Ancient teachers of rhetoric recognized the importance of opening words, indicating that the function of the *exordium* (Latin *proemium*) was to introduce the topic and make the audience favorably disposed. In a letter intended to unify the community under threatening circumstances, Paul also knows the critical importance of opening words. With his adaptation of the opening greeting, he sets the tone for his appeal to the community, establishing a relationship with the listeners and introducing the themes of the letter. With the introductory **Paul and Timothy** as **slaves** (*douloi*, NRSV "servants") **of Christ Jesus**, he introduces the countercultural mind-set that he will establish in the letter. Over against the Philippians' quest for honor, Paul and Timothy are models of an alternative set of values (cf. Tite 2010, 65). Paul anticipates the reminder that the one they now worship as Lord came "in the form of a slave" (2:7) and that Timothy served (*edouleusen*) with Paul in the gospel (2:22).

The address **to all the saints** (*hagioi*) **in Christ Jesus who are in Philippi** establishes the collective identity of the listeners, who are not, like other communities, united by ethnicity, social class, age, or gender but by their incorporation in Christ. By identifying the gentile readers of Philippians as saints, Paul indicates that they are the heirs of ancient Israel, the people who were called to be holy (*hagios*) as God is holy (cf. Lev. 19:2) and separate from the larger society (cf. Lev. 18:1–5). Unlike other heirs of ancient Israel, however, they exist "in Christ," as Paul indicates repeatedly in the letter (1:13, 26, 29; 2:1–5; 3:3, 9, 14; 4:7, 19, 21). Believers have been baptized "into Christ" (*eis Christon*, Rom. 6:3; Gal. 3:27; cf. 1 Cor. 10:2; 12:13) and died "with Christ" (*syn Christō*, Rom. 6:8; cf. 6:6; 8:17; Gal. 2:19; 2 Tim. 2:11). As a result, they now exist "in Christ" (*en Christō*), "in him" (cf. 2 Cor. 5:21; Phil. 3:9), and "in the body of Christ" (Rom. 12:3–8; 1 Cor. 12:12–27; cf. Thompson 2014, 52–77). By addressing "all of the saints," Paul may be anticipating his exhortations to unity (cf. 1:27–2:4; Tite 2010, 76–77). While Paul addresses "all" of the community in the letter, he includes **the overseers** (NRSV "bishops") **and servants** (NRSV "deacons") in the salutation without suggesting their specific roles.

Grace to you and peace from God our Father and the Lord Jesus Christ is not only the customary introduction but also a prayer to God, which sets the tone and anticipates themes in the letter. The readers are partners in God's grace (1:7), who have been "graciously granted" (*echaristhē*) the privilege of suffering for Christ (1:29). Paul promises those who overcome anxiety that "the peace that passes all understanding" will rule their hearts in Christ Jesus (4:7).

The Thanksgiving: Between Past and Future (1:3–11)

1:3–6. *Partnership in the past.* Like the opening salutation, the introductory thanksgivings are not merely common literary conventions but a means to make the audience favorably disposed and introduce the themes that follow. Before Paul gives ethical instructions to the church, he builds a relationship with the hearers by recalling both his gratitude for them and his constant prayers for them. He establishes ethos and pathos by recalling his feelings for the Philippians and his actions on their behalf (Davis 1999, 68). His gratitude for their moral progress, a consistent feature in Paul's letters, is implicitly an exhortation to continue on the path that the church has begun and an anticipation of the moral advice that follows (Jewett 1970, 53).

The elevated style in 1:3–11 is appropriate for the *exordium*. The report of Paul's prayers is composed of two sentences in Greek, which includes a thanksgiving (1:3–6), an expression of intimacy with the readers (1:7–8), and a petition on their behalf (1:9–11). **I give thanks** (*eucharistō*) **to my God** introduces the main clause of the thanksgiving followed by that for which Paul is thankful (1:3–6). Distinctive features of this thanksgiving are **for your memory** (*epi tē mneia*, v. 3; NRSV "every time I remember you") and **for your partnership** (*epi tē koinōnia*) **in the gospel** (1:5), each of which employs *epi* with the dative. Some interpreters have rendered the phrases as parallel, suggesting that both are the objects of Paul's thanksgiving; that is, Paul is thankful for (a) their memory of him (v. 3; cf. Holloway 2006, 420–22) and (b) their participation (*koinōnia*) in the gospel (v. 5). Two factors raise issues of translation. *Epi* with the dative can express either the basis for something (BDAG 364) or the time during which something occurred (BDAG 367; NRSV "every time"). "Your memory" (*mneia hymōn*) can be rendered either "my memory of you" (cf. NRSV "every time I remember you") or "your memory of me." The parallels with Paul's other introductory thanksgivings suggest that Paul is thankful for his memory of them (see Rom. 1:9; 1 Thess. 1:2; Philem. 4) every time (BDAG 367) he prays. Thus Paul expresses gratitude for their partnership (*koinōnia*) in the gospel (*eis to euangelion*, 1:5) only after he employs two adverbial phrases to describe the manner of this thanksgiving: "every time I remember you" (1:3) and **in every one of my prayers** (*en pasē deēsei*, 1:4) **for you** with the participial phrase **constantly praying with joy** (*meta charas tēn deēsin poioumenos*).

Paul does not indicate the reason for the thanksgiving (1:5) until he has strengthened his relationship with the readers. Verse 4 is a parenthesis indicating the nature of his thanksgiving. The redundancy of "every" (*pasē*), "constantly" (*pantote*), and "every" (*pasē*) in 1:3–4 is intended to strengthen Paul's relationship with the readers and prepare the way for the requests that he will make later (1:27–2:18; 4:1–9). Indeed, his prayer for all of the readers anticipates his encouragement to stand together in one spirit (1:27). Only in Philippians does Paul indicate that he prays for his churches with joy (*chara*), as he introduces a dominant theme of the letter. In reporting that he prays with joy (*meta charas*, 1:4), Paul introduces another major concern of the letter. He orients his life with the attitude that the OT commends (Lev. 23:40; Deut. 12:7, 12; Zech. 9:9) for those who serve the Lord. As he indicates in other letters, his churches are his joy (Rom. 15:32; 2 Cor. 2:3; 7:4, 13; 1 Thess. 2:19; 3:9; Philem. 7), and he can instruct his churches to share his joy (1 Thess. 5:16), which is the evidence of the presence of the Spirit (Gal. 5:22; cf. Rom. 14:17).

This theme is especially prominent in Philippians, as Paul's joy comes in the midst of imprisonment and deprivation as he challenges his readers, even in the midst of their own duress, to rejoice (2:18; 3:1; 4:4). This joy is not a temporary happiness, but the experience that believers have in all circumstances (K. Berger, *EDNT* 3:454). As he prays with joy, he is a model for the joy that he desires from his listeners (3:1; 4:4).

What is striking is that Paul twice uses *deēsis* to describe his thanksgiving. *Deēsis* refers to an urgent request to God (BDAG 213; cf. Rom. 10:1; 2 Cor. 1:11; 9:14), an urgency that is probably related to Paul's present circumstances. The twofold reference to his prayers (*deēsei*) strengthens Paul's relationship with the readers and anticipates his expectation that they will offer prayers for him (1:19) in his imprisonment (cf. 4:6).

In 1:5 Paul finally indicates that for which he is thankful: **because of the** Philippians' partnership (*epi tē koinōnia*, NRSV "sharing") in the gospel **from the first day until now**. Partnership (*koinōnia*) involved the sharing of gifts, as Paul indicates in 4:15, when he recalls that "no one participated [*ekoinōnēsen*] in giving and receiving" except the Philippians. The Philippians had sent gifts to him repeatedly (cf. 2 Cor. 11:7–11) and had sent Epaphroditus (2:25–30) to assist in his ministry. *Koinōnia* was a common term for a financial partnership. The Philippians were probably among the Macedonians who begged for the "privilege of sharing" (*charin kai tēn koinōnian*) their resources with the Jerusalem church (2 Cor. 8:4; cf. 9:13). As Paul writes to the Romans, "The Macedonians have been pleased to share their resources" (Rom. 15:26, *koinōnian . . . poiēsasthai*), having previously shared (*ekoinōnēsan*) spiritual blessings (15:27).

Interpreters have observed the pervasiveness of the language of friendship throughout Philippians, recalling the ancient description of friendship in which friends have all things in common (*koina*). While this *koinōnia* involved the sharing of property, it also involved the partnership in all areas of life. According to Aristotle (*Eth. nic.* 9.8.2), *koinōnia* is essential to all forms of friendship. Friends shared leisure time but also assisted one another in shared projects (Stowers 1991, 109) and shared with each other in sorrow and joy (cf. Phil. 2:18). Thus *koinōnia* means more than a financial partnership. Paul himself experiences the "partnership [*koinōnia*] in the sufferings of Christ" (3:10). The Philippians are partners (*synkoinōnoi*) in God's grace (1:7, NRSV "share in God's grace"), engaged in "the same struggle" (1:30) with Paul. Related to the use of *koinōnia* are the compound words with *syn*. The Philippians "struggle side by side" (*synathlountes*) in the gospel (1:27) and rejoice with (*synchairein*) Paul (2:18). Euodia and Syntyche struggled together (*synēthlēsan*) with Paul in the gospel (Phil. 4:3). Thus the *koinōnia* in the gospel (*eis to euangelion*) involves the total participation in the marginalization that Paul experiences. Paul mentions his own ministry *eis to euangelion* (2 Cor. 2:12) and Timothy's service with him *eis to euangelion* (Phil. 2:22). They share with Paul in suffering on behalf of Christ (1:28–30) and imitate Paul in his total investment in the gospel by sharing their resources, proclaiming Christ, and suffering for it.

The gospel (*euangelion*) is Paul's one-word summary of the Christian message. Paul probably derives the word from the prophetic announcement of the "good news" of the return from exile (Isa. 52:7; 61:1). In the context of Roman Philippi, however, the word had a different meaning. To proclaim the gospel is the equivalent of "speaking the word" (1:14) and "preaching Christ" (1:18). Paul defends it (1:7, 16), and believers live according to its norms (1:27). It is a force that advances (1:12) as believers struggle in it.

This partnership has existed "from the first day until now" (Phil. 1:5). The first day recalls the founding of the church, a common theme in the letters (see 1 Cor. 1:18–2:5; 2 Cor. 3:3–6; 1 Thess. 1:5), and "the beginning of the gospel" (Phil. 4:15), meaning when no other church shared with him as well as the moment when God "began a good work" among the Philippians. The reference to the first day (1:5) leads Paul to reflect on the entire narrative of the community's existence and their continuing relationship with Paul. Undoubtedly they shared his sufferings when he was mistreated in Philippi (cf. 1 Thess. 2:2). As Paul says later (4:15), in Thessalonica "no one partnered [*ekoinōnēsen*, NRSV "shared"] in the gospel" except the Philippians, who sent once and twice to his need (4:16). He probably has the Philippians in mind when he says to the Corinthians, "I robbed other churches . . . for your ministry" (2 Cor. 11:8) and when he says that the Macedonians desired to have *koinōnia* (2 Cor. 8:4).

The Philippians' partnership "from the first day until now" (Phil. 1:5) is the basis for Paul's confidence that **the one who began a good work among you will bring it to completion at the day of Christ** (1:6). Paul is **confident** (*pepoithōs*, "being persuaded") because of a deep conviction based on faith in God (cf. *peithō, pepoithēsis* in 2 Cor. 1:9; 2:3; Gal. 5:10; Phil. 1:6, 14; 2:24; 3:3–4) rather than faith in his own calculations. The first day was the occasion when God "began a good work" among the Philippians. Paul speaks frequently of the beginning of the church as the occasion when God's power was evident (cf. 1 Cor. 1:18–2:5; 3:10; 2 Cor. 3:2–3; Gal. 3:1–5; 1 Thess. 1:5). Thus "the one who began a good work among you" was God, who is still at work in the community (2:13). In contrast to the Galatians, who "began in the Spirit and ended in the flesh" (Gal. 3:3), the Philippians will continue to completion through God's work. Paul's imprisonment and the Philippians' distress will not prevent God from bringing the community to the ultimate goal.

Paul knows from the Hebrew Scriptures that God completes what God begins (Thompson 2006, 38). The same combination of the verbs *archomai* . . . *epiteleō* appears in 1 Sam. 3:12, when God promises to bring to an end the priestly line of Eli, saying, "I begin [*archomai*] and I will bring to completion [*epitelesō*]." This emphasis on God who is present at the beginning and draws to a conclusion echoes the emphasis of Deutero-Isaiah, according to which

God is the beginning and the end (Isa. 41:4; 44:6; 48:12), who will soon do a "new thing" for Israel that is analogous to the primordial act of creation (Isa. 42:5, 8–9). Paul indicates the collective identity of the church, declaring that God began a good work "among you." He writes to the whole church, and he suggests that the church has a communal narrative that has a beginning, a middle, and an end. This communal identity separates them from the competing narratives of the larger society. The church lives **now** (1:5) between the beginning and the end (Miller 2010, 17).

God will bring the church to an end at the day of Christ (1:6; cf. 1:10). In the present, the church is being transformed into the image of God's son (cf. Rom. 12:1–2; 2 Cor. 3:18) and sanctified by the Holy Spirit (cf. 1 Thess. 3:11–13). The occasion for the completion is the day of Christ, a term that NT writers adapt from the "day of the Lord" in the OT (see Isa. 13:6–9; 34:8–12; Jer. 46:9–12; Ezek. 30:1–9; Joel 3:14–21; Mal 4:5) to speak of the return of Christ (see Matt. 7:22; 10:15; 12:36; 24:36, 42; 25:13; John 6:39; 12:48; 14:20). Paul frequently speaks of the "day of wrath" (Rom. 2:5) and of judgment (Rom. 2:16; cf. Rom. 13:12; 1 Cor. 1:8; 3:13; 2 Cor. 1:14; 6:2; 1 Thess. 5:2, 4; 2 Thess. 1:6–9; 2:1–3; cf. Heb. 10:25). In Philippians Paul speaks of his boast at the day (2:16). He envisions that God is at work in the community now and will complete the work when they are "blameless" at the end (1:10; cf. 1 Cor. 1:8; 2 Cor. 1:14). The threatening forces surrounding Paul and the Philippians will not prevent their ongoing transformation, which continues until the time when they will be conformed to the image of the resurrected Lord (3:21).

1:7–8. *Affections and partnership.* Contrary to most English translations, the thanksgiving does not end in 1:6 but continues with the added clause that begins with **insofar as** (*kathōs*, BDAG 494), which indicates that Paul goes on in 1:7–8 to justify the thanksgiving (Fee 1995, 89), speaking directly to the readers and appealing to what is **right** (*dikaios*), that is, fair or equitable (cf. BDAG 247). The nature of this *koinōnia* is evident in the reciprocity of affection between Paul and the church. Here in the *exordium* of the letter he indicates that he **thinks about all** of them, while in the *peroratio* (4:2–23) he expresses gratitude that they "think about" him (4:10, *hyper emou phronein*). Forms of *phronein*, a major theme in the letter, appear twenty-two times in the undisputed Pauline letters, of which ten are in Philippians and eight are in Romans. The verb *phronein* and the noun *phronēsis* are difficult to render into English because no single word captures the nuance of the Greek word. Fowl (2005, 28) describes it as a pattern of judgment that involves thinking, feeling, and acting. As a result, many people incorporate the Greek word *phronēsis* to describe this disposition. That is, Paul seeks to establish a communal moral reasoning (*phronēsis*) in which believers look to the interests of others (2:4–5), "have the same mind-set" (*to auto phronein*, 2:2; 4:2), and "have this mind" (*touto phroneite*) because they are in Christ (2:5; cf. 3:15), in contrast to those who have their minds on earthly things (*ta epigeia phronountes*, 3:19). Here

Paul is a model of this *phronēsis*, for he thinks about all of the believers in Philippians.

Translations differ on the reason for his thoughts about them, for one can translate either **because I have you in my heart** (NIV, RSV) or "because you hold me in your heart" (NRSV). Because of the Greek word order and the reaffirmation in 1:8, the NIV and RSV are probably correct (cf. O'Brien 1991, 68; Bockmuehl 1998, 63). One may compare Paul's statements to the Corinthians, "Our hearts are wide open to you" (2 Cor. 6:11) and "you are in our hearts to live together and die together" (2 Cor. 7:3; cf. 2 Cor. 3:2). The heart, both here and in other Jewish and Christian writings, is the seat of the emotions.

Paul elaborates on the nature of this partnership (*koinōnia*, 1:5) and affection, describing the Philippians as **partners** (*synkoinōnoi*) in **God's grace** (NRSV "all of you share in God's grace"), even in his **imprisonment** (*desmos*, lit. "fetters") and **defense** (*apologia*) **and confirmation** (*bebaiōsis*) **of the gospel** (1:7). For the first time in the letter he mentions his imprisonment, the occasion for the letter (see also 1:13, 14, 17). The forensic terms "defense" and "confirmation" suggest that Paul anticipates a trial (1:16). Here Paul experiences God's grace, just as he regularly receives God's grace in the midst of his weakness and suffering (cf. 2 Cor. 1:12; 4:15; 8:1–2; 12:9). The Philippians have been partners in his tribulation (4:14, *synkoinōnēsantes mou tē thlipsei*), they shared in his distress, and now they continue to share both suffering and God's grace as they participate in the same struggle with Paul (cf. 1:28–30).

To affirm his affection in the strongest possible terms, Paul calls God as witness (cf. Rom. 1:9; 2 Cor. 1:23; 1 Thess. 2:5) to declare that he **longs for** them with the "compassion of Christ Jesus" (1:8). Such expressions of affection are common in Paul. Epaphroditus, whom the Philippians have sent to Paul, "has been longing for all of [them]" (2:26). Paul addresses the Philippians as beloved (*agapētoi*) family members whom he "longs for" (*epipothētoi*, 4:1). To the Romans, whom he has never met, he declares, "I am longing [*epipothō*] to see you" (1:11).

This language of intimacy in 1:7–8 suggests the larger significance of *koinōnia* between Paul and his churches, and it elaborates on the theme of friendship. A common topic in antiquity was friends' concern for each other and their longing to be together (Stowers 1991, 110). Demetrius writes, "I am genuinely concerned about your affairs" (cf. Stowers 1991, 110). This is no ordinary friendship, however, for Paul adds the christological dimension, **with the compassion** (*splanchna*) **of Christ** (1:8). *Splanchna* (lit. "intestines") is a synonym for love or affections (BDAG 938). Paul invites the Corinthians to "widen [their] affections" (*splanchna*, 2 Cor. 6:13). He recalls that Philemon has "refreshed the hearts [*splanchna*] of the saints" (Philem. 7), describes Onesimus as his "own heart" (*splanchna*, v. 12), and urges him to "refresh [his] heart" (*splanchna*, v. 20). He assumes that these affections (*splanchna*) already exist within the community (Phil. 2:1). Both their affections and their *koinōnia* originate in Christ and overflow to the community.

1:9–11. *Petition for the future.* Paul's deep affection for the Philippians (1:7–8) is the context for the petition in 1:9–11. Having expressed confidence that God will bring to completion what God began at the day of Christ, he prays for the community's continued formation in two parallel purpose clauses: **so that your love may overflow more and more** and **so that in the day of Christ you may be pure and blameless,** adding a modifying elaboration in each clause describing their abounding love. Love stands at the center of Paul's ethical instruction in all of the letters (e.g., Rom. 12:9–16; 13:8–10; 1 Cor. 13; Gal. 5:22; 1 Thess. 4:9–12). Believers are recipients of God's love (e.g., Rom. 5:8; 2 Cor. 5:14). As the petition indicates, love is not human effort but the work of God (1 Thess. 3:12; cf. Gal. 5:22). Nor is love a static possession but overflows more and more. Thus Paul both acknowledges the presence of the "consolation in love" (2:1) and instructs the readers to "have the same love" (2:2). In 1:9 Paul does not mention the direct object of their love but describes the manner of love: in **full knowledge** (*epignōsis*) and **full insight** (*aisthēsis*). In a similar passage, he prays that the Thessalonians will "increase and abound in love for one another and for all" (1 Thess. 3:12). *Epignōsis* is used regularly by Paul for knowledge of the divine will (Rom. 3:20; 10:2; Eph. 1:17; Col. 1:9; BDAG 369). Just as knowledge without love is not edifying (see 1 Cor. 8:1; 13:2), love without knowledge is not beneficial (cf. Bockmuehl 1998, 67), for formation involves continued conceptual understanding of the will of God. Paul expresses gratitude that Philemon has a "knowledge of everything good" (v. 6). *Aisthēsis* is the capacity to understand, especially in moral understanding (BDAG 29). Thus the work that God is bringing to completion (1:6) is the maturation of love within the community.

Paul elaborates on this moral formation with the purpose clause **that you determine what is best** (*eis to dokimazein hymas ta diapheronta*), using the language of the Stoics, who distinguished *ta diapheronta* ("that which really matters," L. Oberlinner, *EDNT* 1:315) from the *adiaphora* (indifferent matters). Paul argues that his Jewish interlocutor in Romans "determine[s] what is best" (Rom. 2:18, *dokimazeis ta diapheronta*) and urges believers to "discern what is the will of God" (Rom. 12:2, *dokimazein . . . to thelēma tou theou*). Unlike the Stoics, however, Paul envisions love as "what is best" that the community discerns.

The second purpose clause indicates the ultimate goal of the believers' formation: that at the day of Christ they may be **pure and blameless** (*eilikrineis kai aproskopoi*). *Eilikrinēs*, a term that means literally "without mixture" (*TLNT* 1:420), could be used for gold that is unalloyed or air that is not polluted. It took on the ethical connotation to describe the person who has no hidden motives or pretense (BDAG 282). *Aproskopos* is one of several synonyms used by Paul for ethical blamelessness. In 1 Cor. 1:8 he prays that the community will be "blameless [*anenklētos*] at the day of Christ" (cf. Col. 1:22). The **fruit of righteousness** (1:11, *karpos dikaiosynēs*) is the moral formation of the community (the "fruit which is righteousness"), which occurs, not through their own efforts, but **through Jesus Christ** (cf. 2:13). The ultimate outcome of their formation is **the glory and praise of God**. While the community lives now between the beginning and the end, God is at work to bring about the moral behavior. Paul's comment elsewhere that he hopes to present the church blameless to Christ indicates his ultimate goal for his churches (2 Cor. 1:14; 11:1–4). Before Paul instructs his communities to be "blameless and innocent" (*amemptoi kai akeraioi*, 2:15), he offers a prayer for their moral formation. This petition is implicitly moral advice, anticipating the community formation that follows in the ethical instructions.

Theological Issues

Although the salutation resembles the opening words of most ancient letters, the words reflect Paul's deep theological convictions. The identification of himself and Timothy as slaves of Christ reflects a challenge to the values of a society based on honor and personal advancement. With this singular title, he gives a statement of his personal identity. As he says later, "To live is Christ" (1:21).

The identification of the readers as saints not only places them within Israel's story but also indicates that their marginalization is not an unfortunate circumstance but a divine calling. The saint is not the individual spiritual hero; rather, the entire community is called to be a counterculture. As Gerhard Lohfink observes, this usage dropped from the vocabulary in the second century, as it increasingly became a term for only the few, including the martyrs. "To us the early Christian self-designation as 'the saints' is almost embarrassing" (Lohfink 1984, 131). In a post-Christian society, as in a pre-Christian society, the term suggests the badge of identity of a people whose Christian confession and way of life separates them from the values of the larger society. As the words "grace to you and peace" suggest, a marginalized community lives by the grace of God.

Paul's theology is nowhere more evident than in his prayers for the church. Through both thanksgiving (1:3–8) and petition (1:9–11) he indicates what is ultimately important for him. Although the word "church" does not appear in 1:3–11, Paul's major concern is the ecclesial identity of the community. The second-person plural "you," which is lost to English translations, dominates the prayer, appearing in all but one verse (1:11). Four times Paul adds emphasis with the words "all of you" (1:4, 7 [2×], 8). Paul writes neither to individuals nor to a select few but to a diverse community that includes men and women who have nothing in common but their allegiance to Christ.

Paul describes this communal consciousness twice with forms of *koinōnia* (1:5, 7), a term that was familiar to readers who would have probably associated the term with a partnership among friends. As Paul's usage throughout Philippians indicates (see 3:10; 4:14–15), the term takes on a new meaning in Christ. It is not the normal partnership between friends who choose each other but a partnership only through Jesus Christ. As Dietrich Bonhoeffer declares, "Christianity means community through Jesus Christ and in Jesus Christ. No Christian community is more or less than this. Whether it be a brief, single encounter or the daily fellowship of years, Christian community is only this. We belong to one another only through and in Jesus Christ" (1954, 21). As Paul indicates, partnership involves participating in the sufferings of Christ (cf. 3:10; 4:14), which is inseparable from partnership in his grace (1:7). It results in the warm affections (1:7–8; 4:1) within the community and the sharing of financial resources (1:5; 4:15).

The solidarity of believers is evident in the corporate formation of the community as it lives between the time when "God began a good work" among them and the conclusion, when God will bring the church to completion. It lives between the times—between the day of its birth and the final day. In the middle is the joint participation in sorrow and joy, the participation in the story of Christ. Spiritual formation is not the quest of isolated individuals but of a community that lives out a corporate narrative. The goal of the church, as Paul's prayer indicates, is to be a community that has progressed from the self-seeking manners of its culture to ever-increasing love for others.

PART 2

Philippians 1:12–26

Narratio: *The Present and Future Advance of the Gospel*

Introductory Matters

The body of the ancient letter frequently began with the disclosure formula, "I want you to know" (cf. Rom. 1:13, "I want you to know"; 2 Cor. 1:8, "I do not want you to be ignorant"). Paul adopts this formula in Phil. 1:12 to inform the readers of recent developments. "What has happened to me" (*ta kat' eme*) is an oblique way of referring to Paul's imprisonment (*desmoi*, lit. "bonds, fetters"), to which he alludes elsewhere (1:7, 13–14, 17). The Philippians have heard about his imprisonment, which, along with their own sufferings (1:28–29), is a source of anxiety. Paul indicates in 1:18–26 that he is uncertain of the outcome—that a death sentence is possible. The references to the praetorian guard (1:13) and Caesar's household (4:22) indicate his encounter with Roman power.

The letter gives no clear indication of the place or conditions of Paul's imprisonment. Prison conditions varied widely, often depending on the status of the prisoner (Wansink 1996, 41–43). Some prisons were dark dungeons, while others included the house arrest described in Acts 28:16–31. Paul's prison, like many others in the Roman world, was a holding place for those who

Figure 5. Rembrandt's depiction of Paul in prison

were awaiting trial. He probably did not suffer the worst abuses associated with imprisonment, as evidenced by his reception and sending of messengers and writing activity. Nevertheless, he was under the watchful eye of the praetorian guard (NRSV "imperial guard") and known to those of Caesar's household (4:22).

Both Acts and the letters indicate that Paul was imprisoned multiple times (Acts 16:22–24; 24–26; 28:16–31; 2 Cor. 6:5; 11:23). The references to the praetorium (*praitōrion*) and to Caesar's household (4:22) provide no clear indication, for both could have been used for Roman outposts. The term *praitōrion* is used in a variety of ways—for the governor's residence in localities such as Judea (cf. Matt. 27:27; John 18:28, 33; 19:9) or the imperial palace in Rome. In other ancient texts it refers to the body of troops which comprised the praetorian guard (cf. Lightfoot 1888, 101). The reference to "everyone else" suggests that Paul is referring to Roman soldiers rather than to a specific location. His reflections about life and death (1:20–24) suggest that Paul is in Rome awaiting the verdict on his life.

Interpreters have debated the identity of those who preach Christ from envy and rivalry and selfish ambition (1:15, 17) and those who wish to increase Paul's suffering in imprisonment (1:17). Some have identified them with the Judaizers in 3:2 or other opponents. However, the carefully balanced contrasts between those who preach from goodwill and love and those who preach out of envy, rivalry, and selfish ambition—all common vices (2:3–4; Gal. 5:19–21)—correspond to Paul's style throughout the letter. He employs contrasting models of good and bad behavior to emphasize the appropriate models (cf. 2:21–22; 3:2–3; 3:18–21) throughout the letter (cf. Davis 1999, 66). They are "brothers in the Lord" (1:14), and they "preach Christ" (1:15, 17). Thus the focus is not on the identity of the opponents but on the advance of the gospel.

In comparing the two potential outcomes of his imprisonment (1:18–26)—life or death—Paul "verges on soliloquy" (Dailea 1990; Croy 2003, 518) that is filled with echoes of ancient discussions of the topic. In the OT, Jonah cries out, "Now, O Lord, please take my life from me, for it is better for me to die than to live" (Jon. 4:3 NRSV). Both Moses (Num. 11:14–15) and Elijah (1 Kings 19:4) cry to God to take their lives (Gupta 2008, 257). The comparison of life

Public Domain/Wikimedia Commons

Figure 6. Artist's depiction of the death of Socrates

and death was a familiar theme in philosophical discussion. *Synkrisis* was a common rhetorical device in which the speaker compared either individuals or subjects, distinguishing either between the good and the bad or between the good and the better. The anthologist Stobaeus gathered sayings under the title "About Life and Death." Here Paul compares the good and the better, introducing the topic with the assurance that "Christ will be magnified" in his "body, whether through life or death" (1:20). The passage suggests his uncertainty over the outcome of his imprisonment: whether he will be executed or set free.

Paul elaborates on the way in which Christ will be magnified in 1:21–26. "To live is Christ and to die is gain" (1:21) expands on the reference to life and death in 1:20. Paul further expands this alternative, indicating that "to live is Christ" is to live in the flesh (1:22) and remain with the Philippians (1:24–26); "to die is gain" is to "depart and be with Christ" (1:23).

"To die is gain" (*kerdos*) recalls numerous sayings in antiquity in which death is a gain. Telemachus cries out at the evils in the palace of his parents, "But if you are minded even now to slay me myself with the sword, even that would I choose, and it would be better [*kerdion*] far to die than continually to behold these shameful deeds" (Homer, *Od.* 20.16, A. T. Murray, LCL). According to the collection in Stobaeus (4.53.27), "It is better to end this life than to live wickedly." Isocrates (*Archid.* 89) says, "To end this life is better than to live in dishonor."

The death of Socrates was known everywhere. Socrates says, "And if there is no consciousness, but [death] is like a sleep, when the sleeper does not even see a dream, death would be a wonderful gain" (Plato, *Apol.* 40c–d). He adds, "So if that is the sort of thing death is, I count it a gain" (Plato, *Apol.* 40e). Death is a gain because it is preferable to a hateful life (Euripides, *Medea* 145–47), a life of trouble (Euripides, *Medea* 798–99), or a life that is useless (Euripides, *Hercules furens* 1301–2). Death is a gain because it brings freedom from misery. To die in battle is a gain (Pausanias 4.7.11; cf. Josephus, *Ant.* 15.158) compared to the alternative. Death can either be a "gain" because the alternative is a life of shame or misery or because of the anticipation of future bliss (Vollenweider 1994, 248–49). While Paul employs the Greek topos on life and death, his perspective is different. Unlike the ancient writers, he does not regard death as a gain in comparison with a dishonorable or miserable life, but the choice between the good and the better.

Paul's statement, "I do not know what I will choose" (*hairēsomai*, NRSV "prefer") recalls the numerous statements in which individuals choose between life and death (Vollenweider 1994, 250), claiming that death is preferable to life. The rendering of *hairēsomai* as "choose" (ASV, RSV, NIV) corresponds to ancient Greek usage, suggesting that Paul has a decision between life and death. Some interpreters (e.g., Droge 1988, 262–86), therefore, maintain that Paul contemplates suicide. Indeed, suicide was a common choice among prisoners in antiquity (Wansink 1996, 58–59). Vollenweider cites a variety of ancient passages that use forms of *haireō* to describe a choice between life or death (1994, 250). While no evidence exists that Paul contemplated suicide, he did, however, have a choice between a rigorous defense and the passive acceptance of his death. One of the great examples of such a choice is that of Socrates, who says, "I will choose [*hairēsomai*] to die rather than to live begging meanly and thus gaining a life far less worthy in exchange for Death" (Xenophon, *Apol.* 9; cf. Plato, *Apol.* 38e, cited in Wansink 1996, 121). Similarly, the four Gospels report the trial and death of Jesus, who chose not to answer his accusers. Thus Paul's choice is likely between defending himself or living to serve others.

Paul formulates his personal preference of dying, echoing widely disseminated aphorisms that were deep in the consciousness of his contemporaries (Vollenweider 1994, 255). Using these aphorisms, he hopes to gain understanding from the Philippians and reconcile them to his death. The basic tone of the citations introduced is pessimistic: dying and death are better in comparison with pain and suffering, which darken life (Vollenweider 1994, 255). Paul does not proceed from general thought about negativity of existence but places his reflections in the shadow of the cross (Vollenweider 1994, 255). The gain of death for Paul is not simply the redemption from earthly life but life with Christ. Thus, while Paul takes up the language of his culture, he distinguishes himself from the Greeks in that he does not denigrate earthly life or flee from it (Gnilka 1968, 74).

Ancient readers would probably have heard in Paul's "desire to depart and be with Christ" (1:23) an echo of Socrates's desire to die and "be with the gods" (*Phaed.* 69c; cf. 81a). Interpreters have debated how Paul's statement is consistent with his eschatological views elsewhere. According to 1 Thess. 4:13–18, Paul anticipates the return of Christ in his own lifetime. The dead in Christ will arise and Christians who are alive will be caught up with him. Similarly, in 1 Cor. 15:50–58 he anticipates the end when all will be changed, and the perishable body will put on the imperishable. Many scholars have explained the tension between Paul's expectation in Phil. 1:23 and his hope for the return of Christ assuming that, with the delay of the parousia, Paul altered his views from the apocalyptic expectation of the end of the world to the individualized view of the future existence reflected in 2 Cor. 5:1–10 and

> **Philippians 1:12–26 in the Rhetorical Flow**
>
> *Exordium*: **Thanksgiving and prayer for moral formation (1:1–11)**
>
> ▶ *Narratio*: **The present and future advance of the gospel (1:12–26)**
>
> The advance of the gospel in the present (1:12–18a)
>
> The advance of the gospel in the future (1:18b–26)
>
> Paul's imprisonment and ultimate salvation (1:18b–20)
>
> Living and dying (1:21–24)
>
> Paul's continuing presence and the joy of faith (1:25–26)

Phil. 1:23. This would be the turning away from Jewish apocalyptic to a Greek view of the immortality of the soul. Others have suggested that Paul assumes an intermediate state of the dead before the return of Christ. However, this development in Paul's eschatology is unlikely, for Paul refers at numerous points in Philippians to the "day of Christ," using language that is consistent with the other letters (Phil. 1:6, 10; 2:16). Paul anticipates a time when God will "transform the body of our humiliation that it may be conformed to the body of his glory" (Phil. 3:21).

Jewish apocalyptic writers frequently spoke both of individual eschatology and the end of the world without demonstrating the consistency of these concepts. In the same way, Paul does not attempt to provide a detailed description of the end-time, for his concern is not to describe how the end takes place, but to affirm his hope (cf. G. Barth 1996, 339; Schapdick 2009, 33).

Tracing the Train of Thought

The Advance of the Gospel in the Present (1:12–18a)

1:12–18a. With the disclosure form **I want you to know, brothers [and sisters]** (1:12), Paul turns from his prayer for the church to his own situation as a prisoner, which was undoubtedly a cause for anxiety among the Philippians. His report has little resemblance to ancient prison letters, which described in detail the self-centeredness, suffering, and isolation of the prisoner (Bloomquist

1993, 69). Paul says little about his own situation, however, but counters their fears with the conviction that **what has happened to [him] will, to the contrary** (*mallon*, NRSV "actually"), result in "the advance [*prokopē*] of the gospel" (NRSV "helped to spread the gospel"). *Mallon* here is rendered "to the contrary" because it indicates that Paul is correcting the expectations of the Philippians. This claim would have been a surprise to the Philippians, who would have judged from appearances that the gospel was in jeopardy. *Prokopē* (advance) was used synonymously with *auxēsis* (growth), and was commonly used for the individual's advancement in knowledge or ethical sensitivity (cf. 1 Tim. 4:15). It became a technical word among the philosophers for the individual's moral advancement. It was also used for the advancement of an army (cf. Josephus, *Ant.* 3.42; 2 Macc. 8:8) and for the increase in military power (Polybius, *Hist.* 3.4.2). Among the undisputed letters of Paul, the word appears only in Phil. 1:12, 25, forming the frame for 1:12–26 and providing the essential focus for this section. The advance of the gospel evokes the image of a movement that, like an advancing army, continues to go forward. With Paul's imprisonment the gospel will reach more people than would have been possible otherwise (Giessen 2006, 232).

With the disclosure form, "I want you to know," Paul is not informing the Philippians about his imprisonment, to which he has already referred (1:7), but offering his own perspective on his suffering. This autobiographical section prepares the way for the exhortation in 1:27–2:18, as Paul describes his own attitude toward suffering before he instructs the readers on their response to suffering. In Philippians, as in other letters, autobiographical reflections precede the exhortations (cf. 1 Cor. 1:18–2:5; 2 Cor. 1:15–2:13; Gal. 1:11–21; 1 Thess. 2:1–11).

Autobiography plays an especially important role in Philippians, as Paul presents himself as a model for his readers to imitate (3:17; 4:9). Consistent with ancient rhetorical theorists, Paul knows that the appeal to his own ethos is a persuasive argument. The argument from ethos indicates that speakers exemplify what they commend to others. Thus Paul is a model of the hope and joy that sustain him. His positive evaluation of suffering prepares the way for his instruction urging them to accept the suffering that necessarily accompanies faith (Wojtkowiak 2012, 270).

As the *inclusio* in 1:12, 25 indicates, Paul's focus is the **advance** (*prokopē*) **of the gospel** (1:12) and the Philippians' "advance and joy of faith" (1:25). Paul delineates this assurance of advancement in two ways. In 1:12–18a he speaks of recent events and their impact on the present, concluding his thought with **in this I rejoice**. In 1:18b–26 he turns to the future tense, introducing his thought with "I will continue to rejoice" (1:18b). Thus Paul employs a rhetorical strategy that was well known in antiquity by interpreting every negative fact in a positive way (Vos 2005, 279–81). Like military leaders who instilled courage in the midst of desperate conditions by claiming that the other side was in retreat, Paul argues that the gospel is advancing, with the difference that Paul is confident of ultimate victory. He looks to recent events and concludes with thoughts on the future as a response to the Philippians' fears for the future. He is sure that recent events are evidence not of the failure of the gospel but of its advance in both the present and the future. Despite current appearances, the advance of the gospel is already taking place.

Paul offers evidence that his imprisonment will result rather in the advance of the gospel (1:12). In the first place, his **bonds have become known throughout the whole praetorian guard** (1:13). This hyperbole suggests that, by Paul's imprisonment, Roman authorities have become aware of his mission. He does not mention the success of this public awareness but says only that his bonds have become manifest. **All of the others** probably refers to the wider circles around the praetorian guard. Thus the advance of the gospel is the spread of the word even among Roman authorities.

The advance of the gospel is further evidenced in the fact that **most of the brothers [and sisters] in the Lord have been persuaded** by Paul's **bonds to speak the word of God without fear** (1:14). Paul's imprisonment has given them the courage to speak and to follow his example. To speak the word of God (1:14) is the equivalent of preaching Christ (1:15) or proclaiming Christ (1:17–18). What follows is a reflection on the motives from which they preach. Paul neither names anyone nor indicates that their preaching is false. In fact, he offers this as an example of the advance of the gospel. In a chiastic manner (*ABBA*), Paul reflects on those who proclaim the gospel.

A   **Some preach Christ because of envy** (*phthonos*) **and strife** (*eris*),
  B   **while others preach from goodwill** (*eudokia*),
  B′   **Some preach from love, knowing that I am destined for the defense of the gospel,**
A′   **Others preach Christ from selfish ambition** (*eritheia*), **not sincerely, thinking that they will add affliction in my chains.**

The description corresponds to the vices and virtues that Paul frequently contrasts (cf. Gal. 5:19–23; Phil. 2:3–4). His hortatory strategy throughout Philippians is to describe contrasting models of behavior, hoping that his readers will choose the appropriate behavior (3:2–3, 17–21). Envy (*phthonos*) is among the vices that Paul lists in Rom. 1:29 as characteristic of unrighteous humanity, and it is a vice to be put away as one of the works of the flesh (Gal. 5:21; cf. also 1 Tim. 6:4; Titus 3:3; 1 Pet. 2:1). Strife (*eris*) is also among the vices of unrighteous humanity (Rom. 1:29) and appears frequently in Paul's vice lists (Rom. 13:13; 2 Cor. 12:20; Gal. 5:20; cf. 1 Tim. 6:4; Titus 3:9). The term was used in Greek literature for political strife and is frequently used with lists of synonyms (LSJ 689). Selfish ambition (*eritheia*) appears in 2 Cor. 12:20. Except for two references in Aristotle (*Pol.* 5.3.1302b4, 1303a4), where it is used for the self-seeking pursuit of political office, it is unknown in Greek prior to Paul (*TLNT* 1:70) but is commonplace in Pauline ethical instruction (2 Cor. 12:20; Phil. 1:17; 2:3; cf. James 3:14). In Philippians these vices are not compatible with the mind of Christ (Phil. 2:3–5). Love is the predominant ethical value (1:9–11; cf. 2:1). *Eudokia* here is parallel to love (cf. God's goodwill in 2:13; God's goodwill in Eph. 1:5, 9; human goodwill in 2 Thess. 1:11). Paul does not refer to a false teaching but mentions only motives. Ambitious people with impure motives (*ouch hagnōs*, NRSV "not sincerely") suppose that they will increase Paul's suffering in his chains (NRSV "imprisonment"). However, as Paul indicates, they are mistaken in their assumption, for the end result of his imprisonment is that **Christ is preached** (1:18a). Thus the advance of the gospel is seen not in the results of the preaching but in the gospel's now becoming known to Roman power and the broader public.

Despite his imprisonment, Paul rejoices (see also 1:4; 2:2, 17; 4:1 for Paul's rejoicing) because of the advance of the gospel. As he indicates to the Corinthians, he experiences joy in his afflictions (2 Cor. 7:4; cf. Col. 1:24), and he can rejoice when he is weak (2 Cor. 13:9) when he receives good news of the progress of his churches (2 Cor. 2:3; 7:7, 13; 1 Thess. 2:19; 3:9; Philem. 7), his "joy and crown" (Phil. 4:1; 1 Thess. 2:19). This should be an encouragement for the Philippians (Böttrich 2004, 99) and an example to emulate (cf. 2:1–4). Paul is not defeated by his imprisonment or by people who preach with bad motives.

The Advance of the Gospel in the Future (1:18b–26)

1:18b–20. *Paul's imprisonment and ultimate salvation.* Paul turns from the recent events that have made him rejoice in 1:12–18a to his anticipation of future rejoicing in 1:18b–26 as he moves from "I rejoice" in 1:18a to "I will continue to rejoice" in 1:18b, introducing the future tense that dominates 1:18b–26. The basis for this joy, as the explanatory **for** (*gar*, v. 19) indicates, is his knowledge (**I know**) about the future that is based on what God has done in the past. Just as he is confident that God will complete his work among the Philippians (1:6), he knows that **this** (i.e., his imprisonment) will result in **salvation**. The salvation is not release from prison but the triumph of the gospel, which is advancing through his present circumstances. Paul elaborates on this salvation in 1:18b–20, which is a single sentence in Greek.

Two prepositional modifiers clarify Paul's reason for rejoicing. First, he indicates the means of this favorable outcome: **through** (*dia*) their **petition** (*deēseōs*) **and the supply of the Spirit of Jesus Christ.** The community reciprocates Paul's petition (*deēsis*, 1:4) with their own prayers, and they receive the supply (*epichorēgias*, NRSV "help") of the Spirit of Jesus Christ. In both Greek and English, the supply of the Spirit is ambiguous, since it can either mean "the supply, which is the Spirit" (objective genitive) or "the supply that comes from the Holy Spirit" (subjective genitive). The parallel in Gal. 3:5 ("The one who supplies [*epichorēgōn*] you with the Spirit"; cf. Eph. 4:16; Col. 2:19;

2 Cor. 9:10) indicates that the supply of the Spirit is the Spirit himself (objective genitive) rather than the supply that the Spirit gives (Bockmuehl 1998, 84). In secular Greek the term *epichorēgia* is used for generous public service (BDAG 387) or a husband's support for his wife (cf. *1 Clem.* 38.2; MM 251). Only here does Paul speak of the Spirit of Jesus Christ, which is equivalent to references elsewhere to the Spirit (Rom. 8:4–5; Gal. 3:5; 5:22, 25), Spirit of God (Rom. 8:9), Spirit of Christ (Rom. 8:9), and Holy Spirit (1 Thess. 4:8).

The second prepositional phrase indicates that what Paul knows (cf. 1:25) is not an expression of his calculation (Gnilka 1968, 65) but is **according to** (*kata*) **his eager expectation and hope.** Eager expectation (*apokaradokia*) is linked with hope in its only other appearance in the NT. In Rom. 8:18–29 Paul describes the "eager expectation" of the creation and the hope in which believers live (cf. H. Balz, *EDNT* 1:132). Together the two words suggest the intensity of Paul's expectation, which is a positive model for the Philippians as they worry about the future.

The confidence that "this will result in salvation" is an echo of Job 13:16, to which Paul alludes without indicating that he is citing Scripture. Paul's imprisonment probably caused him to identify with Job. Both Job and Paul have confidence in the future salvation (*sōtēria*). Job anticipates *sōtēria* from illness and death, while for Paul the *sōtēria* is the ultimate triumph of God when Christ, the Savior (*sōtēr*), returns (cf. 3:21).

Parallel expressions **I will not be ashamed** and **Christ will be magnified in my body, whether in life or death** (1:20) express the future hope in language derived from the Psalms. The psalmist cries, "Do not let those who wait for you be put to shame; let them be ashamed who are wantonly treacherous" (Ps. 24:3 LXX [25:3 NRSV]). According to Isa. 28:16 (cf. Rom. 9:33), "those who believe in him will not be put to shame." Paul uses the terminology of shame in Rom. 5:5, "Hope is not ashamed, because the love of God has been poured into our hearts." Shame is not a sense of guilt but, as in the Psalms, the failure to reach the goal (Gupta 2008, 26). Used as an antonym four times in Paul is *kauchaomai*. When Paul boasts to Titus of the church at Corinth, he is not put to shame (2 Cor. 7:14; A. Horstmann, *EDNT* 2:258); when he boasts to the Macedonians of their goodwill in the collection, he does not want to be put to shame (2 Cor. 9:4). His ultimate boast will occur when he presents his people blameless before God (cf. 2:16; 2 Cor. 1:14; 1 Thess. 2:19).

Paul knew the OT expression "Let the Lord be magnified" (*megalynthētō ho kyrios*). The psalmist says,

> Let all those who rejoice in my calamity
>   be put to shame and confusion;
> let those who exalt themselves against me
>   be clothed with shame and dishonor.

> Let those who desire my vindication
>   shout for joy and be glad,
>   and say evermore,
> "Great is the LORD,
>   who delights in the welfare of his servant."
>   (Ps. 35:26–27 NRSV [34:26–27 LXX])

The people say, "May those who love your salvation / say continually, 'Great is the LORD!'" (40:16 NRSV [39:17 LXX]; cf. 69:30 [68:31 LXX]: "I will magnify him in praise"). Paul says to the Corinthians that God has shamed the wise so that they cannot boast before him (1 Cor. 1:27–29). For Paul, the words of the psalm become a reality in the preaching of Christ, which will occur **in all boldness** (*en pasē parrhēsia*, 1:20). As other passages in the NT indicate, *parrhēsia* is the absence of concealment (cf. 2 Cor. 3:2) and the courage to speak unpopular words to people in power (Acts 2:29; 4:13, 29; cf. 1 Thess. 2:2).

The future hope and Paul's present ministry are intertwined. When Paul declares that Christ will be magnified **now and always** (1:20), he speaks both of his present circumstances and the future hope. That Christ is magnified in his body, even in the context of suffering, is a theme elsewhere (cf. 2 Cor. 4:10–11, 16–18). The ultimate salvation is when Christ is magnified in the life beyond death.

1:21–24. *Living and dying.* Mention of life or death leads Paul to reflect on life and death in 1:21–24. Here he employs motifs that were common in Hellenistic literature. We observe the contrasts:

life or death (1:20)

to live . . . to die (1:21)

to live in the flesh . . . remain in the flesh (1:22, 24) . . . **depart and be with Christ** (1:23)

"To live" in verse 21 is "to live in the flesh" (v. 22) and "remain in the flesh" (v. 24). To die (vv. 20–21) is "to depart and be with Christ" (v. 23). While Paul echoes Greek reflections on life and death (see under "Introductory Matters"), he does not share the Greek view that death is desirable because it brings an end to an unbearable existence. Nor does he compare the evils of life with the good of death. Instead, he compares the good with what is **better**, which is an increase in what he has already experienced (Gnilka 1968, 71).

To live is Christ is an epigrammatic way of expanding on the claim that Christ is magnified in his body, whether in life or death, for Christ is the orientation point of his life. The image recalls his statement, "I have been crucified with Christ, . . . and the life that I live in the flesh I live in faith in the Son of God" (Gal. 2:19–20). In Philippians he speaks of sharing in the afflictions of Christ (Phil. 3:10) and of discarding all achievements for the sake of Christ.

In the phrase **to die is gain** (*kerdos*), Paul employs the commercial image in anticipation of 3:7–10. Having lost all that he had achieved, the ultimate **gain** is to depart and be with Christ (Giessen 2006, 215).

After describing the two options of life and death (1:20–21), Paul comments on each of them in 1:22–25, elaborating on the first option (to live) with the phrase "to live in the flesh" (1:22). A debate on the syntax and punctuation of 1:22 is reflected in the translations:

> But what if my living on in the body may serve some good purpose?
> Which then am I to choose? (NEB)

> If I am to live in the flesh, that means fruitful labor for me;
> and I do not know which I prefer. (NRSV)

> If I am going to go on living in the body, this will mean fruitful labor for me.
> Yet what shall I choose? I do not know! (NIV)

> If it is to be life in the flesh, that means fruitful labor for me.
> Yet which I shall choose I cannot tell. (RSV)

> If I am to live in the flesh, that means fruitful labor for me.
> Yet which I shall choose I cannot tell. (ESV)

Because of the comparison of life and death, the reader expects the conditional clause, **If I am to live in the flesh** (1:22 [protasis]) to be followed by a *then* clause (apodosis). The logic of Paul's argument suggests that he should continue with a comparison to the benefits of dying (i.e., "if I am to die"; cf. Bockmuehl 1998, 90). Instead, he breaks off the comparison in 1:22, exclaiming, **I do not know what I shall choose**, elaborating on the choice in 1:23. The benefit of his life in the flesh is **fruitful labor** (*karpos ergou*). *Karpos* (lit. "fruit") is the term for ethical conduct (cf. 1:11; Gal. 5:22; Rom. 6:19, 22) and also a term for the results of Paul's ministry (Rom. 1:13). Thus Paul envisions continued missionary effectiveness if he remains in the flesh.

The passage also has other puzzling issues of translation. The translation of *hairēsomai*, rendered "choose" in the NIV and RSV and "prefer" in the NRSV, is a question inasmuch as interpreters conclude that Paul has no choice in the matter. However, the most common meaning of *hairēsomai* is *choose*, a term that Paul has selected for rhetorical reasons, suggesting that he patterns himself after the preexistent Christ, who chose to empty himself (2:7; see under "Introductory Matters"). Although the term *gnōrizō* normally means "make known" in Paul (see Rom. 9:22–23; 1 Cor. 12:3; 15:1; 2 Cor. 8:1; Gal. 1:11; Phil. 4:6) rather than "know" (BDAG 203), here Paul is using the term in the classical sense to indicate that he does "not know" what he will choose (note the translations above).

Paul's difficult choice is stated in 1:23. **I am hard pressed** (*synechō*) between the two options. In its literal sense the verb *synechō* refers to people, diseases, or powers that "press hard and leave little room for movement" (BDAG 971; cf. Matt. 4:24; Luke 8:37, 45; 19:43; Acts 28:8). According to 2 Cor. 5:14, the love of Christ compels (*synechei*) Paul to proclaim the message. In Phil. 1:23 Paul is hard pressed between the choice of life and death. The decision is not between good and bad but between what is **better** (*kreisson*) for Paul and what is more necessary (*anankaioteron*) for the church (Gnilka 1968, 73): to depart and be with Christ or to remain in the flesh (v. 24).

The image of a departure (*analysis*) as a euphemism for death is commonplace in Greek literature. The literal meaning "untie" or "loosen" was a metaphor drawn from the ships that were set loose from their moorings (LSJ 112). The image is used in 2 Tim. 4:6 for Paul's departure from life, suggesting that death is a journey (cf. Tob. 3:6 BA). While Paul employs an image that appears frequently in Greek and Roman literature (Plato, *Phaed.* 67a; Epictetus, *Diatr.* 1.9.16; Cicero, *Tusc.* 1.74), he does not accept the ancient idea of the soul's departure from the imprisonment in the body (Gnilka 1968, 73) that is associated with this image. Paul neither elaborates on the details of being with Christ after his death nor indicates how this expectation coheres with his references to the day of Christ (1:6, 10; 2:16) when the Savior returns (3:20–21), for his primary concern is pastoral and rhetorical (see under "Introductory Matters"). He is a model for the Philippians, who are threatened with the possibility of death for the sake of Christ. In keeping with his exhortations to think of others more than oneself (e.g., 2:4), Paul indicates that his choice is for their sakes (1:24, *di' hymas*). That is, he recalls the story of Christ in 2:6–11, knowing that Christ gave himself for others. As one who chooses to remain with the Philippians, he exemplifies the life that does not look to its own interests but to the interests of others as he places the interests of the Philippian church above his own. Thus Paul will imitate Christ and serve as a model for the Philippians (Engberg-Pedersen 1995, 275).

1:25–26. *Paul's continuing presence and the joy of faith.* Paul elaborates on how his continued existence in the flesh is "more necessary" (1:24) for the Philippians. It is the basis of a conviction about God's ultimate purposes. **Being persuaded of this** (*touto pepoithōs*), **I know** recalls the earlier statement, "being persuaded of this very thing, that the one who began a good work among you will bring it to completion" (1:6) and the affirmation, "I know that this will turn out for salvation" (1:19). Thus Paul is persuaded because of his faith that God is bringing the church to completion. Indeed, the focus is not on Paul, but on the community, as the predominance of the second-person plural indicates. Paul's continued existence in the flesh is more necessary "for you" (1:24); consequently he will "remain with all of you" for **your advancement and joy of faith** (1:24). That is, the benefit to the church is of ultimate importance for Paul, who demonstrates his cruciform love (Gorman 2001,

211). Because God is bringing the church to completion, Paul's continued ministry is necessary. In a play on words, Paul promises, **I will remain** (*menō*) and **I will continue** (*paramenō*) **with all of you**, indicating that he will both live and be present with this church. In mentioning all (cf. 1:3), he emphasizes the unity of the community. Because the community has not yet reached its goal (cf. 1:6), their "advancement [*prokopē*] and joy in faith" requires his continuing presence. At the beginning of this section (1:12), Paul affirms that his imprisonment serves the advance (*prokopē*) of the gospel, and now he concludes with a focus on the advance of the community. *Prokopē* is not the progress of the individual, as it is among the Stoics, but the formation of the community, about which Paul prays in 1:9–11 and to which he gives the ethical instructions that follow (1:27–2:18; 4:1–9). The joy in faith, a major topic in the letter (see 2:18; 3:1; 4:4) and a critical dimension of formation, is a reality for those who look beyond present circumstances to the triumph of God.

In view of the uncertainty about his fate that he expresses in 1:18b–24, Paul's confidence is surprising. If his more immediate purpose is the advancement and joy of their faith (1:25), his ultimate aim is that their **boast** (*kauchēma*) **may increase in Christ Jesus** through Paul's presence. This boasting does not have the negative connotations present elsewhere (cf. Rom. 3:27; 4:2; 2 Cor. 10:13; 11:12, 16, 18) but has the positive significance derived from Jeremiah, according to which the believer "boasts in the Lord" (Jer. 9:24; cf. Rom. 5:2–3, 11; 1 Cor. 1:31; 2 Cor. 10:17). Paul's ultimate ambition is that his churches will be his boast at the end (2:16; cf. 2 Cor. 1:14; 1 Thess. 2:19), and he hopes that his churches will boast in Christ through his presence.

Theological Issues

The transition from Paul's prayer for the Philippians (1:3–11) to the news of his situation (1:12–26) is not a break in the argument but an expression of confidence that no obstacles—neither the imprisonment of the leader nor the preaching by people who have impure motives—can prevent the completion of God's work. As the *inclusio* of *prokopē* (1:12, 25) indicates, the progress is twofold. It occurs in the continued preaching of the gospel (1:12–18) and in their continued formation (1:25; cf. 1:6). Paul's hopeful outlook is a demonstration of the *phronēsis*—the disposition and way of seeing the world—that he hopes to instill in the Philippians. Paul hopes that his perception of his own circumstances will be a model for their response to their own suffering.

Paul assures ancient and modern readers that the progress of the gospel does not depend on having ideal conditions. As Tertullian observed the impact of persecution on the Christian movement, he declared, "We become more numerous every time we are hewn down by you: the blood of Christians is seed" (Tertullian, *Apol.* 50). Kierkegaard observed the opposite situation in

The Donatists

The Donatists broke away from the church in North Africa in protest against the presence of clerics who had betrayed their faith during persecution in 303–305. Insisting on the purity of the church, they considered any sacraments administered by a cleric in a state of sin to be invalid.

a Christian society, complaining that a Christian society trivializes any sense of discipleship (Kierkegaard 1944, 127; cf. Migliore 2014, 47). While Christian faith declines in the context of economic prosperity in Europe and North America, it grows under oppressive governments and conditions of extreme poverty in Asia and the global South.

Paul is confident that the progress of the gospel does not depend on the purity of the proclaimers. Since the Donatist controversy of the fourth and fifth centuries, believers have debated whether the power of the gospel depends on the purity of the proclaimer. Anticipating the outcome of the later debate, Paul's joy that "Christ is preached," even by those whose motives are impure, is a reminder that God works not only through ideal proclaimers but also through those who are weak or have mixed motives.

In his declaration that the progress of the gospel can occur whether he lives or dies, Paul presents one of the earliest reflections on a Christian view of death. He does not welcome death because of the misery of life, as some ancient people did, but because he participates in the story of Christ that progresses from death to life. To die is to continue to be "with Christ." In his attitude toward death (1:20–26), Paul is a model both for the Philippians and for contemporary believers, both of whom may be shaped by the attitudes of the surrounding culture. Paul challenges a culture that denies death and employs technology to extend life indefinitely with his confidence that death is a gain for those who trust God.

Paul's desire to depart and be with Christ has puzzled interpreters who have questioned how this hope is consistent with his frequent references to the final day (1:6, 10; cf. 3:20–21). Paul is not concerned to answer questions about the time of the end or the intermediate state of the dead, but to express a confident expectation of the end result when God's work will be complete. For Paul, as for Jesus (see Mark 13:32), the time of the end is not the major concern. What matters is faithful living until the end (cf. Migliore 2014, 61).

PART 3

Philippians 1:27–30

Propositio: *Citizens United in an Alternative Commonwealth*

Introductory Matters

In 1:27–2:18 Paul turns from "the things about me" (1:12) to the "things about you" (1:27)—from questions about his presence or absence (1:25–26) to their conduct, whether he is present or absent (1:27). In the imperative "live your life in a manner worthy of the gospel" (1:27 NRSV), Paul employs a verb that he uses nowhere else in his letter. His most common verb for ethical conduct is *peripatein* (lit. "walk around"), a term drawn from Jewish ethical discourse (cf. Rom. 6:4; 8:4; 13:13; 1 Cor. 3:3; 7:17; Gal. 5:16; Phil. 3:17; Col. 2:6; 4:5; 1 Thess. 4:1, 12). Here, however, he employs the verb *politeuesthai*, which is drawn from political life and means literally "conduct yourselves as citizens" (U. Hutter, *EDNT* 3:130) or "administer a government." It is used for someone who lives according to the norms of the *polis*. The verb anticipates the noun *politeuma* (3:20), which indicates that the community's citizenship (*politeuma*) is in heaven.

A *politeuma* is a community or civic body or political entity; the word is frequently used for citizens of the same place in the midst of a foreign state (*TLNT* 3:130). Josephus speaks of the Jewish *politeuma* of Cyrenaica and

Antioch (*Ant.* 12.28–33; *J.W.* 7.441), and the *Letter of Aristeas* (310) speaks of the "delegation of the *politeuma* of Alexandrian Jews (cf. Philo, *Flacc.* 74–80; *Legat.* 194; *TLNT* 3:131). It often refers to a colony of foreigners or relocated veterans. This term, used only in Philippians, may suggest that believers, living in the Roman colony of Philippi, are colonists in an alternative commonwealth (Geoffrion 1999, 43).

While Paul probably chose the verb *politeuesthai* and the noun *politeuma* because the Philippians lived in a Roman colony where the image would resonate, he employed metaphors that also had a significant history in Hellenistic Judaism. Philo spoke of the heavenly *politeuma*, in which the righteous are citizens. Joseph says, "I am not a slave, but as highly-born as any, one who claims enrollment among the citizens of that best and greatest state [*politeuma*], this world" (*Jos.* 69). The Jews are "enrolled in the greatest and most perfect commonwealth [*politeuma*]" (*Opif.* 144). Philo speaks of two kinds of cities—one based on justice and the other based on injustice. Good people are enrolled in the former type of state (*politeuma*), while the evil are enrolled where injustice prevails (*Conf.* 109).

Philo uses the verb to describe rulers who conduct government (*politeuomenois*) as they should (*Flacc.* 81) or live according to the standards of their commonwealth. He claims that, for the wise, the heavenly regions, where their citizenship is (*ton ouranion chōron en hō politeuontai*), is their native land (*Conf.* 77–78; cf. *Agr.* 81) and that Moses gave laws to direct their civic life (*politeusontai*, *Decal.* 14). "With such instructions he tamed and softened the minds of the citizens of his commonwealth [*politeuomenōn*] and set them out of the reach of pride and arrogance" (*Virt.* 161). He speaks of the law (*Spec. Leg.* 4.226), declaring, "Indeed so great a love of justice does the law instill into those who live under its constitution [*politeuomenois*] that it does not even permit the fertile soil of a hostile city to be outraged by devastation or by cutting down trees to destroy the fruits." He speaks of living "with our fellow citizens [*politeusasthai*] in peace and law observance" (*Mut. Nom.* 240). Elsewhere he says that the law is accepted "by those who enjoy their citizenship" (*politeuomenōn*, *Prob.* 47; cf. *Conf.* 109).

A *politeuma* has its own laws and obligations. The image played an important role in Jewish consciousness. To be citizens of a *politeuma* is to be involved in a certain way of life corresponding to the *politeuma* of which one is a part (*TLNT* 3:131). Thus Paul's imperative *politeuesthe* means literally "engage in public life" or "live out your citizenship." To live one's life by the standards of the alternative commonwealth is to come into conflict with the way of life of the majority culture. As the Maccabean literature indicates, those who conduct themselves according to the laws of an alternative state run into conflict with the dominant state. According to 2 Maccabees, "the king sent an Athenian senator to compel the Jews to forsake the laws of their ancestors and no longer to live by the laws [*mē politeuesthai*] of God" (6:1

NRSV). King Antiochus V writes to Lysias, having heard that the Jews have not adopted Greek customs, requesting that the Jews be allowed to "live according to the customs [*politeuesthai*] of their ancestors" (2 Macc. 11:25 NRSV). Earlier, when Antiochus IV urged the Jews to eat pork, Eleazar replied, "We, O Antiochus, who have been persuaded to govern our lives [*politeuesthai*] by the divine law, think that there is no compulsion more powerful than our obedience to the law" (4 Macc. 5:16 NRSV). This usage occurs in Paul's speech before the Sanhedrin, when he says, "I have lived my life [*pepoliteumai*] with a clear conscience before God" (Acts 23:1 NRSV).

For Roman authorities, Paul's instruction, "Live out your citizenship worthily of the gospel," would have been a revolutionary demand (Pilhofer 1995, 137), suggesting the disloyalty of people who were expected to live "worthily" of the Roman state. The residents of a Roman colony recognized the importance of living worthily (*axiōs*) of their citizenship. Peter Pilhofer (1995, 137) offers examples from epigraphic sources for the use of *axiōs* to describe the responsibilities of the citizens of a state. In an inscription from Gazoros (about 50 km from Philippi) are the words "worthy of the king and the citizens" (*axiōs tou te basileōs kai tōn politōn*; cf. Wojtkowiak 2012, 128). From other regions he finds the words *axiōs tēs hēmeteras poleōs* ("worthy of our city"; Pilhofer 1995, 137; *IG* IV 7, 387, line 6). Thus Paul employs common usage to describe the life worthy of a city. To live worthily of the gospel was, therefore, the alternative to the life worthy of the Roman colony of Philippi. Their norms are not those of the Roman state, according to which they once conducted themselves, but those of the alternative commonwealth (Wojtkowiak 2012, 129). This alternative way of life brought believers inevitably in conflict with Romans, who required that they live "worthily of the colony" of Rome.

This conflict is reflected in the description of the obligations of citizenship in 1:27–30, which has a concentration of terms reflecting a community engaged in a difficult struggle. Images drawn from athletics (*agōn*, 1:30) were commonly employed to describe the personal struggle of the individual, military conflict, and the struggle of those who were persecuted. Paul's imagery may be compared to Philo's description of instruction in the law (*Praem.* 4), "Having schooled the citizens of his polity [*tous politeuomenous*] with gentle instructions and exhortations . . . they advanced into the sacred arena and showed the spirit in which they would act bared ready for the contest [*agōn*]." He adds (*Praem.* 5) that it was found that the true athletes of virtue did not disappoint the high hopes of the laws that had trained them. For Philo, as for Paul, those who receive instruction in good citizenship in God's commonwealth enter the arena and engage in the contest (*agōn*).

Paul employs athletic images that were used metaphorically in antiquity for the struggle. The purpose clause "that you stand firm" (*hoti stēkete*) is a military image for the unit that forms a line together in the face of the enemy in contrast to those who flee in the presence of opposition (Geoffrion 1999, 55). Paul uses

Early Criticism of Christians

Minucius Felix, a third-century apologist, complained about Christians:

"You do not go to our shows, you take no part in our processions, you are not present at our public banquets, you shrink in horror from our sacred games." (Octavius 12)

the term always in the imperative (see 1 Cor. 16:13; Gal. 5:1; Phil. 4:1), commonly indicating that one stands firm in the midst of opposition.

Two participial phrases provide the positive and negative dimensions of standing firm. "Striving side by side with one mind in the faith of the gospel" (1:27) is the positive aspect. "Striving side by side" (*synathlēsan*) is an athletic image that Paul employs again in 4:3 but nowhere else in his correspondence. The related athletic image is found in Heb. 10:32 for the "hard struggle" against opposition that the readers had endured. Philosophers employed the image for the struggle for self-mastery. Paul's imagery is probably derived from the portrayals of the martyrs in the Maccabean literature.

The negative side of standing firm is not to be intimidated by the opponents (*antikeimenoi*). Paul nowhere else uses the verb *ptyromai*, a word that was commonly used for the frightening of horses in the midst of battle (LSJ 1549). As the language of martyrdom suggests, the opponents are not believers (i.e., the opponents of 3:2) but the local populace, who are now persecuting believers. They are probably the same as those who abused Paul when he was in Philippi (1 Thess. 2:2). Like the Thessalonians, the Philippians share in various forms of persecution (cf. 1 Thess. 1:6; 3:3). Indeed, Acts probably reflects accurately the common charges against Christians: "These men are disturbing our city; they are Jews and are advocating customs that are not lawful for us as Romans to adopt or observe" (Acts 16:21 NRSV). Believers who live out their citizenship in another *politeuma* inevitably come into conflict with the local government. As Paul indicates, the surrounding society is "a crooked and perverse generation" (Phil. 2:15). As in Paul's other churches, the believers face persecution in their local communities (cf. 1 Thess. 3:2–5) as the consequence of their alternative way of life (De Vos 1997, 263).

Because citizens are expected to conduct themselves worthily of their citizenship, that is, to conform to the norms of their *politeuma*, Paul instructs those whose commonwealth is in heaven to live worthily of the gospel. Elsewhere he challenges readers to live worthily of God (1 Thess. 2:12; cf. Eph. 4:1; Col. 1:10). Here the good news has its own norms, which Paul will describe in 1:27–2:18; 4:1–9. These norms have already been alluded to in 1:9–11. Whether he is present or absent alludes to the two possibilities that he has mentioned in 1:23–24.

Paul is probably recalling the Maccabean literature, in which the martyrs were the noble athletes. The image is developed at length in 4 Maccabees when the author describes the torture and persecution of the martyrs in athletic terms: "The tyrant was the antagonist, and the world and the human race were the spectators" (17:14 NRSV). God gave the crown to the noble athletes (17:15–16). This image continues among the Apostolic Fathers to describe martyrdom (Ign. *Pol.* 1.3; 3.1; *1 Clem.* 5.1).

Peter Oakes (2001, 89–95) has described the various ways that the local church was marginalized and persecuted by the local populace. Withdrawal from the emperor cult could cause social and economic consequences. Alienation from families undoubtedly also played a role, as it did elsewhere in the early churches. Pilhofer indicates also that the international character of these communities was perceived as a threat to Roman order (1995, 137). While the cults in

> **Philippians 1:27–30 in the Rhetorical Flow**
>
> *Exordium*: Thanksgiving and prayer for moral formation (1:1–11)
>
> *Narratio*: The present and future advance of the gospel (1:12–26)
>
> ▶ *Propositio*: Citizens united in an alternative commonwealth (1:27–30)

Philippi were local in nature, the Philippian church was connected to other communities throughout the empire. Although Paul gives no indication of arrests or incarceration in the city, the members were the subject of ostracism and various forms of harassment, even sporadic violence (Oakes 2001, 106–7). The statement that "it has been granted to you not only to believe, but also to suffer" (1:28) indicates the reality of persecution in Philippi.

Paul assumes that the readers will share in his sufferings as he participates in the sufferings of Christ (2 Cor. 1:5–7; Phil. 3:10). In his catechetical instruction to new converts, he indicates that "we are destined" for suffering (1 Thess. 3:3). As Phil. 1:28–30 indicates, to imitate Paul is to imitate him in suffering.

The parallel phrases "in one spirit" and "in one soul" (1:27) and the compound *synathlountes* ("striving side by side") indicate the solidarity of the community as it engages in the difficult struggle. Paul conjures up the notion of soldiers standing side by side, ready to face the opponent as a single unit (Geoffrion 1999, 62) as the natural component of standing firm.

The focus on unity raises the question about the presence of division within the church. Paul refers later to the conflict between Euodia and Syntyche (Phil. 4:2–3). Some interpreters have suggested that the outward threats are the source of division within the church, maintaining that some wish to accommodate to the larger society, while others choose to be a direct challenge to the larger society (cf. Peterlin 1995, 55). However, the call for unity is not occasioned by division within the community but is the obvious necessity for a community that faces an external threat.

Tracing the Train of Thought

1:27–30. The thanksgiving (1:3–11) and the autobiographical reflection (1:12–26) lay the foundation for the letter's *propositio* (1:27–30), the basic thesis of this letter of encouragement. Having prayed for their moral formation (1:9–11) and offered his own example (1:12–26) of faithfulness in the midst of suffering, Paul instructs his community to **live out your citizenship** in the heavenly commonwealth **worthily of the gospel** (1:27). The *propositio* in 1:27–30 is one compound sentence in Greek. Paul elaborates on the main clause "live out your citizenship" (1:27) with two participial phrases, giving the positive and negative dimensions of this existence (**contending together . . . not being intimidated by the adversaries** [1:27–28]) and a theological reason for this conduct (**For** [*hoti*] **it has been graciously granted you the privilege not only of believing, but also of suffering for him as well** [1:29]). As the *propositio* indicates, living out the heavenly citizenship brings conflict with the citizens of the Roman commonwealth. Paul elaborates on this conduct in 2:1–18.

Paul's use of the verb *politeuesthai* rather than the usual *peripatein* to describe ethical behavior is no coincidence. He elaborates on the norms for this new existence in the remainder of the letter. The gospel is the narrative of Christ described in 2:6–11. Thus the life worthy of the gospel conforms to this narrative.

Only (*monon*, 1:27) focuses the attention on the most urgent matter in this difficult situation, indicating that "only this matter is important" (Landmesser 1997, 554). The image of an army closing ranks, standing **in one spirit** and contending together **with one soul** (*mia psychē*) introduces the theme of unity that will dominate the letter (Krentz 1993, 120). A breaking in the ranks or panic among some would be devastating for the community. The specific content of this behavior is introduced by **so that**, which is then interrupted by the parenthetical statement, **whether I come to see you or am absent**, a continuation of the presence-absence theme of 1:23–24. Paul hopes **to hear** that they **stand firm** in one Spirit, and elaborates on this with two participial phrases: "contending together in one spirit . . . and not being intimidated by the adversary" (1:27–28). The images suggest the severe struggle that the church faces against opposition. Paul regularly uses the verb *stēkō* (stand firm) in the imperative (1 Cor. 16:13; Gal. 5:1; Phil. 4:1; 1 Thess. 3:8). The verb normally refers to standing firm in the midst of a threat (Gnilka 1968, 99; Krentz 1993, 120). Interpreters debate whether "one spirit" refers to the human spirit and is parallel to "one soul" (NRSV "one mind"). However, "one spirit" is also used elsewhere for the Holy Spirit (1 Cor. 12:13). Paul also speaks of the "help of the Spirit" (1:19) and the "sharing in the Spirit" (2:1) Thus he probably describes the need to stand firm in the Holy Spirit, the source of strength for the distressed community. This unity in the community will be the result of Paul's prayer that they love each other more and more (1:9–11). Paul elaborates on this conduct in 2:1–5, describing the "sharing of the Spirit" (2:1) and the "one mind" (2:2, 5) in which no one behaves from selfish ambition.

Interpreters have recognized in Paul's words the echoes of the ancient conversations on friendship (Fitzgerald 1996, 144). According to Aristotle, friends are of "one soul" (*mia psychē, Eth. nic.* 9.8.2). Friends are so similar that they are two bodies sharing one soul (Diogenes Laertius, *Lives* 5.20). Paul encourages believers to meet this challenge by striving with one mind (*mia psychē,* lit. "one soul"). Luke describes the ideal community as "one soul" (Acts 4:32), and Paul challenges the Philippians (2:2) to be "souls together" (NRSV "being in full accord," *sympsychoi*). The church meets the challenge with unity.

Greeks and Romans could not conceive of friendship without the presence of enemies (Stowers 1991, 113). In the Greco-Roman social system, there were no neutral parties, for friends shared not only their possessions and time together but also their enemies. Thus for the Philippians, the threats from opponents necessitated that the believers come together as friends. However, they are more than friends, for they are a new family of brothers and sisters.

Paul's challenge is to place the believers' suffering in a new light (1:28), declaring first that their suffering is a **sign** of their **salvation** (*sōtēria*), but of the opponents' **destruction** (*apōleia*). ("Which" [*hētis*] refers to their suffering.) He assumes the common theme of eschatological reversal, according to which the suffering people will ultimately be saved, while the oppressors will be destroyed. As he points out in Phil. 2:6–11, Jesus's death on the cross was the prelude to his exaltation (cf. 2 Cor. 13:3–4). At the center of his proclamation is "Christ crucified" (1 Cor. 1:23; 2:2). He himself participates in the sufferings of Christ (Phil. 3:10; cf. 2 Cor. 1:3–7; 4:10–11; Gal. 6:17; 1 Thess. 2:1–2; cf. Col. 1:24) in the physical abuse he receives from his proclamation (cf. 2 Cor. 6:4–10; 11:23–30) and in his imprisonment (Phil. 1:7, 14, 17). He does not suffer alone, however, for suffering is a part of Christian existence (cf. Rom. 5:2–5; 8:18–30) and the prelude to glory. His churches are in his heart, "to live together and die together" (2 Cor. 7:3). His converts receive the gospel in the midst of persecution, imitating him in his sufferings (1 Thess. 1:6; cf. 3:3–4). The salvation (*sōtēria*) here is eschatological salvation when the Savior (*sōtēr*) returns (Phil. 3:20), and those who inhabit the body of lowliness will be transformed. The destruction (*apōleia*) is the eschatological wrath of God on the oppressors. Those who put their minds on earthly things will face destruction (Phil. 3:19). Paul expresses this view also in 1 Thess. 2:14–16. One may compare the day of wrath in Rom. 2:5, 9. Because of the assumption of eschatological reversal, the present suffering is a sign (*endeixis*) of the Philippians' future salvation (Fowl 2003, 174).

Because the necessity of suffering for one's religion was totally foreign to ancient religiosity, it was undoubtedly a disorienting factor for new converts in Philippi (Wojtkowiak 2012, 238–39). Paul offers further motivation for the readers, declaring, "It has been graciously granted [*echaristhē*] you the privilege not only of believing in Christ, but of suffering for him as well" (1:29). To believe is a gift (cf. Rom. 12:3; 1 Cor. 12:9), but to suffer for Christ is also a gift. The passive *echaristhē* suggests that God is the one who grants the suffering. The God who graciously gives suffering is the one who gave (*echarisato*) to

---

Kierkegaard on Playing at Christianity

"There is that which is more contrary to Christianity, and to the very nature of Christianity, than any heresy, any schism, more contrary than all heresies and all schisms combined, and that is, to play Christianity. But precisely in the very same sense that the child plays soldier, it is playing Christianity to take away the danger . . . , and in place of this to introduce power (to be a danger for others), worldly goods, advantages, luxurious enjoyment of the most exquisite refinements." (Kierkegaard 1944, 8)

---

the exalted Christ a name above every other name (2:9). To suffer for Christ is the equivalent of participating in the sufferings of Christ (3:10), to be crucified with Christ (Gal. 2:19). As Paul indicates in 1 Thess. 3:3, suffering is the destiny of believers. To suffer for Christ is to participate in the **same struggle** (*agōn*, 1:30) in which Paul is involved (Wolter 2009, 233). Paul has provided a model for the believers' understanding of suffering (1:12–26), and in his frequent autobiographical statements in Philippians, he calls on the community to imitate him (see 3:17; 4:9; cf. 1 Thess. 1:6). The community shares in the sufferings of Christ, imitating Paul in what it **sees** and **hears** in him. Indeed, imitation of Paul is a major theme of Philippians.

This suffering is an *agōn*, a term drawn from athletics to describe the struggles of the people of God in times of conflict. The Philippians have observed Paul's *agōn*, and his imprisonment is another dimension of the struggle. The Philippians share the struggle with Paul. Their suffering is neither unexpected nor a sign of failure. To suffer for religion was unheard of in ancient society. Paul places their suffering in a different light by indicating that he shares suffering and that it is the prelude to glory.

Theological Issues

Paul's choice of the verb *politeuesthai* (lit. "live as citizens") rather than his customary *peripatein* (lit. "walk") as the verb for moral conduct suggests the political implications of the gospel. Paul does not mention the community's obligation to the civic institutions but suggests only that the ultimate loyalty of believers is to an alternative commonwealth (cf. 3:20). From the time when Jesus was asked about obedience to Caesar (Mark 12:13–17) until now, believers have attempted to determine their place within two kingdoms. Augustine wrote of the two cities—the city of God and the city of humankind—that had separate responsibilities. The Reformers spoke of the separate responsibilities of the two kingdoms in which the believer could be loyal to both. Paul's exhortation to "stand firm in one spirit," his acknowledgment of the suffering of believers (1:28), and his reference to their *agōn* ("struggle," 1:30) indicate that living "worthily of the gospel" evokes the hostility of the wider populace. H. Richard Niebuhr describes the constant tension between Christ and culture (1951, 8), concluding that "the political problem such monotheism presents to the exponents of a national or imperial culture has been largely obscured in modern times, but became quite evident in the anti-Christian and especially anti-Jewish attacks of German national socialism." He adds,

> The Christ who will not worship Satan to gain the world's kingdoms is followed by Christians who will worship only Christ in unity with the Lord whom he serves. And this is intolerable to all defenders of society who are content that many gods should be worshipped if only Democracy or America or Germany or the Empire receives its due, religious homage.

The hostility from the larger society to believers who will not bow down to the gods of nationalism, pluralism, or political ideologies has been a consistent factor in the history of Christian faith and remains a reality today. When the facade of Westminster Abbey was removed in 1998, niches that had been empty since the Middle Ages were filled with the sculptures of ten martyrs of the twentieth century, including Dietrich Bonhoeffer, Oscar Romero, and Martin Luther King Jr. These sculptures represent only a fraction of Christian martyrs throughout the centuries (Migliore 2014, 75). Because those who have "lived out their citizenship worthily of the gospel" have rejected the values of the larger society, they have been rejected in their own community.

When Paul declares that "it has been granted [*echaristhē*] to you" not only to believe, but also to suffer for Christ (1:29), he does not suggest that all suffering is a gift, but only the suffering that believers freely choose as they participate in the destiny of the one who suffered first. This dimension of grace (*charis*) is largely ignored in the consumer-driven Christianity of the twenty-first century. As Dietrich Bonhoeffer argued in *The Cost of Discipleship*, the biblical doctrine of grace becomes "cheap grace" that dispenses benefits for the believer without making demands. Bonhoeffer speaks of grace without discipleship. True grace "is costly because it calls us to follow Jesus Christ. It is costly because it costs a man his life, and it is grace because it gives a man the only true life" (1963, 47).

PART 4

Philippians 2:1–4:1

Probatio: *Examples of Faithful Living*

The thesis statement (*propositio*) in 1:27–30 requires a supporting argument (*probatio*), which Paul offers in 2:1–4:1. This section consists of imperatives (2:2, 5, 12–13, 14) elaborating on the call for unity expressed in the *propositio* and the proofs motivating the readers to live "worthily of the gospel" (1:27). The centerpiece of the proofs is the poetic narrative in 2:5–11, which resonates throughout the argument (Landmesser 1997, 551–52). The *probatio* consists primarily of an argument from example, which played an important role among ancient rhetorical theorists. According to Aristotle, "examples [*paradeigmata*] are most suitable for deliberative speakers, for it is by examination of the past that we divine and judge the future" (*Rhet*. 1.9.40; cf. Cicero, *De or*. 2.335). Examples provide a basis for imitation (Witherington 1994, 58). The story of Jesus in 2:6–11 shapes the mind-set of Timothy (2:19–23), Epaphroditus (2:25–30), and Paul (3:1–4:1). In challenging the Philippians to imitate him (3:17), Paul hopes that the Philippians will also be persuaded to adopt the disposition and values of the exemplars of faith. Over against the Philippians' values of self-serving behavior, Paul presents examples of the self-denial that will result in a unified community.

Philippians 2:1–11

The Ultimate Example

Introductory Matters

Paul gives no concrete description of the life that is worthy of the gospel in 1:27–30, but describes it with images suggesting that this existence involves a conflict requiring a united front. In 2:1–11 he describes in more detail the value system that runs contrary to that of the citizens of Philippi. Paul has a special focus on the development of an alternative *phronēsis* that unites the community. His joy will be complete when they "think the same thing" (*to auto phronein*), "have the same love," are "in full accord" (*sympsychoi*, lit. "united in spirit"; BDAG 961), and are "of one mind" (*to hen phronountes*, 2:2). Similar terminology is used in Paul's paraenesis elsewhere. In 2 Cor. 13:11, he urges the readers to "agree with one another" (*to auto phronein*). The instruction in Philippians is parallel to the paraenesis in Rom. 12:1–15:13 (Sandnes 1994, 152; Engberg-Pederson 2003, 206).

Philippians	Romans
"standing firm in one spirit" (1:27)	"together . . . in one voice" (15:6)
"of the same mind" (2:2)	"live in harmony" (15:5)
"look not to your own interests" (2:4)	"not to please ourselves" (15:1–2)
Jesus as example (2:5)	"For Christ did not please himself" (15:3)

In Rom. 12:16 (NRSV), Paul instructs the community to "live in harmony with one another" (*to auto eis allēlous phronountes*), and in 15:5 (NRSV) he prays that God will enable them to "live in harmony with one another [*to auto phronein en allēlous*], in accordance with Christ Jesus." Thus *phronein* is commonplace in Pauline paraenesis in Romans and Philippians.

This command would have resonated with a Greco-Roman audience, which associated it with friendship, a frequent theme among ancient writers, who maintained that "friends think the same thing" (*to auto phronein*) and are "one soul" (Fitzgerald 1996, 145). According to Cicero (*Amic.* 15, W. A. Falconer, LCL), the essence of friendship lies in "the most complete agreement in policy, in pursuits, and in opinions." Dio Chrysostom writes on civic concord to a city torn by factions, challenging his hearers to adorn themselves "with mutual friendship and concord" (*Or.* 48.2). He asks, "Is it not disgraceful that bees are of one mind [*homonousi*] and no one has ever seen a swarm that is factious and fights against itself, but on the contrary, they both work and live together, providing food for one another and using it as well" (*Or.* 48.15, H. L. Crosby, LCL). According to Dio Chrysostom (*Or.* 34.20), "There are not two people in Tarsus who think alike" (*to auto phronountes*). Following civil strife in Nicea, Dio delivered a speech in which he appealed to the citizens to maintain peace and friendship toward one another (*Or.* 39). After complimenting the city on its antiquity and renown (Welborn 1997, 59), he observes, "I rejoice at the present moment to see you having one voice, and desiring the same things." He adds, "What spectacle is more enchanting than a city with the same mind [*homophrosynē*]? . . . What city is less liable to failure than that which deliberates the same things?" Then he prays to the gods that

> from this day forth they implant in this city a yearning for itself, a love, a single judgment [*mia gnomē*], and that it desires and thinks the same thing [*kai tauta boulesthai kai phronein*]; and on the other hand that it cast out discord and contentiousness. (*Or.* 39.8 LCL, cited in Welborn 1997, 60)

While the terminology would be familiar to a Greco-Roman audience, the content of this moral reasoning (*phronēsis*) would have been contrary to the Greco-Roman values. *Eritheia*, already mentioned in 1:17, is a vice that Paul refers to elsewhere (2 Cor. 12:20; Gal. 5:20; cf. James 3:14). In Aristotle (*Pol.* 5.2.3; 5.2.9), *eritheia* designates the use of influence in an election with the goal of attaining office, frequently through fraud. *Kenodoxia* ("vanity," "excessive ambition," BDAG 538) appears elsewhere in Paul's vice lists (Gal. 5:26). The compound refers to the possession of a military post for the purpose of personal advancement. Paul uses the term in vice lists in Gal. 5:19–21 and 2 Cor. 12:20. *Tapeinophrosynē* (humility) normally has a negative connotation that associates it with service, weakness, obsequious groveling, or mean-spiritedness. In secular Greek it is used for the person who is base, ignoble, and of low birth or works at a low occupation (cf. P.Oxy. 74, "nothing humble or ignoble or despised"). According to Aristotle (*Eth. nic.* 4.3.1125a2), the *tapeinoi* are flatterers who grovel before others, hoping to gain an advantage. Epictetus frequently lists the adjective *tapeinos* among the common vices (*Diatr.* 1.3.4; 3.2.14; 3.24.43) as a synonym for "ignoble" (1.3.4), "cowardly" (1.9.33), or the status of the slave (3.24.43). This clash of values is evident in Paul's conflict with the Corinthians, who charge him with being humble (*tapeinos*) when he is present (2 Cor. 10:1).

The value that Paul places on *tapeinophrosynē* is rooted in his Christology, for he responds to the charge that he is humble (*tapeinos*) by appealing to the "meekness and gentleness of Christ" (2 Cor. 10:1). When he encourages his readers to adopt *tapeinophrosynē* as a way of life, he offers the christological motivation that the preexistent Christ "humbled himself" (Phil. 2:8) at the incarnation (Thompson 2011, 106). Paul's use of *tapeinophrosynē* reflects a sharp contrast with the values of Greco-Roman culture, as his debate with the Corinthians suggests. In their eyes he is *tapeinos* (2 Cor. 10:1) insofar as he does servile work (2 Cor. 11:7) and lacks the boldness to speak openly to his readers.

One does not need to conclude that Paul's instructions are a response to the problems at Philippi (contra Peterlin 1995, 59). They are probably an essential aspect of community formation that would have been necessary throughout the Mediterranean world, where the quest for honor and status was a paramount value. Cicero observed this central value: "By nature we yearn and hunger for honor, and once we have glimpsed, as it were, some part of its radiance, there is nothing we are not prepared to bear and suffer in order to secure it" (*Tusc.* 2.24.58). The exhortation "not to look to [one's] own interests, but to the interests of others" (2:4) is common in Pauline paraenesis (cf. Rom. 12:10; 1 Cor. 10:33; 13:5) and an alternative to Roman values, which would have been especially prominent in Philippi. Paul faces the fundamental tension between common Roman values and the conduct that is worthy of the gospel (1:27; cf. Wojtkowiak 2012, 149).

Paul follows the imperative "Make full my joy" (2:2) with the second imperative, "Have this mind among you" (2:5, *touto phroneite en hymin*), indicating that to "have the same mind" (*to auto phronein*) and to "mind one thing" (*hen phronountes*) is to have "this mind" that he will describe in the narrative that follows. Because no verb is present in the following clause (lit. "which also in Christ Jesus"), translators supply either the verb "is" or "was." The NRSV renders it, "the same mind . . . that was in Christ Jesus," suggesting that the following narrative is a call for imitating Christ. The RSV (cf. NIV) renders the phrase "this mind . . . which is yours in Christ Jesus." Thus interpreters debate the extent to which Paul articulates an ethic of imitation in this passage. Inasmuch as "in Christ" is commonly described as the sphere in which believers live (cf. 1:1; 2:1), the most probable conclusion is that Paul describes a moral reasoning (*phronēsis*) that belongs to the community that is in Christ. Michael Gorman renders the phrase appropriately: "Have this mindset in your community, which is indeed a community in Christ, who . . ." (Gorman 2001, 43).

"This mind" (2:5) points forward to the narrative of 2:6–11, introduced by "who, being in the form of God." The main verbs "counted not equality with God," "emptied himself," and "humbled himself" describe two stages in the narrative: a downward spiral of descent followed by the third event when "God highly exalted him" (2:9). Paul's portrayal of Jesus consists of three progressively degrading positions of social status, as Jesus descends from equality with God (status 1) to "the form of a slave," the equivalent of the "likeness" (*homoiōma*) and "form" (*schēma*) of a man (2:7; status 2) to the public humiliation of the cross (status 3; Hellerman 2005, 130). Although almost every line of 2:6–11 is disputed, the basic narrative of descent and ascent is not in question.

The theme of the descent and ascent of Christ appears elsewhere in Paul as a motivation for ethical conduct. He motivates the Corinthians to participate in the collection, reminding them that though Christ was rich, for our sakes he became poor, in order that we might become rich (2 Cor. 8:9). He appeals to the Romans not to please themselves, adding "for Christ did not please himself" (Rom. 15:1, 3). According to Rom. 8:3, "God sent his son in the likeness of sinful flesh," but Christ is now at the right hand of God above all cosmic powers (8:32–38). Paul develops the theme of the triumph of the exalted Christ over the cosmic powers in 1 Cor. 15:20–28. These themes are also present in John 1:1–18; Heb. 1:1–4; and Col. 1:15–20, all of which tell the story in a poetic style of the descent and ascent of the exalted Christ.

The poetic qualities and the vocabulary of 2:6–11 distinguish it from both its context and other Pauline writings. The rhythm is evident in the parallelisms and the alternation between participles and main verbs. The words *harpagmos* (NRSV "something to be exploited"; RSV "a thing to be grasped," 2:6), "form" (*morphē*, 2:6, 7), and "highly exalted" (*hyperypsoō*, 2:9) do not appear elsewhere in Pauline literature. Other words are used in a way that they are not used elsewhere (e.g., *schēma*, "form" [cf. 1 Cor. 7:31]; *kenoō*, "empty" [cf. Rom. 4:14; 1 Cor. 1:17; 9:15; 2 Cor. 9:3]). Taken together, this usage has suggested to many scholars that Paul is not the original author of 2:6–11 (Tobin 2006, 91–92) but has adapted a preexistent hymn into his letter.

In 1928 Ernst Lohmeyer noted these distinctive features and argued that the passage is a pre-Pauline hymn (Lohmeyer 1961), which Paul incorporated into the letter. Lohmeyer set the agenda for the subsequent discussion of the passage. Three issues have occupied scholarship on Phil. 2:6–11.

1. *The structure and genre of the passage.* Lohmeyer maintained that the passage is a hymn consisting of six strophes, each with three lines, and that each strophe contains a main verb. The six strophes are divided into two equal parts, with *dio* (therefore) dividing the two halves of the passage (Lohmeyer 1953, 90). Joachim Jeremias observed the use of parallelism, arguing that the poem consists of three strophes, each with four lines (1963, 186–87). Jeremias

correctly noted that the first two strophes begin and end with participles ("being in the form of God . . . taking on the form of a slave") and that the third line in each is the main verb ("he emptied himself," "he humbled himself"). While his third strophe has two main verbs ("God highly exalted him," "he gave to him a name"), it does not fit the pattern of the first two strophes. The absence of unanimity on the arrangement suggests that one must be cautious in calling this passage a hymn. Undoubtedly it has a rhythm, which consists of the alternation between participles and main verbs. It elaborates on the narratives that are present in other passages. The passage may be described more appropriately as a poetic narrative.

2. *The conceptual world of the passage.* Scholars also debate the conceptual world to which the poetic narrative belongs. Ernst Käsemann proposed the existence of a Gnostic redeemer myth (1968, 45–50), according to which the primal man descends to earth to rescue humanity, a view that has been largely abandoned. Vollenweider has observed that the theme of deities who change their form and visit the earth is common in the Greco-Roman world (2002a, 289). The *locus classicus* for this view is the statement in Homer's *Odyssey* that "the gods in the guise of strangers from afar put on all manner of shapes, and visit the cities" (*Od.* 17.485–86). Dionysus, appearing in the mask of his own prophet, says, "I exchange my form for that of a human" (Euripides, *Bacch.* 4). Jupiter and Mercury visit the world "in mortal form" (Ovid, *Met.* 8.626–724). Especially noteworthy are the stories in which the gods must serve among mortals. Apollo and Poseidon suffer this fate under Laemedon (Ovid, *Met.* 11.202–3). These stories have only a superficial resemblance to the narrative of the one who "emptied himself," took the form of a slave, and submitted himself to public humiliation.

A common theme in Greco-Roman literature is the transformation of a god into a man and his subsequent exaltation. Horace combines the ruler's equality with God with an epiphany on earth, identifying Octavian with the epiphany of Mercury, who becomes transformed and appears as a young boy (Horace, *Carm.* 1.2.41; cited in Wojtkowiak 2012, 90). Ovid speaks of Caesar as one who spent his allotted time on earth, but then as a god entered heaven and his place among the temples on earth (*Met.* 15.815–20). Ancient readers would probably have recognized the parallel themes of the transformation into a human followed by the deity's return to heaven and worship on earth.

More likely is the proposal that the OT and Jewish wisdom literature play a role, as they do in the other narratives of descent and ascent. Wisdom is the "image of God" and "reflection of God" (cf. Wis. 7:25–26). Philo identifies wisdom with the logos, the image of God (*Conf.* 97, 147; *Fug.* 101). This theme probably originated among Hellenistic Jews. The "image of God" and the "reflection of God" are equivalent to the "form of God" (cf. R. Martin 1997, 108).

Richard Bauckham has observed echoes of the suffering servant songs (Isa. 52–53) in this poem. The descent and humiliation of the servant followed by exaltation (Isa. 52:13–53:12) parallels the sequence in Phil. 2:6–11 (Bauckham 1998, 135; Gorman 2001, 90). Indeed, the narrative of Phil. 2:6–11 concludes with the acclamation that "every knee shall bow . . . and every tongue confess" as Lord the one who once suffered the humiliating death on the cross (Phil. 2:10–11).

3. *The meaning of* harpagmos: *A possession to exploit or an object to grasp?* A major debate among interpreters concerns the meaning of *ouk harpagmon hēgēsato*, which the NRSV renders "did not regard . . . something to be exploited" and the RSV renders "did not count . . . a thing to be grasped." *Harpagmos*, which is not used elsewhere in the Septuagint or the NT, can mean "a violent seizure of property" or a grasping of something that one already has (BDAG 133). Some interpreters have suggested that the imagery indicates that Christ was less than equal to God and, in contrast to Adam, chose not to grasp it. R. W. Hoover maintains that the classical parallels indicate that *harpagmon hēgēsato* is an idiom that consistently refers to something that is already present and at one's disposal (Hoover 1971, 118). Dio Chrysostom uses the verb *harpazō* to describe improper ways of using authority in contrast to the behavior of the ideal ruler (*Or.* 4.95). Both the linguistic evidence and the larger context indicate that Christ chose not to grasp what he already had but "emptied himself" of this status. As N. T. Wright has argued, "Over against the standard picture of oriental despots, who understood their position as something to be used for their advantage, Jesus understood his position to mean self-negation, the vocation described in vss. 7–8" (Wright 1991, 83).

4. *The political significance of the passage.* Recent scholars have noted the political implications of this narrative. The description of one who was "equal to God" and "did not count equality with God a thing to be exploited" has echoes of Roman emperors, who were recognized as "equal to God" and exploited this status. Nearly every description of the emperors of the first century depicts them as "grasping their power through self-assertion, greed, rivalry, violence, and murder" (Tellbe 2001, 256). Thus ancient readers would have thought the idea of a ruler's abandonment of his privileges strange (Wojtkowiak 2012, 155). The self-emptying of Christ is the antithesis of the self-exalting Hellenistic ruler (Vollenweider 2002b, 283).

Both the OT and Greco-Roman sources describe arrogant rulers who exalt themselves to divine status. Isaiah announces the fall of the king of Babylon, who had said, "I will ascend to heaven; I will raise my throne above the stars of God. . . . I will make myself like the Most High" (Isa. 14:13–15 NRSV). Ezekiel proclaims the fall of the prince of Tyre, who had compared his mind to the mind of God (28:6) and had said, "I am a god" (28:1, 9).

Rulers in the ancient world claimed divine prerogatives and were honored as "equal to God." A second-century papyrus asks, "What is a god? Exercising power. What is a king? One who is equal to God" (Pap. Heid. 1716.5; Hellerman 2005, 133). According to Aeschylus, Darius is described as "equal to the gods" (*isotheos*, *Pers.* 857). Cassius Dio (51.20) reports that the senate decided that the name of Caesar "would be written in the hymns alongside the gods" (*auton ex isou tois theois esgraphesthai*; *TLNT* 2:231–32; Standhartinger 2006b, 370–71). Philo describes Caligula's claim to divine honors. He first identified himself with the demigods Dionysus and Heracles (*Legat.* 77). "Filled with envy and covetousness, he took possession wholesale of the honors" of the deities themselves (*Legat.* 80). He identified himself with Hermes, adorning himself with a herald's staff, sandals, and a mantle (*Legat.* 94). He also dressed as Apollo, his head encircled with garlands of the sun rays (*Legat.* 95). Philo objects to Caligula's claims, concluding that "a divine form [*morphē*] cannot be counterfeited as a coin can be" (*Legat.* 110; cited in Wojtkowiak 2012, 90).

Conflict between the new community and Rome is nowhere more present than in the confession that "Jesus Christ is Lord" (Phil. 2:11). The acclamation, drawn from Isa. 45:23, applies to the exalted Christ the term that the prophet and other OT writers use for God. This identification of Christ with the *kyrios* (Lord) of the OT began in the earliest days of the Aramaic-speaking church (Hellerman 2005, 151) and continued as the Christian confession (cf. 1 Cor. 8:6; 2 Cor. 4:5). New Testament writers frequently cited LXX Scriptures referring to God as the *kyrios* as references to Christ (cf. Joel 3:5 [2:32 Eng.]; Acts 2:21, 34–39; Rom. 10:13) while also citing passages where the *kyrios* is God. Indeed, as the confession in Phil. 2:11 indicates, the church continued to distinguish the exalted Lord from God, inasmuch as it was God who exalted the one who had "emptied" and "humbled" himself.

By the time that Paul wrote Philippians, *kyrios* had become a common title for the emperor. This confession played a vital part in creating opposition between the Christian community and the Roman populace. Inscriptions attest to the use of the term for Claudius (P.Oxy. 1.37.5–6) and Nero (*SIG* 2.184.30–31, 55). The claim that every knee will bow and every tongue confess that Jesus is Lord (2:10–11) conflicts with the claims of the emperor's universal sovereignty.

The passage undoubtedly had political implications. The community that has formed its own commonwealth as an alternative to the Roman state worships the one who is *kyrios*, a term that was widely used for the emperor. This *kyrios*, however, is the antithesis of the

---

Philippians 2:1–11 in the Rhetorical Flow

Exordium: Thanksgiving and prayer for moral formation (1:1–11)

Narratio: The present and future advance of the gospel (1:12–26)

Propositio: Citizens united in an alternative commonwealth (1:27–30)

Probatio: Examples of faithful living (2:1–4:1)

▶ The ultimate example (2:1–11)

    A reversal of values (2:1–4)

    The mind of Christ (2:5–11)

Roman *kyrios*. He did not exploit his status as one equal to God, as Roman emperors did, but emptied himself of his prerogatives.

Tracing the Train of Thought

A Reversal of Values (2:1–4)

2:1–4. In the first of the proofs (2:1–11), Paul reiterates the thesis statement (2:1–4) and develops the argument, as **therefore** (*oun*) indicates (2:1). Two imperatives (2:2, **make my joy complete**; 2:5, **have this mind among you**) indicate the behavior that is necessary for the alternative *polis*, which Paul describes in greater detail in two highly poetic sections (2:1–4; 2:6–11), with 2:5 functioning as a bridge between them.

In 2:1–4 Paul describes the behavior in the alternative *polis* in a poetic form composed of three strophes, which constitute one sentence in Greek:

> If there is any encouragement (*paraklēsis*) in Christ,
> if there is any consolation (*paramythia*) of love,
> if there is any partnership (*koinōnia*) in the Spirit,
> if there is any compassion (*splanchna*) and mercy (*oiktirmos*)
> make my joy complete, in order that
> > you have the same mind (*to auto phronēte*),
> > having the same love (*agapē*),
> > being of full accord (*sympsychoi*),
> > having one mind (*hen phronountes*),
> > > A not with selfish ambition (*eritheia*) or conceit (*kenodoxia*),
> > > B but with humility considering one another better than yourselves,
> > > A' not looking to your own interests,
> > > B' but to the interests of others.

This section is distinguished by the carefully arranged parallelism (2:1) and antitheses (2:2–4; cf. 1:15–18; 3:2–4, 17–19). The first strophe, with the four parallel *ei tis/ti* ("if there is any") clauses (the NRSV omits all but the first *ei tis*), provides the foundation for the appeal that follows. "If" in this clause means "since"; thus it should be read, "If, as indeed the case is . . ." (cf. the similar construction in Gal. 5:25; Black 1985, 301). The four parallel clauses, of roughly equal length, indicate the present reality of the community and the basis for the requests that follow. "Encouragement" (*paraklēsis*) has connotations of both comfort (cf. 2 Cor. 1:3–7) and exhortation (Rom. 12:8; 15:4–5; 1 Thess. 2:3). The term is related to the verb *parakaleō*, Paul's usual word for making a polite request (cf. Rom. 12:1; 1 Cor. 1:10; 2 Cor. 6:1–2; Phil. 4:2). Although the emphasis may vary in different contexts, the aspects of comforting and encouraging cannot be rigidly distinguished (Thompson 2011, 55–57). This comfort comes only from being in Christ.

Paul probably includes the phrase "in Christ" first in this list because existence "in Christ" is central to the believers' identity. This phrase forms an *inclusio* with 2:5, the description of the believers' existence in Christ. Although "in Christ" can be used in a variety of ways by Paul, the most basic meaning is that Christ is the realm in which believers live because they have been baptized into Christ, died with Christ, and now live in Christ. As Paul develops this theme elsewhere (see 1 Cor. 12:12–26), to be in Christ is to be in the body of Christ.

Consolation (*paramythion*) often appears alongside encouragement (*paraklēsis*, 1 Cor. 14:3; 1 Thess. 2:12; cf. 2 Macc. 15:8–9), overlapping with *paraklēsis* but also having the additional connotation of consolation for those who are grieving (cf. John 11:19) or the support for the fainthearted (1 Thess. 5:14). This consolation grows out of the love that is already in the community and for which Paul prays (Phil. 1:9–11).

The partnership in the Spirit (*koinōnia tou pneumatos*) establishes solidarity in the community. The Spirit is the gift of the new age and the empowerment for ethical living (cf. Rom. 8:1–17; Gal. 5:16–25). Paul assumes that compassion and mercy (*splanchna kai oiktirmos*) already exist in the community, just as his compassion (*splanchna*) extends to them (1:7).

On the basis of their progress, for which Paul has already given thanks (1:3–11), Paul urges the response when he adds "make my joy complete" (2:2). He has already expressed his joy in the Philippians (1:4), and he has expressed both his present and future joy in the context of his imprisonment and possible death sentence (1:18). The church is his joy (4:1), and he finds special joy in the moral progress of his congregations. His pastoral ambition, as he says on numerous occasions, is the transformed community (cf. 2 Cor. 1:14). In this instance he indicates the nature of this transformation in the four qualities mentioned in 2:2, introduced by the purpose clause (*hina*, "so that you may be," 2:2). Once more, Paul employs parallelism (cf. 2:1) to emphasize the moral qualities he encourages. As the use of *phron-* in the first and fourth items in the list indicates (*to auto phronēte . . . hen phronountes*), a community with a shared *phronēsis* (moral reasoning) is his goal. They are of "the same mind" and of "one mind," living up to the highest ideals of friendship. Between these references to the shared *phronēsis*, Paul includes "the same love" alongside compassion and mercy. He has already prayed that their love will increase (1:9), and now he encourages the same love, a phrase he uses nowhere else. Compassion and mercy are almost indistinguishable in Paul. These qualities are directed to the community's common life.

In the *ABAB* pattern of 2:3–4, Paul alternates the negative and positive qualities that either destroy or unite the community, using two participial phrases. Selfish ambition (*eritheia*) and conceit (*kenodoxia*), which appear elsewhere in Paul's vice lists to describe the conduct that undermines community, are contrasted to humility (*tapeinophrosynē*). This contrasts Greco-Roman values of self-aggrandizement with a quality that was widely considered a vice in the ancient world. In the second participial phrase, "looking not to your own interests but to the interests of others" (cf. 1 Cor. 10:24; 13:5), Paul offers one of his most familiar ethical instructions. Thus this common *phronēsis*, or moral reasoning, subverts the values of the Greco-Roman world.

The Mind of Christ (2:5–11)

2:5–11. The second imperative, **Have this mind among you,** is a bridge connecting the ethical instructions of 2:1–4 and the poetic narrative in 2:6–11. "This mind" recalls the encouragement to "have the same mind" and "one mind" (2:2) and anticipates the following section, indicating that "having the same mind" (2:2) consists of having the mind that Paul will now describe. This is the mind that is "among you" rather than the mind "in you" (NRSV), "this mindset in your community" (Gorman 2001, 43). That is, Paul desires a shared mind-set (*phronēsis*).

The absence of verbs in 2:5 creates problems, as the alternative readings indicate. According to the NRSV, Paul encourages the readers to have the mind "that was in Christ Jesus," while the RSV renders the statement "which is yours in Christ Jesus." Thus translators supply either "was" or "is" to complete the sentence: either the mind that was in Christ Jesus, or the mind that is among the members because they are in Christ Jesus. The past tense suggests that Paul is giving a call for imitation, while the present tense indicates that the focus is not on imitating Christ but on recognizing that the people in Christ have a mind that is rooted in the poetic narrative that follows. While imitation is a dimension of this passage, its focus is the common *phronēsis*, or moral reasoning, that those in Christ have. "In Christ" forms an *inclusio* with the same phrase in 2:1 and recalls the earlier identification of the readers as "the saints in Christ Jesus" (1:1). The term signifies the communal life of the people who have been incorporated in Christ (Gorman 2001, 43).

The poetic narrative places before the readers the qualities enjoined in 2:1–4 (Black 1985, 304).

en Christō (2:1)	*en Christō* (2:5)
in Christ	in Christ
to auto phronēte, hen phronountes (2:2)	*touto phroneite* (2:5)
have the same mind, mind one thing	have this mind
hēgoumenoi (2:3)	*ouch harpagmon hēgēsato* (2:6)
consider	consider a thing to be grasped
kenodoxian (2:3)	*heauton ekenōsen* (2:7)
conceit, vainglory	emptied himself

tapeinophrosynē (2:3)	*etapeinōsen heauton* (2:8)
humility	humbled himself

Three strophes describe the stages in the story of Christ. Marked by the alternation between participles and verbs in the first two strophes, the poem describes the downward spiral of the preexistent Christ in two stages. The first stage describes the incarnation (2:6–7):

> Being in the form of God,
>> He did not count equality with God a thing to be exploited
>> But emptied himself,
> Taking the form of a slave,
> Becoming in the likeness of a human.

The parallel verbs describe the action, and the participles indicate the change in status from the form of God/equality with God to the form of a slave/human likeness. The parallelism offers valuable insight into the meaning of the terms. Although *morphē* in most instances refers to the outward appearance or shape (BDAG 659), here the form of God (*morphē tou theou*) is the equivalent of equality with God (Marshall in Donfried and Marshall 1993, 132). Thus "form of God" actually refers to the divine nature. The parallel with "form of a slave" (2:7) indicates that the term refers not to outer shape or form but to the nature of the existence. That is, in the initial stage, Christ was equal to God. This appears to be the equivalent of "image of God" in the wisdom literature. The phrase "equal to God" establishes the contrast to Hellenistic rulers, who also claimed to be equal to God.

In the first act of the narrative "he emptied himself," exemplifying the conduct of one who looks to the interests of others (2:4). The parallel phrases "taking the form of a slave" and "becoming in the likeness of a human" highlight the sharp contrast between the divine and human status, indicating the manner of his sacrifice. This is no Hellenistic story of a deity who made an appearance on earth. The "form of a slave" suggests the abject depth of the descent, for slaves were at the bottom of the social hierarchy. While not all slaves endured the same brutalized existence, those who were free considered slavery as "the most shameful and wretched of estates" (Dio Chrysostom, *Or.* 14.4). The likeness (*homoiōma*, cf. Rom. 8:3) of humankind, which can mean "similarity" or absolute likeness (BDAG 707), indicates the participation in the total human condition. Thus two main verbs describe the extent of the descent. Unlike Hellenistic rulers, who exploited their prerogatives, "he did not count equality with God a thing to be exploited." The absolute humanity of the preexistent Christ is also evident in the phrase "he emptied himself."

The second strophe has the same alternation of participles and main verbs, indicating the movement from one status to another (2:7–8):

> Being found in human form,
> He humbled himself to death,
> Even death on a cross.

The first line of the second strophe, "being found in human form," builds on the last line of the first strophe, "becoming in the likeness of man," in a sorites. As in the first strophe, the status provides the setting for the action: "he humbled himself to death," the second stage in the descent. That "he humbled himself" (*etapeinōsen heauton*) recalls the encouragement to the readers to adopt humility (*tapeinophrosynē*) as a way of life (2:3). The added phrase, "even death on a cross," indicates the absolute nadir of the descent and the epitome of shame (Hellerman 2009, 784; Williams 2002, 133). As Paul indicates in 1 Corinthians, the message of the cross is "foolishness" to the Greeks and a "scandal" to the Jews (1:18, 23). John Chrysostom wrote, "Not every death is similar. Jesus's death seemed more disgraceful than all the others . . . his was accursed" (*Hom. Phil.* 8, trans. Allen 2013). As Roman writers indicate, it is the most shameful form of death. According to Cicero (*Rab. Perd.* 5.16), the word *cross* should be far removed from the "thoughts, eyes, and ears" of Roman citizens.

In the first two strophes the preexistent Christ is the subject of the action who chooses to empty himself and humble himself. In the third strophe God is the subject, and the crucified one is the object. **Therefore** (*dio*) marks the radical break in the downward spiral. The subject is no longer Christ who made decisions to empty himself and humble himself, but God who now exalts him. Because the preexistent Christ emptied and humbled himself, **God highly exalted** (*hyperypsōsen*) him in a radical reversal of his status (Kampling 2009, 20–21).

The poetic narrative speaks in superlatives, indicating that God has not only exalted Jesus, but has "highly exalted" (*hyperypsōsen*) the Christ who "emptied himself." *Hyper*, both in the compound word and in the claim that the exalted one is over (*hyper*) every name, indicates that he is in the highest place, the place of God. In the OT this terminology is used only for God. The psalmist exclaims, "For you, O LORD, are most high [*hypsistos*] over all the earth; you are exalted [*hyperypsōthēs*] far above all gods" (Ps. 96:9 LXX [97:9 NRSV]). Thus God has exalted the one who chose not to exploit his status as equal to God.

At the exaltation God also conferred **the name that is above every other name**. *Echarisato* recalls God's many acts of grace (*charis*). This acclamation also occurs in Heb. 1:4, which describes the descent of the preexistent Christ and the exaltation, when he received a "more excellent name" than the angels.

In the OT the name that is above every other name is that of God. The conferring of a name presupposes the ancient view that the name is something real, an aspect of the person whom it designates (BDAG 712). The psalmist speaks of God's "great and awesome name" (99:3; cf. Deut. 28:58). In Neh. 9:5 the people pray, "Blessed be your glorious name, which is exalted above all blessing and praise" (NRSV). According to *Midrash on the Psalms* 6, God's name is "above all names." Thus God gives Jesus the name that he, in his preexistent state, did not try to grasp. Greek-speaking Jews employed the term *kyrios* as a reverential substitute for the divine name (Bauckham 1998, 131). Jesus is given the divine name because he participates in the divine sovereignty (Bauckham 1998, 131).

> **Sorites**
>
> In the study of logic, "sorites" refers to a chain of syllogisms. In rhetoric, the term is used for a reduplication in which the last word in one clause is repeated, forming the first phrase of the next clause.

The poem appeals to Isa. 45:23 in 2:10b–11a to support the claim. This passage belongs to the larger context of God's claim in Deutero-Isaiah, "I am God, and there is no other" (45:22). To the prophetic claim **that every knee will bow,** the poem adds **in heaven and on the earth and under the earth.** Whereas the original passage (Isa. 45:23) has "every tongue will confess," the poem has **every tongue will confess that Jesus Christ is Lord to the glory of the Father.** The *kyrios* of the OT is now the preexistent Christ who emptied himself of divine prerogatives.

The elevation of Christ above cosmic powers is a theme elsewhere in the NT, often in comments on Ps. 110:1, which declares the victory of God over the enemies. Alluding to Ps. 110:1 (Rom. 8:34), Paul declares that "neither angels nor principalities nor things to come" will separate believers from the love of Christ (Rom. 8:38–39). Reflecting on Ps. 110:1, he declares to the Corinthians that the resurrected Christ "will rule until he puts all enemies under his feet" (1 Cor. 15:25), when he destroys "every ruler and authority and power" (15:24). Similarly, in Ephesians Jesus is at the right hand of God (1:20; cf. Ps. 110:1), "far above all rule and authority and dominion, and every name that is named" (1:21). Only in Philippians do all worship the exalted Christ and call him Lord. In Rev. 5 all creatures worship the lamb.

The narrative of Christ as the one who humbled himself (*heauton etapeinōsen*) and was then highly exalted conforms to a common theme in the OT that God will exalt those who are humble (*tapeinoi*) and bring down the mighty. According to Ps. 74:8 LXX (75:7 Eng.), God exalts (*hypsoi*) the humble (*tapeinoi*). God grants favor to the *tapeinoi* (Prov. 3:34), gives justice to the *tapeinoi* (Ps. 81:3 LXX [82:3 Eng.]), and delivers the *tapeinoi* (Ps. 17:28 LXX [18:27 Eng.]). The three young men in the fiery furnace describe themselves and their people as the *tapeinoi* (Dan. 3:37 LXX), whom God will rescue. The suffering servant is the ultimate example of the triumph of the humble. The servant was taken away "by oppression [*en tē tapeinōsei*] and judgment" (Isa. 53:8), and he "poured himself out to death" (Isa. 53:12). Nevertheless, he will prosper "and be lifted up [*hypsōthēsetai*], and shall be very high" (52:13). As a result, all nations will recognize God's sovereignty (Isa. 52:15) and see the salvation of God (Isa. 52:10; cf. 40:5; 45:22; 49:6).

Figure 7. Artist's depiction of Christ as Pantocrator, the one who rules over all

The poetic narrative has a pastoral and paraenetic significance for the readers, for it indicates a reversal of the situation in which they now live (Williams 2002, 146). In a letter that consistently argues from positive and negative examples (1:12–26; 2:19–30; 3:2–21; 4:10–20), Christ is the ultimate example. Those who, like Paul, risk death will be vindicated. As believers worship the one who died a humiliating death, they acknowledge a deity who stands in sharp contrast to ancient rulers, and they take on the values of the one who looked to the interests of others. What the church now confesses will ultimately be recognized throughout the world.

The political significance of this claim would have been apparent to the ancient readers. To the church in Philippi, the passage indicates the cosmic victory described in Deutero-Isaiah. The community that is marginalized by the Roman populace now participates in the humiliation of Christ, but will ultimately be the victors. This claim is a challenge to Roman power.

Theological Issues

The presence of the poetic narrative of 2:6–11 within a sequence of imperatives (2:2, 5, 12, 14, 18) indicates that conduct worthy of the gospel (1:27) cannot be reduced to a series of rules but is inseparable from the community's defining narrative. The Philippian society, like other societies, had its own narrative

---

John Chrysostom on Phil. 2:6–8

"If a human washed humans, he didn't empty himself, he didn't humble himself; if, being a human, he didn't seize equality with God, he's not praiseworthy. I mean, for someone who is God to become a human is a huge act of humility, unutterable, indescribable." (Hom. Phil. 7, trans. Allen 2013)

---

that unified the people under Roman rule, gave the citizens an identity, and provided the foundation for moral obligations. Paul recalls a narrative that may be already known to the believers, convinced that behavior "worthy of the gospel" will be radically different from that of the Roman citizens of Philippi. Countercultural behavior requires an alternative narrative.

Throughout Scripture, narrative is inseparable from moral obligation. Israelites recited their story (cf. Deut. 26:5–11) as they recalled their covenantal obligations. The gospels challenge reigning narratives and invite the hearers to participate in the story of Jesus. While Paul does not write a gospel, he consistently appeals to the founding narrative that is the basis for the identity of his communities (e.g., 1 Cor. 15:1–3; 2 Cor. 5:14–15). The founding story is the basis for a new creation—a new way of knowing (cf. 2 Cor. 5:17). According to Phil. 2:5, it is the basis for a new *phronēsis*—a new mind-set and new habits.

Narrative is also the basis for further theological reflection. Philippians 2:6–11 has stood at the center of theological debates since ancient times. Interpreters have debated the relationship between "being in the form of God" (2:6) and "he emptied himself" (2:7), seeking to determine the extent of the divine self-emptying (*kenōsis*). The church fathers insisted on maintaining both the humanity and deity of Christ. The one who emptied himself did not cease to be divine. In challenging the Arians, who claimed that the Son was a created being, John Chrysostom declared that "Christ took on what he wasn't and, when he became flesh, remained God the Word" (*Hom. Phil. 8*, trans. Allen 2013). The church fathers found a resolution to the mystery in its declaration at the Council of Chalcedon (451 CE) that Jesus Christ is "truly God, truly human, two natures united into one person, without confusion, change, or separation."

It is not Paul's purpose to answer the multiple christological questions that subsequent generations have raised but to offer a revolutionary view of God and a new *phronēsis*—a new way of thinking and acting. "Against the age-old attempts to make God in their (arrogant, self-glorifying) image, Calvary reveals the truth about what it meant to be God" (Wright 1991, 84). In the incarnation, the self-emptying of Christ, both in his human existence and his shameful death, was the ultimate expression of God. Over against the rapacious and self-seeking gods of antiquity, Paul describes a deity who does what we think God is unwilling to do or incapable of doing (Migliore 2014, 85). Thus Paul challenges the imperial claims of the Caesar, confronting believers with a decision: "Do not live as Augustus and the rulers before and after him do. Do not orient yourself to the Caesar and his veterans, but to the Messiah Jesus" (Hecking 2009, 30).

Ernst Käsemann, who lived through the Nazi horrors, said, "One cannot say, as in Nazi times, that one believes in God. It is necessary to be precise who God is" (2010, 175). In shaping the communal consciousness of the Philippians, Paul depicts one who was "equal to God" but, unlike the deities of ancient culture, did not exploit divine prerogatives. Those who worship this deity reject the quest for status and look to the interests of others as their theology shapes their ethics.

Philippians 2:12–18

Following the Example of Christ

Introductory Matters

"Therefore" (*hōste*) in 2:12 introduces the resumption of the ethical teachings that began in 1:27, indicating that the narrative of Christ's descent and exaltation (2:6–11) shapes the mind-set (2:5) and the behavior of the Philippians. Paul's imprisonment and uncertainty over the outcome gives him a special concern for the Philippians' conduct, whether in his presence or absence (2:12; cf. 1:27). Paul concludes the ethical exhortations that began in 1:27 with two imperatives (2:12, 14), to which he offers support.

The initial phrase, "as you have always obeyed," and the first imperative, "work out your own salvation with fear and trembling" (2:12), has puzzled interpreters, who have seen here a conflict with Paul's repeated insistence that salvation is not by works (e.g., Rom. 3:20; Gal. 2:16; 3:2). To "work out your own salvation" has no close parallel in Paul's letters. Indeed, Ernst Lohmeyer (1953, 102) suggests that this imperative has the basic marks of Pharisaic piety. "Fear and trembling" is the common response of humankind to God in the OT and Jewish literature (cf. Exod. 15:16; Deut. 2:25; 11:25; Isa. 19:16; Jdt. 2:28; 15:2; 4 Macc. 4:10; *Jos. Asen.* 16.7). Paul speaks of his own preaching "in weakness and fear and trembling" (1 Cor. 2:3) and of the Corinthians' obedience "in fear and trembling" (2 Cor. 7:15).

While the instruction "work out your own salvation" has no precise parallel elsewhere in Paul, the apostle speaks of faith working through love (Gal. 5:6), and he frequently speaks of obedience in positive terms. His goal is "the obedience of faith" (Rom. 1:5) among the nations, and he recalls that the

Romans "obeyed from the heart" the teaching they had received (6:17) but laments that not all have "obeyed the gospel" (Rom. 10:16).

The basis for this imperative is the fact that it is "God who works among you both to will and to do according to his good pleasure" (2:13). This passage summarizes a theme that Paul develops at length elsewhere. The imperative "work out" (*katergazesthe*) is literally "to achieve" or "accomplish" (BDAG 531). The term is used in Romans when Paul, speaking for the person under the law, says, "I do not know what I am accomplishing" (7:15, 17) because of the conflict between the will to do the good and the actual deeds (7:15–16, 18–19), a theme that was well known among philosophers in antiquity. According to Rom. 8:1–11, this conflict no longer exists for those who have the Spirit since the "just requirement of the law" (Rom. 8:4) is fulfilled among those who are empowered by the Spirit. Whereas sin once dwelled (*oikei*) in the person under law (Rom. 7:20), the Spirit now dwells (*oikei*) among those who are in Christ (Rom. 8:9), enabling believers to meet God's demands. Similarly, Paul assumes that the Philippians can "work out [their own] salvation" because it is "God who is at work" (*ho energōn*) among believers. Paul speaks elsewhere of a variety of activities (*energēmatōn*), but "the same God who is at work" (*energōn*) for the common good (1 Cor. 12:6). He describes faith that works (*energei*) through love (Gal. 5:6). Similarly, he speaks in 1 Thess. 2:13 of the word that is active (*energeitai*) among the believers. Thus the affirmation that it is "God who works among you" is the equivalent of his claim that the Spirit dwells in the community (Rom. 8:9) and that Christ is among believers (Rom. 8:10). As a result of the divine activity, the community has overcome the conflict between willing and doing that was the subject of the ancient conversation. To do the will of God "with fear and trembling" connects the readers with Israel as the renewed people of God who can keep God's demands. As in Rom. 7–8, Paul envisions the church as the people who are now empowered to keep God's demands.

The second imperative, "Do nothing with murmuring [*gongysmōn*] and quarreling [*dialogismōn*]," clarifies the meaning of the first imperative, "work out your own salvation," evoking a comparison between the church and Israel. "Murmuring" (BDAG 204, lit. "to express oneself in low tones of disapprobation") was associated with Israel's response to adversity in the wilderness (Exod. 16:7–9, 12; Num. 17:20, 25). Israel's murmuring became the dominant theme in the memory of the wilderness period and a negative example for the early church (1 Cor. 10:10; cf. Acts 6:1; Heb. 3:7–4:11). While *dialogismos* has the literal meaning of the "process of reasoning" (BDAG 232), it has the negative connotation in the Bible of reasoning with the thoughts that are not subject to God (Ps. 55:6 LXX [56:5 Eng.]; Ps. 93:11 LXX [94:11 Eng.]; Isa. 59:7) or the hostile thoughts of Jesus's opponents (Matt. 15:19; Luke 5:22; 6:8; 9:46–47). The command continues the focus on maintaining a united front.

The purpose clause introduced by *hina* ("so that") maintains the association with Israel as Paul employs words commonly used in the OT for keeping the commandments. Paul uses three terms that are indistinguishable from each other. "Blameless" (*amemptoi*) is used in the OT for those who are upright in keeping God's commandments. It is used in the LXX for Abraham (Gen. 17:1; Wis. 10:5), Moses (Wis. 18:21), and the holy people (Wis. 10:15). Paul employs the term in this sense when he describes himself as "blameless" in keeping the law before his conversion (Phil. 3:6). He prays that his communities will be blameless at the end (1 Thess. 3:13; Thompson 2011, 185–86). He also wants his churches to be "innocent" (*akeraioi*, lit. "unmixed," BDAG 35; cf. Matt. 10:16, "innocent as doves"; Rom. 16:19, "innocent in regard to evil"), a term that was used in antiquity for city walls that remained in their pristine condition and then was used figuratively for moral purity. The word is synonymous with "unblemished" (*amōma*), a term that was used for unblemished sacrificial animals (Lev. 1:3, 10; 9:2–3; 22:19; 23:18; Num. 29:8, 13; Ezek. 43:25; cf. Ps. 101:6), for people who kept the commandments (Pss. 14:2 LXX [15:2 Eng.]; 18:14 LXX [19:13 Eng.]; 36:18 LXX [37:18 Eng.]; 118:1 LXX [119:1 Eng.]; Prov. 11:5, 20; 20:7; 22:11), and for Christ as the unblemished sacrifice (1 Pet. 1:19).

The "blameless children of light" are what Israel was meant to be. Just as God called Israel to be the "children of God" and separate from the nations (see Lev. 18:2–3), Paul employs two parallel images to indicate the separation of the community from the environment in Philippi. The unified believers are "the children of God . . . in the midst of a crooked and perverse generation" and lights "in the world" (2:15). Thus he hopes that they become what God intended for Israel to be. Whereas Israel is the "crooked and perverse generation" in the OT (Deut. 32:5), because of the situation of the church in the hostile climate of Philippi, Paul describes the people of the city as "a crooked and perverse generation" and the world in which the community shines. This claim indicates the sharp distinction between their conduct and that of the world. As they live out their citizenship in the alternative *polis* (cf. 1:27) and are subject to the hostility of the city, they are the lights to the world. This indicates the relationship between the church and the world. The minority community in Philippi is the light, "holding on to the word of life." Contrary to James P. Ware (2011, 256–70), "holding on" (*epechontes*) refers not to extending the gospel through evangelism but to grasping (BDAG 362) the word in difficult circumstances (Peterson 2008, 168). Such a community fulfills Paul's pastoral ambition, for they are his "boast . . . that he did not labor in vain." The language is derived from Isa. 49:4, as Paul plays the role of the servant.

The conditional clause, "if I am poured out as a libation" (2:17), reflects Paul's uncertainty over his fate. As he indicates in 1:22–26, he sees two possibilities before him. While death is a possibility, he hopes for a reunion with

Marie-Lan Nguyen/Wikimedia Commons

Figure 8. A Greek youth pouring out a libation

the Philippians (1:25–26; 2:24). Because of the uncertainty over his fate (1:21–26), Paul considers the possibility that he will be "poured out as a libation" (*spendomai*, BDAG 937). Both Jews and Greeks would have recognized the sacrificial imagery of the pouring out of a drink offering to the deity. The practice is attested in Greek literature from the time of Homer and was commonplace in Paul's time (Michel 1971, 529). In the OT the priest poured the drink offering on the altar (Exod. 30:9; Num. 28:24). In the ritual of the second temple, the high priest poured the blood of the animal on the altar (Lev. 16:14–15). In Phil. 2:17 Paul employs the term to describe his death; the term is also used in 2 Tim. 4:6 for martyrdom. Having alluded to his imprisonment (1:12–13) and the possibility of his death (1:22–24), he interprets his death in cultic terms. For readers who are fearful about the outcome of Paul's imprisonment, this interpretation gives positive meaning to Paul's death.

Whereas he earlier described his death as a departure (1:23), he now interprets his death as a sacrifice. One may contrast this image with Paul's use of the cultic terminology in other places. In Rom. 15:16 he describes himself as a minister (*leitourgos*), a term that was used in the OT for the priest (Num. 18:21, 31; Isa. 61:6) who offers the "sacrifice of the gentiles." Believers offer themselves as a "living sacrifice" (Rom. 12:1) to God.

This pouring out is probably not only Paul's death, but the ministry that leads to his death. He is engaged in a struggle (*agōn*) against hostile opponents (1:30) that will lead to death for the sake of Christ, and he participates in the "fellowship of his sufferings" (3:10).

Tracing the Train of Thought

God at Work (2:12–13)

2:12–13. After the exhortation to unity in the midst of adversity in 1:27–2:4 and the poetic narrative of Christ (2:5–11), Paul concludes with ethical instructions in 2:12–18, drawing together motifs from the preceding sections and stating the implications of the story of Christ for the community's own conduct.

He reiterates the theme of presence-absence (2:12; cf. 1:27), his own fate (2:17; cf. 1:30), the anticipation of salvation (2:12; cf. 1:28), and the relationship between the church and the outside world (2:15; cf. 1:28). There-fore (*hōste*) introduces the inference from the preceding paraenesis and the consequences of the story of Christ for believers. **As you always obeyed** suggests that the believers' lives have conformed to the narrative of the one who "became obedient" (2:8) to the cross. Their obedience is an expression of the humility that characterizes believers and the progress the Philippians have made since God began a good work among them (1:6). **Not only in my presence but also in my absence**, repeated from 1:27, indicates Paul's concern for the church in his absence and the uncertainty of whether he will return to them (cf. 1:25–26).

> ## Philippians 2:12–18 in the Rhetorical Flow
>
> *Exordium*: **Thanksgiving and prayer for moral formation (1:1–11)**
>
> *Narratio*: **The present and future advance of the gospel (1:12–26)**
>
> *Propositio*: **Citizens united in an alternative commonwealth (1:27–30)**
>
> *Probatio*: **Examples of faithful living (2:1–4:1)**
>
>   **The ultimate example (2:1–11)**
>
> ▶ **Following the example of Christ (2:12–18)**
>
>   God at work (2:12–13)
>
>   A blameless and pure community (2:14–16)
>
>   Poured out as a libation (2:17–18)

Paul employs imperatives in 2:12, 14, accompanied by the motivation for this conduct, concluding with the imperatives in 2:18, "rejoice" and "join in rejoicing with me." He first instructs the believers, **work out your own salvation with fear and trembling** (2:12). The summons is for a corporate response in which the whole community is involved in a common effort in reaching the goal for which Paul prayed (1:9–11). Fear and trembling is an expression of the community's humility in response to God's saving acts. As Paul indicates in 2:13, those who respond to the story of Christ with humility will attain salvation, following the path of the Savior from humiliation to exaltation. Having mentioned their hope for salvation twice (1:28; 2:12) and their expectation of the day of Christ (1:6, 10), he now challenges them to work out (*katergazesthe*) their salvation (2:12). This is a continuation of the obedience they have already displayed. In this instance, he is challenging them to work out their salvation by living according to the standards enunciated in 1:27–2:11, that is, to work for unity by looking to the interests of others.

The corporate nature of salvation is indicated by the assurance that **it is God who works among you both to will and to do** (2:13). God is at work, not only in individuals, but in the whole community. As Paul declared earlier, God "began a good work among you" (1:6) and later Paul commanded them to "have among you" a common *phronēsis* (2:5). The community is not left to its own resources, as Paul indicated earlier, for God began a good work among them and will bring it to completion (1:6). Paul's focus is not on the individuals, but on the community of faith, where God is active.

Interpreters debate the proper rendering of *eudokia* (2:13), which the NRSV renders "for [God's] good pleasure." *Eudokia* (lit. "goodwill," BDAG 405) can mean either "God's goodwill" (e.g., Matt. 11:26), referring to the favor granted by God, or the goodwill of humans (e.g., Luke 2:14; Phil. 1:15). Since the Greek has no possessive pronoun in Phil. 2:13, translators must choose between rendering for his goodwill or the goodwill of others. The NRSV rendering that it is God who works for his goodwill is probably correct.

A Blameless and Pure Community (2:14–16)

2:14–16. While the first imperative, "work out your own salvation," is a general injunction, the second imperative, **do all things without murmuring and arguing** (2:14), elaborates on the first imperative. To act without murmuring and arguing is to have the unified front that Paul describes earlier. Unlike Israel, the church does not respond to adversity with dissent but shares a harmonious mind-set. As in 2:2, so here Paul elaborates on the command with a purpose clause introduced by **so that** (*hina*). Three words, all with the alpha-privative (the alpha prefix indicating a negative), state the goal of the community's existence (cf. 1:6, 9–11) in alliterative terms. Like Israel, they will be **children of God** (2:15). A unified church will be **blameless** (*amemptos*), **pure** (*akeraioi*), and **unblemished** (*amōma*). A blameless and pure community will be separate from the hostile environment in Philippi (1:28), which is **a crooked and perverse generation.** Against this dark background of the environment around them, **they shine like stars in the world** when they demonstrate the unity that Paul encourages. This world, or "wicked generation," is the culture of Philippi, with its values of selfish ambition and honor. While the countercultural existence of the church may have an evangelistic impact, Paul's primary concern is their endurance in the midst of the hostile climate. Indeed, the participial phrase **holding on** (*epechontes*) **to the word of life** (2:16) suggests the need for endurance. *Epechontes* (lit. to "hold on" or "maintain one's grasp," BDAG 362), suggests the challenges that the community faces in the context of adversity. Just as he had earlier encouraged the community to "stand firm" (*stēkete*) against opposition (1:27; see also 4:1), here he encourages them to hold on to the word of life, which is the equivalent of the good news that shapes their moral conduct.

Such a community is the fulfillment of Paul's pastoral ambition, his **boast** (*kauchēma*) at **the day of Christ.** As Paul's prayer in 1:6 and 10 indicates, he envisions the completion of God's work at the day of Christ. As he indicates elsewhere, his churches will be his boast at the day of Christ (2 Cor. 1:14; 1 Thess. 2:19). However, he considers that he, like the servant in Isaiah 49:4, might **run in vain** (cf. Gal. 2:2; 4:11). If his churches are not his boast, he will have run in vain and labored in vain.

Poured Out as a Libation (2:17–18)

2:17–18. Paul elaborates on his investment in the community's transformation in 2:17, using cultic sacrificial metaphors to describe his labor on behalf of the church. **If I am poured out as a libation**, which evokes images of the sacrificial libation (see under "Introductory Matters"), is the protasis of a conditional sentence that concludes, **I rejoice and I rejoice with you.** Just as he rejoiced in the context of his imprisonment (1:18), he rejoices at the prospect of his impending martyrdom, knowing that it has been for the sacrifice and joy of their faith.

Both Jewish and Greek readers were familiar with the pouring out of wine as part of the sacrifice. This image is employed in 2 Tim. 4:6 for Paul's impending martyrdom. In Philippians it describes not only Paul's martyrdom, which remains a possibility, but also his participation in suffering on behalf of others in the present.

Paul pours out the libation **on the offering and sacrificial service of your faith** (2:17). This imagery anticipates references to the sacrifices offered by the Philippians. Epaphroditus is their minister (*leitourgos*, 2:25) to his needs, and his gifts are "a pleasing sacrifice, acceptable to God" (4:18). Their many deeds are acts of faithfulness, for which Paul exhausts himself. When his pastoral ambition is fulfilled, he rejoices and joins in rejoicing with the Philippians (2:17). In the final imperative of this section, he encourages the Philippians for the first time, **rejoice and join in rejoicing with me** (2:18), anticipating the subsequent encouragement to "rejoice in the Lord" (3:1; 4:4). Paul is their example of one who can rejoice and suffer at the same time, knowing that ultimate salvation follows the present distress. Just as they join Paul in suffering (1:29–30), they rejoice with him (2:18).

Theological Issues

The exhortation "work out your own salvation" (2:12) is likely to be problematic for all who have been influenced by Paul's repeated claim that salvation is not by works (cf. Rom. 3:20, 27; 9:12; Gal. 2:16; 3:2). The juxtaposition of this imperative with the assurance "it is God who is at work among you" (2:13) further complicates the matter, raising the issue of synergism, the view that human and divine works complement each other to effect salvation. Indeed, Paul's reference to obedience is a disturbing feature not only to those who place grace and obedience in opposition, but also to modern people who see here a conflict with their ideal of the autonomous individual. For Paul, however, the imperative is the logical response for believers who participate in the narrative of 2:6–11, as "therefore" (2:12) indicates. Paul called for a specific conduct whether he is present or absent (1:27) before reciting the narrative of Christ, and he concludes the narrative with the imperative "work out your own salvation with fear and trembling, not only when I am present, but much more in my absence" (2:12).

Paul does not suggest that human and divine works complement each other. Consistent with his ethical instruction elsewhere, Paul places the indicative and the imperative in a paradoxical relationship. God requires obedience but empowers believers to obey. Paul does not distinguish between the empowering work of God, Christ, or the Spirit in the letters. While he speaks of the work of God in 2:13, he speaks elsewhere of the dwelling of both Christ and the Spirit among believers (cf. Rom. 8:10–11; 1 Cor. 3:16; Gal. 4:19) and the empowerment they provide for the moral life (Rom. 8:1–11; Gal. 5:22–29). The God who began a good work among believers (1:6) completes that work as the community conducts itself worthily of the gospel (1:27).

The "fear and trembling" with which believers respond to God's saving acts is a graphic way of describing the urgency associated with the Christian moral life and a sharp contrast to conventional religious expressions. John Chrysostom captured the significance of fear and trembling in a homily on this passage: "Tell me, if you were continually standing next to the ruler, wouldn't you be standing in fear? How come, when you're standing next to God, you're laughing and laid back and neither afraid nor shuddering? Don't despise his forbearance: his patience is leading you toward repentance" (*Hom. Phil.* 9, trans. Allen 2013).

English translations obscure the corporate nature of God's work. As the plural "you" indicates in 2:12–13, the community works out its salvation together, just as God works in the community (lit. "among you") to bring it to completion (1:6). The corporate response is evident in the imperative "do all things without grumbling or quarreling" (2:14), which elaborates on the command "work out your own salvation." Paul's prayer for a blameless community at the final day (1:10) will become a reality in a unified community. Just as Jesus emptied himself for the sake of others, Paul will be poured out as a libation for the sake of this community (2:17).

Paul anticipates that the community will not only be transformed at the end but also live "worthily of the gospel" (1:27) in the present. Such a countercultural community will not retreat from the world but will "shine like stars in a crooked and perverse generation" (2:15). The image of stars shining in a darkened world suggests both the community's differentiation from the world and their impact on it. While Paul never encourages believers to evangelize in their local communities, he assumes that they will continually interact with nonbelievers. The countercultural conduct of a unified community will have an impact on others. Indeed, the moral behavior of Christians influenced many pagans and resulted in their conversion.

Philippians 2:19–30

The Examples of Timothy and Epaphroditus

Introductory Matters

A consistent feature of Paul's letters is the parousia, the announcement of his impending visit to his churches (see Rom. 15:22–29; 1 Cor. 4:14–21; 16:5–9; 2 Cor. 12:14–13:10; Philem. 22). In some instances he announces the visit of his coworker Timothy (1 Cor. 4:14–21; 16:5–9). In Philippians he announces the visits of Timothy, his coworker, and Epaphroditus, the emissary from the Philippians, who had recently delivered their gifts to Paul (4:18). Paul also hopes to visit them (2:24). Because of his imprisonment, however, his future plans remain uncertain. Although he mentions Timothy's visit first (2:19–24), he probably intends to send Epaphroditus first, for he must wait until he finds out about his fate before he sends his trusted coworker (2:23).

Paul probably mentions Timothy first because of his importance in the Pauline mission. Timothy has been Paul's companion from the time that he first encountered Paul (Acts 16:1–5; 17:14–15; 18:5; 19:22; 20:4). He is present with Paul at the writing of 2 Corinthians (1:1), 1 Thessalonians (1:1), and Philippians (1:1), and he is listed as Paul's companion in Colossians (1:1) and 2 Thessalonians (1:1). In 1 Corinthians and 1 Thessalonians he is Paul's emissary who "explains [Paul's] ways" (1 Cor. 4:17), continues Paul's catechetical work (1 Thess. 3:2–6), and brings reports to Paul (1 Thess. 3:6). His role as Paul's spokesman in 1 and 2 Timothy is consistent with the portrayal in the undisputed letters.

Epaphroditus is unknown outside Philippians. His name, derived from the goddess Aphrodite, indicates that he is a gentile. Paul describes him as the Philippians' messenger (*apostolos*, 2:25) to his needs. He brought the gifts from the Philippians to Paul (4:18), placing himself at great risk. We do not know if he is the deliverer of the letter.

The travel plans in 2:19–30 have been central to the debates about the place and condition of Paul's imprisonment. He indicates here the frequent interactions he has had with the Philippians. As he writes, he does not mention the place of his imprisonment. He mentions frequent interactions with the Philippians: (1) Epaphroditus became ill (2:27); (2) the Philippians heard that Epaphroditus was ill (2:26); and (3) Paul is aware that the Philippians have heard of the illness of Epaphroditus. The number of interactions has raised questions about the place of Paul's imprisonment. Many scholars conclude that Ephesus is the most likely place of Paul's imprisonment, but since no mention is made of an Ephesian imprisonment, the argument that Paul is in prison there is not compelling. The distance from Rome does not preclude the interactions that are described in 2:25–29. The two-year imprisonment in Acts, the possibility of a death sentence, and the interaction with messengers correspond to the description of Paul's imprisonment in Acts 28:17–31.

Tracing the Train of Thought

The Example of Timothy (2:19–24)

2:19–24. Paul concludes the ethical instruction with the affirmation that a blameless community, free of division and self-seeking, is the goal of the ministry for which he sacrifices himself (2:14–18). Interpreters have debated the relationship between the ethical instructions in 2:12–18 and the travel plans in 2:19–30 (see Holloway 2008, 552–53), noting that travel plans do not ordinarily appear in the middle of a letter. In this instance, however, Paul's travel plans are an expression of his concern for the Philippians, which he describes in 2:16–18. He indicates his continuing concern in 2:19–30, announcing the impending visits of Timothy and Epaphroditus. Having reassured the Philippians about his situation (*ta kat' eme*), he hopes to be cheered (*eupsychō*) when he hears the news about them (*ta peri hymōn*) because they are his boast (2:16) and his "joy and crown" (4:1).

Paul begins with Timothy's visit because of the importance of Paul's younger coworker to the Philippians. While 2:19–24 has the formal appearance of the traditional announcement of a visit (cf. Rom. 15:22–29; 1 Cor. 16:5–9; Philem. 22), the extended description of Timothy indicates that Paul's coworker is an exemplary figure. Verses 19 and 23 provide a frame for the announcement:

> I hope in the Lord to send Timothy to you soon (*tacheōs*),
> in order that I may be encouraged, knowing the news about you (*ta peri hymōn*, 2:19).

> I hope to send [Timothy] to you as soon as I know the news about me (*ta peri eme*, 2:23).
> I am persuaded in the Lord that I myself will come quickly (*tacheōs*, 2:24).

Paul wants to send Timothy to learn the news about the church and will do so as soon as he knows how things will turn out for him. Enclosed within this frame is the recommendation of Timothy (cf. Harvey 1998, 238). Paul has **no one like** (*isopsychon*) Timothy (lit., "of like soul/mind," BDAG 481), who **will be genuinely concerned for [their] welfare** (2:20). The statement **they all look to their own interests, not those of Jesus Christ** (2:21) provides a sharp contrast between Timothy and others. Indeed, only Timothy has the mind of Christ (2:5) that is embodied in the poetic narrative of 2:6–11. Here, as elsewhere in the letter, Paul presents sharp contrasts between good and bad examples (1:15–18; 3:2–3, 18–19). The fact that Timothy has, **like a child to a father** (cf. 1 Cor. 4:17), **served** (*edouleusen*, lit. "slaved") with Paul **in the gospel** (2:22) indicates that he has been shaped by the one who took the form of a slave (*doulos*). Paul **trusts** (*pepoitha*) **in the Lord** that [he] **himself will also come soon** (2:24). Thus despite the uncertainty over his fate (1:12–26), he is confident that he will continue his ministry, devoting himself to their progress (cf. 1:24–26).

The Example of Epaphroditus (2:25–30)

2:25–30. While Paul hopes to send Timothy (2:19, 23), he considers it **necessary to send Epaphroditus** first (2:25). Paul's promise of the visit from Epaphroditus is also more than an announcement of a reunion with the Philippians. He is a **brother** (*adelphos*), a **fellow worker** (*synergos*), and **fellow soldier** (*systratiōtēs*) for Paul, and a **messenger** (*apostolos*) and **minister** (*leitourgos*) from the Philippians for Paul's needs. Like Paul, he was **longing** (*epipothōn*) for **all** of them and **distressed** (*adēmonōn*) that they had **heard that he had been sick** (2:26). The fact that he had **nearly died** (*paraplēsion thanatō*, 2:27) and **came close to death** (*mechri thanatou*, 2:30) indicates the special significance of the possibility of death for the readers, who are also concerned about the verdict on Paul's life. **God had mercy on him** and thus on Paul (2:27), indicating that God's power is present in weakness (cf. Phil. 4:13). As a result, Paul may continue to have joy (cf. 1:4; 18; 2:18) rather than **grief upon grief** in his ministry. He is **sending him** to Philippi **more eagerly** so that they may **rejoice** and Paul may be **without grief** (2:28). The recommendation for Epaphroditus has echoes of the narrative poem in 2:6–11. In recalling that he came "close to death" (*mechri thanatou*, 2:30) **for the work of Christ**, Epaphroditus followed the path of Jesus, who became obedient to death (*mechri thanatou*, 2:8). In this way Paul indicates that Epaphroditus had imitated Christ (Wojtkowiak 2012, 220). Consequently, Paul urges them to **receive him in the Lord with all joy** and to **hold such persons in honor** who follow the path of self-denial (2:29). As a counterculture, they have reversed the concept of honor that is dominant in the society.

Theological Issues

Paul's customary travelogue and commendation of coworkers (2:19–30) indicates that, even in making routine announcements, he offers theological insights to his listeners that elaborate on the central message of the letter. The anticipated visits of his coworkers are necessary to fulfill his pastoral ambitions for the church, reflecting his conviction that the church is unfinished business (cf. 1:6, 9–11). Paul's commendation of Timothy and Epaphroditus indicates that others participate in that ministry, sharing his concern for the outcome of the churches. Christian ministry involves participation in the formation of churches, extending the work initiated by Paul.

The commendation of the two ministers reflects the intense pathos involved in ministry and the challenges involved in the formation of churches. Epaphroditus was distressed (*adēmonōn*, used elsewhere only for Jesus in Gethsemane, Mark 14:33). The death of Epaphroditus would mean "grief upon grief" (2:27), but their reunion with him would bring great joy (2:28–29), sparing Paul such grief (2:28). As Paul indicates throughout the letter, his joy is the well-being and formation of the church into the image of Christ, and his grief emerges when obstacles stand in the way of this outcome.

Paul's commendation indicates that the formation of believers requires exemplars who follow Jesus in emptying themselves of personal ambition for the sake of others. Ministry involves not only the skills appropriate to a profession, but also the personal sacrifice and devotion exhibited by Timothy and Epaphroditus. Not only the Philippians, but subsequent communities as well, tell the stories of past and present believers who have embodied the Christian narrative of self-sacrifice. As Stephen Fowl has concluded, "If Christians are to interpret and embody these texts in the concrete situations in which they find themselves . . . we must attend to those saintly lives around us as well as those saints preceding us who best embody these texts" (2005, 142).

Ancient society, with its emphasis on honor, would have considered odd the imperative "hold such people in honor" (2:29). Epaphroditus is not the only one who has sacrificed himself for the sake of the church, for there are unnamed people who are also worthy of honor. As a counterculture, the church offers an alternative to society's understanding of honor. While ancient people gave honor to those who made major donations or achieved recognition for military success (Fowl 2005, 138), the church honors those who, often behind the scenes, sacrifice for the benefit of others.

Philippians 3:1–4:1

The Example of Paul

Introductory Matters

Since the seventeenth century (cf. Gnilka 1968, 6), interpreters have noted the radical break in the argument that begins with "beware of the dogs, beware of the evil doers, beware of those who mutilate the flesh" (3:2) and concludes with the warning about the "enemies of the cross of Christ" whose "god is the belly" (3:18–19). Indeed, an *inclusio* provides the frame of the chapter, consisting of (a) a warning against false teachers (3:2, 18–19), (b) a contrast to the church ("we" in 3:3; "our citizenship" in 3:20–21), and (c) Paul's autobiographical reflection (3:4–17). Thus 3:2–21 is a rhetorical unit that introduces these dangers for the first time.

Since 3:2–21 is a rhetorical unit, interpreters face the additional question of the place of 3:1 and 4:1 in the argument. Most translations render *to loipon* as "finally" (3:1), suggesting that Paul has reached the conclusion of the letter. As the paragraphing in English translations indicates, the relationship between 3:1a ("rejoice in the Lord") and 3:1b ("to write the same things is not troublesome to me, and for you it is in your best interests") is unclear. Thus the questions emerge: Why does Paul speak of writing "the same things"? Is 3:1a the conclusion of 2:19–30 or the beginning of the next section? Where does the new paragraph begin? At the end of 2:30? At the end of 3:1a? Or at the end of 3:1b? Is 3:1b the introduction of the rhetorical unit 3:2–21? The uncertainty over 3:1 has played a role in the issues that have dominated the interpretation of Phil. 3.

Because of the change of tone and subject matter in 3:2, many scholars have concluded that 3:2–21 is not consistent with the remainder of the letter and is thus a fragment of another letter. They have debated two related issues regarding chapter 3: the integrity of the letter and the identity of the opposition.

Philippians 3 and the Integrity of the Letter

J. Gnilka (1968, 8–10) maintains the following reasons for assigning 3:2–21 to a separate letter.

1. Paul confronts a changed situation in chapter 3. Whereas he refers to his imprisonment in chapters 1 and 2, he is no longer in bonds in chapter 3. While chapters 1 and 2 are an appeal to unity, chapter 3 is a polemic against opposition not mentioned in the first two chapters. While chapter 1 mentions those who preach from envy and selfish ambition (1:15–17), in chapter 3 Paul warns against false teachers—"the dogs, evil workers, and the mutilation" (3:2)—and those who are "enemies of the cross" and "whose god is the belly" (3:19). Those who are the objects of Paul's invective in chapter 3 cannot be identified with those who preach Christ with improper motives (1:15–18).
2. Closely related to the change of situation suggested by Gnilka is the change of tone in 3:2–21. In contrast to the warm expressions of affection in the first two chapters (1:7–8, 25–26; 2:16), chapter 3 is filled with invective (3:2, 18–19) and polemic.
3. Chapter 2 ends with Paul's travel plans (2:19–30), the encouragement to rejoice (3:1), and the word "finally" (*to loipon*, 3:1). Travel plans are common near the conclusion of Paul's letters (cf. Rom. 15:22–33; 1 Cor. 16:5–12; 2 Cor. 12:14–13:10). "Finally" (*to loipon*) and the encouragement to rejoice appear at the end of 2 Corinthians (13:11), and the exhortation to rejoice appears at the end of 1 Thessalonians (5:16). The fact that it appears again in Phil. 4:8 has convinced many interpreters that Phil. 3:2–4:1 is a separate letter.

Because of an apparent break in the argument in chapter 3, interpreters have offered numerous theories about the redactional history of the letter, maintaining that it is a composite of either two or three letters. A widely held view is that a separate letter begins in 3:1b in which Paul engages in polemic for the first time. Gnilka (1968) distinguishes between letters *a* (1:1–3:1) and *b* (the polemic, 3:1b–4:1, 8–9), arguing that Philippians consists of two letters. Others (e.g., Reumann 2008, 15; Bormann 1995, 118) argue for three separate letters, maintaining that 4:10–20 is a thank-you note sent prior to the other sections. Advocates of this view maintain that a thank-you note at the end of the letter appears as an afterthought and that such a delay in expressing gratitude would be inconceivable (see introduction to part 5 and comments on 4:10–20).

Despite the apparent break in the flow of thought at 3:2, arguments for regarding chapter 3 as a separate correspondence are not compelling. Little evidence exists for Gnilka's claim of a changed situation in the chapter. While the beginning and end of the chapter contain warnings and invective, the remainder of the chapter is autobiographical rather than polemical. The presence of "finally" (*to loipon*, 3:1), travel plans (2:19–30), and the encouragement to rejoice (3:1) do not always come at the end of a letter but may appear elsewhere in Paul's letters (Watson 2003, 167–68). "Finally" (*loipon*) appears in 1 Thess. 4:1 to introduce a new section of the letter, and travel plans appear in 1 Cor. 4:14–21. The word can either be a closing formula or a transitional particle (Garland 1985, 149). *To loipon* appears frequently in ancient family letters to introduce a new topic (Alexander 1989, 96). As Philippians indicates, "rejoice" (*chairete*) can appear throughout the letter (2:18, 28; cf. Rom. 12:12, 15).

The case for regarding 3:2–21 as a separate letter is further weakened by the fact that those who maintain this theory do not agree on where the interpolation begins or ends (Garland 1985, 154). Some propose that it begins in 3:1a, others 3:1b, and others with 3:2. This lack of consensus undermines any idea that chapter 3 is an interpolation.

The numerous links between chapter 3 and the first two chapters indicate that chapter 3 fits the flow of the argument and is not a foreign body (see Wojkowiak 2012, 176).

Philippians 2	Philippians 3
doxa (glory, 2:11)	*doxa* (3:19, 21)
epigeios (earthly, 2:10)	*epigeia* (3:19)
epouranios (heavenly, 2:10)	*en ouranois* (3:20)
heuretheis (be found, 2:7)	*heurethō* (3:9)
hēgeisthai (regard, 2:3, 6, 25)	*hēgeisthai* (3:7, 8 [2×])
thanatos (death, 2:8)	*thanatos* (3:10)
kyrios Iēsou Christos (Lord Jesus Christ, 2:11)	*Christou Iēsou tou kyriou mou* (of Christ Jesus my Lord, 3:8)
lambanein (take, 2:7)	*katalambanein* (obtain, make one's own, 3:12, 13)
morphē (form, 2:6, 7)	*symmorphizomenos* (be conformed, 3:10)
stauros (cross, 2:8)	suffering, death (3:11), enemies of the cross (3:18)
schēma (form, 2:7)	*metaschēmatizein* (transform, 3:21)
tapeinoun (to humble, 2:8)	*tapeinōsis* (humiliation, 3:21)
phroneite (have this mind, 2:5)	*phroneite* (3:15), *ta epigeia phronountes* (having a mind on earthly things, 3:19)

These parallels indicate the close relationship between chapters 2 and 3 and the strategic place of chapter 3 in the argument of the letter. This relationship is also evident in the *inclusio* between *politeuesthe* (lit. "live out your citizenship," 1:27) and the *politeuma* ("citizenship") in heaven (3:20). It is especially present in the rhythmic conclusion of chapter 3, which Lohmeyer designated as a hymn (see comments on 3:20–21 below). What is noteworthy is the way in which 3:20–21 echoes the hymn in 2:6–11. The one who was in the form (*morphē*, 2:6) of God was found in human form (*schēma*, 2:7) at the incarnation and "humbled himself" (*etapeinōsen heauton*, 2:8). According to 3:20–21, the Lord will transform (*metaschēmatisei*) the body of our humiliation (*tapeinōsis*) so that it will be conformed (*symmorphon*) to the body of his glory. Thus believers follow the path of the Lord from humiliation to transformation into the body of glory. These terms are rare in the Pauline corpus, but link chapters 2 and 3 (Garland 1985, 158).

The Identity of the Opponents

Closely related to the issue of the place of chapter 3 in the letter is the question of the identity of the opponents, which has been a major focus of attention, especially for those who regard chapter 3 as a part of a separate letter. The harsh words of 3:2, 18–19 are reminiscent of the polemic in Galatians and 2 Corinthians. At the beginning of the chapter, Paul warns against the "dogs, evil workers, and mutilation" (3:2), who comprise one group. Because of the paronomasia *katatomē—peritomē* ("mutilation"—"circumcision"), which offers the most identifiable epithet among the three, interpreters have concluded that Paul engages in polemic against those who demand circumcision. At the end of the chapter, he warns against the "many" who are "enemies of the cross of Christ" (3:18) and "whose god is the belly" (3:19).

Paul's statement in 3:12, "I have not been made perfect" (*teteleiōmai*, NRSV "reached the goal") and the later comment, "Let as many as are 'perfect' [*teleios*, NRSV "mature"] be of the same mind" (3:15) has suggested to many interpreters (e.g., Schmithals 1957, 315) that the apostle is using the terminology of opponents who claim to have reached perfection. Thus, by mirror reading they conclude that Paul is responding to the opponents' claim to perfection.

These scattered statements have resulted in a variety of attempts to synthesize the evidence of chapter 3 and identify the opponents. Because of the differences in the references to the heretics in 3:2, 18–19, some have suggested that Paul is fighting on two fronts—against Judaizers (3:2) and against libertines (3:18–19). H. Koester (*IDBSup* 666) and others have synthesized the warnings in 3:2, 18–19 and the references to perfection (3:15) and concluded that Paul confronts a single group, Jewish Gnostics who insist on circumcision as a path to perfection and discount the significance of the cross.

This variety of interpretations reflects the lack of evidence about the opponents, whose views Paul describes only with invective and polemical characterization. Scholars have employed extended mirror reading and the evidence from the polemic in 1 and 2 Corinthians and Galatians to identify the opponents in Philippians, offering a depiction of views for which there is no evidence elsewhere (i.e., Jewish Christian Gnostics). In contrast to the other letters, however, Paul does not engage in extended argument against opponents. Indeed, apart from 3:2, 18–19, Phil. 3 is an extended autobiography.

The brief warning in 3:2, "beware the dogs, beware the evil workers, beware the mutilation," offers little indication of the identity of the opponents. Although *blepete* can be rendered "observe" (cf. Stowers 1991, 116), the NRSV's rendering "Beware" is correct, for Paul is pointing to the danger of the heretics. The threefold *blepete* ("beware") has a rhetorical effect. The danger comes from "the dogs, the evil workers, and the mutilation"—invectives that shed little light on the identity of the opposition. *Dog* is a common invective in antiquity as an image for aggressiveness, threat (cf. Pss. 21:17, 21 LXX [22:16, 20 Eng.]; 58:7, 15 LXX [59:6, 14 Eng.]), and an unquenchable appetite (Isa. 56:10–11). Wild dogs scavenge and eat human flesh (1 Kings 14:11; 16:4; 21:23–24; 2 Kings 9:10; Job 30:1; Jer. 15:3). Thus the epithet draws sharp lines between insiders and outsiders (cf. Matt. 7:6; Mark 7:27–28) and is a vivid image for one's opponents. The connection with the "mutilation" (*katatomē*) suggests that Paul has taken a common invective, used widely in polemic (cf. Nanos 2009, 476), to describe one's opponents. It is used for the Canaanite woman in her encounter with Jesus (Matt. 15:26). While Paul applies it to those who insist on circumcision (Schinkel 2007, 79), the term provides no insight into the identity of the opponents.

The description of the opponents as evil workers (*kakous ergatas*) also gives no indication of their beliefs. The closest parallel is the reference to the "false apostles, deceitful workers" (*ergatai dolioi*) in 2 Cor. 11:13. This belongs among Paul's common epithets for opponents, but gives no clear indication of their teachings.

The reference to the mutilation (*katatomē*) is the clearest indication of the identity of the opposition. Paul undoubtedly is making a wordplay, describing circumcision (*peritomē*) as mutilation (*katatomē*), equating those who insist on circumcision with those who engage in the pagan practice of self-laceration (cf. 1 Kings 18:28). The specific warning against those who insist on circumcision suggests that Paul has inverted the disparaging reference to dogs to refer to the very people who had used that designation on others. Undoubtedly Paul faces those who insist on circumcision, not only in Galatia, but in many places. Thus the issue is probably a potential problem rather than a present reality in the church at Philippi.

The warning in 3:2 is parallel to the warning in 3:18–19, even if Paul characterizes the threat in different terms. In the latter instance, the opponents are "enemies of the cross of Christ" (3:18), "whose god is the belly" (3:19). Once more, Paul refers to opponents in general terms with harsh language, but gives little indication of their beliefs. The statement "as I have often told you of them" (3:18) suggests that Paul's original catechetical work warned of persistent dangers in Philippi. His warning "with tears" (3:18) indicates the urgency of the situation, which is probably occasioned by the hostile climate in which they live.

The cross stands at the center of Paul's proclamation. The nadir of Jesus's descent in the hymn in Philippians is his death on the cross (Phil. 2:8). According to 1 Corinthians, Paul summarizes his preaching as "the word of the cross" (1:18) or "Christ and him crucified" (2:2), a message that is a "scandal" to others (1 Cor. 1:23; Gal. 5:11), for Jews seek signs and Greeks seek wisdom (1 Cor. 1:22). He maintains that those who are involved in partisan rivalry do not understand the message of the cross (1 Cor. 1:10–2:17), and he accuses the opposition in Galatians of making the death of Christ superfluous (Gal. 2:15–21). Thus the "enemies of the cross of Christ" are probably all who do not share Paul's understanding of the centrality of the cross. "Enemies of the cross of Christ" may refer to the majority culture in Philippi, who shared the common revulsion at the subject of the cross. Because of the repugnance of the cross to the citizens of Philippi, the constant temptation for members was to avoid the message of the cross and their participation in it.

The statement that their "god is the belly" is probably a standard polemic. Belly (*koilia*) is frequently used metaphorically for the seat of the desires (BDAG 550). Paul concludes his Epistle to the Romans, warning against those who cause divisions (16:18), indicating that "such people serve not the Lord Jesus Christ, but their own appetites" (*koilia*). He probably quotes a Corinthian slogan when he says, "Food is for the belly, and the belly for food" (1 Cor. 6:13). Thus the belly in Phil. 3:19 is probably metonymy for the life-orientation toward the flesh (cf. 3:3), which is focused on earthly things (3:19; cf. De Vos 1997, 271).

Paul refers to internal opponents nowhere else in the letter. While he refers to those who "proclaim Christ from envy and rivalry" (Phil. 1:15 NRSV), he does not question their message. The opponents whom Paul mentions in 1:28 are outsiders who have the capacity to intimidate the members (1:28) rather than an internal threat. Inasmuch as Paul does not engage in extended polemic in Phil. 3, as in Galatians and 2 Corinthians, the false teachers are more a potential threat than an actual reality. Undoubtedly Paul's ministry has been plagued by rivals who have insisted on the necessity of circumcision for entrance into the people of God, but the absence of polemic in Philippians suggests that false teaching is not the central concern (cf. deSilva 1994, 30). Morna Hooker is correct to speak of the "phantom opponents" of Philippians (2002, 377–95).

As the sharp contrast between the community and the opponents suggests (3:2–3, 17–21), the opponents serve as rhetorical foils for Paul's larger purpose. Paul uses the opponents as a negative example to provide a contrast to the appropriate response (Schinkel 2007, 77). Stowers shows that "the fundamental architecture of the book is one of contrasting models" (Stowers 1991, 115). In 1:15–18 he contrasts those who preach Christ from envy and rivalry to those who preach from love. He contrasts those who seek their own interests to Timothy, who is concerned for the welfare of others (2:20–21). Such a contrast establishes collective identity and creates boundaries. David deSilva (1994, 30) has observed that a sectarian group needs confirmation of its identity in order to maintain group cohesion and group boundaries. A reference to enemies strengthens the commitment to the community. Thus in chapter 3 the "phantom opponents" provide the rhetorical foil to create a sharp contrast to Paul's autobiography. Despite the apparent differences in the description of the opponents in 3:2, 18–19, they have in common that they represent the values of the dominant culture. They place their confidence in the flesh (3:3) and their minds are on earthly things (3:19). Paul's autobiography, like the Christ hymn in 2:6–11, presents a mind-set that stands in contrast to that of the larger society (Wojtkowiak 2012, 175).

The Rhetorical Purpose of Paul's Autobiographical Writing

Interpreters who have argued that Phil. 3 is a foreign body in the letter have not recognized the rhetorical purpose of the chapter. This passage is one of several autobiographical sections in the Pauline letters, each of which serves a rhetorical purpose. Second Corinthians, Paul's most autobiographical letter, is a defense against rivals and a response to charges against him (see 10:1–11; 11:7–11). In 1 Thessalonians the autobiographical section (2:1–12) demonstrates Paul's character and lays the foundation for Paul's ethical advice in chapters 4 and 5. Beverly Gaventa (1986, 319–20) has shown that the autobiography in Galatians 1:10–2:21 presents Paul as a model for others. Thus autobiographical sections in Paul can serve either as a defense against attacks or as an example for imitation. As Paul indicates in Phil. 3:17, his task in this chapter is to present himself as an example to the readers. Indeed, his personal example plays a major role throughout the letter. In 1:12–26 he offers his example to those who are anxious about his fate, and in 4:10–20 he is an example of one who can trust God in all circumstances.

The focal point of the chapter is not the opponents but Paul as an example (3:17). The opponents provide the contrasting backdrop for Paul's presentation of himself. After offering Timothy and Epaphroditus as examples of looking to the interests of others, Paul has followed the path of Christ in abandoning his high status and participating in the sufferings of Christ. Paul demonstrates that his own life embodies the abandonment of selfish ambition, as in the Christ hymn. He gave up his privileges and conformed himself to the cross of Christ.

The argument from the speaker's character (*ēthos*) was one of the three proofs suggested by Aristotle (*Rhet.* 1356a), who said that "it is more fitting that a virtuous man show himself good than that his speech be painfully exact" (*Rhet.* 1418b; 3.12.13). According to Aristotle, "the orator persuades by moral character when his speech is delivered in such a manner as to render him worthy of confidence; for we feel confidence in a greater degree and more readily in persons of worth in regard to everything in general" (*Rhet.* 1.2.4, trans. J. H. Freese, LCL; cf. Quintilian, *Inst. or.* 4.1.7–10). Paul embodies the mind of Christ, which he commends to the Philippians. The argument from ethos was recognized among the rhetoricians as a compelling argument.

The customary autobiographical topics include the speaker's (1) immediate and remote ancestry, native city or country (*genos*), and noteworthy facts about their birth; (2) upbringing, education, and choices revealing their character; (3) presentation of the person's deeds (*praxeis*) that illustrate moral character; and (4) comparison with other exemplary persons, usually with an appeal for imitation (Lyons 1985, 28). In *The Life*, Josephus traces his genealogy through five generations of eminent priests on his father's side (1–6), recalls his upbringing and education (7–12), claims to have investigated the various sects, and even reports a time with the Jewish ascetic Bannus (Lyons 1985, 47). Similar topics are present in 2 Corinthians (11:22–25), Galatians (1:10–24), and Phil. 3:3–6.

Autobiographical reflection also had a major place in philosophical literature, much of which was devoted to the topic of moral formation (Gaventa 1986, 324). Seneca's *Epistulae morales* offers abundant evidence of the importance of imitation in moral development. Seneca insists that learning occurs by example, precept (*Ep.* 7.6–9; 11.9–10), and exercise (*Ep.* 16.1–2; 78.16; cf. *Auct. Her.* 1.2.3). On numerous occasions he describes his own struggle to live the virtuous life (*Ep.* 1.4–5; 2.4–5; 6.1–6; 54.1–6) in order to provide an example for his friend (see Cancik 1967, 75). He describes moral progress toward the goal and concedes that he has not arrived (*Ep.* 6.1; 87.5). One who is "short of perfection" (*imperfecta*, 72.1) must "press on and persevere" (*instemus itaque et perseveremus*; 71.35). Seneca consistently urges his friend to pursue the goal with all of his strength, often speaking with images from athletics. He is delighted that his pupil is in the race (*Ep.* 34.2), and he urges his friend, "Strive toward a sound mind at top speed with your whole strength" (*Ep.* 17.1; cf. 78.16). Moral philosophers strengthened their examples by pointing to negative examples of conduct. Seneca warns his friend "not to act after the fashion of those who desire to be conspicuous rather than to improve" (*Ep.* 5.1).

Unlike Galatians and 2 Corinthians, the chapter is not a polemic but an autobiographical summary used for rhetorical purposes. Employing the antithesis that is familiar in the letter (1:15–18; 2:21), Paul uses the opponents as a foil to highlight his own example. Paul's autobiography has points of contact with his autobiographical report in 2 Cor. 11:16–32 and Gal. 1:10–2:14. As in 2 Corinthians (11:22), he declares that he is an Israelite and a Hebrew (3:5). He describes his advancement in Judaism, including his zeal, in both Philippians (3:6) and Galatians (1:14). The autobiography in Philippians is distinctive, however. In 2 Corinthians his autobiography has an apologetic purpose, while in Philippians Paul presents himself as a model (see 3:17), describing both his past (3:4–11) and his anticipated future (3:12–21). Like his readers,

---

Seneca on Self-Improvement

"I feel, my dear Lucilius, that I am being not only reformed, but transformed. I do not yet, however, assure myself, or indulge the hope, that there are no elements left in me which need to be changed. Of course there are many that should be made more compact, or made thinner, or be brought into greater prominence. And indeed this very fact is proof that my spirit is altered into something better,—that it can see its own faults, of which it was previously ignorant.

"I therefore wish to impart to you this sudden change in myself; I should then begin to place a surer trust in our friendship—the true friendship which hope and fear and self-interest cannot sever, the friendship in which and for the sake of which men meet death. . . . You cannot conceive what distinct progress I notice that each day brings to me. And when you say: 'Give me also a share in these gifts which you have found so helpful,' I reply that I am anxious to heap all these privileges upon you, and that I am glad to learn in order that I may teach." (Seneca, Ep. 6.1–4, trans. R. M. Gummere, LCL)

---

he now lives between the past, when he made a radical change (3:4–11), and the anticipated future (3:12–21).

Philippians 3:3–6 has some of the common characteristics of the ancient autobiography. Of the seven personal claims, the first four describe Paul's status from infancy, while the last three describe his own achievements. This distinction corresponds to the categories of ascribed honor and acquired honor (Hellerman 2005, 124) that were common in antiquity. The former includes honors conferred at birth, while the latter describes achievements.

Among Pauline autobiographical claims, only in 3:5 does Paul mention circumcision and his people (*genos*); he mentions his tribe (*phylē*) elsewhere only in Rom. 11:1. His claim that he was "circumcised on the eighth day" refers to the badge of identity for Jews, especially in the period of the second temple, but for Paul it was also the topic for boasting (cf. 3:2–3; Rom. 4:1–2). This claim was analogous to ancient references to the circumstances of one's birth. The claim to be of the "people [*genos*] of Israel," which he also makes in other instances (see Rom. 9:4; 11:1; 2 Cor. 11:22), is parallel to ancient authors' pride in their *genos* (Lyons 1985, 28; cf. Josephus, *Life* 1.1; 2.2). The claim that he was from "the tribe of Benjamin" and a "Hebrew of Hebrews" is also an appeal to his ancestry, a frequent theme in ancient encomia. A common feature of ancient inscriptions is the identification of the individual's tribe (Hellerman 2005, 114). Like his namesake Saul, the first king of Israel, he was from "the tribe of Benjamin," named for one of Jacob's favorite sons. To be from the tribe of Benjamin, whose ancestor was the son of Jacob's favorite wife, was a special honor. Benjamin was the only one of the sons of Jacob born in the land of promise (Gen. 35:16–18). A "Hebrew of Hebrews" was apparently a special claim (cf. 2 Cor. 11:22), probably indicating that he had not assimilated to Greek culture.

Paul proceeds from his status from birth to his own achievements, further indicating his advancement in the Jewish tradition. In ascending order of significance, he lists his achievements. As a Pharisee, he belonged to the school of thought that attempted to preserve the identity of the Jewish people by applying the purity laws to all of Israel. Not only was Paul a Pharisee, but he apparently belonged to the wing that identified itself with zeal for the law and attempted to force it upon others (cf. Gal. 1:14). Those who had zeal for the law looked back to Phinehas, whose zeal led him to enforce God's commands (Num. 25:11) by executing those who had engaged in idolatrous practices. During times when Israel was threatened, devout Jews appealed to zeal for the law as a motivation for action. The aged Mattathias urged the people, "Let everyone who is zealous for the law and supports the covenant come out with me!" (1 Macc. 2:27 NRSV). Paul reaches the climax of his boasting in the flesh, claiming that he was "blameless" (*amemptos*, 3:6), a term used frequently in the OT for those who are fully obedient to God (e.g., Gen. 17:1; Job 1:1, 8; 2:3; 4:17; 11:4; 15:14; 22:3, 19; 33:9; Wis. 10:5, 15).

Although Paul lists achievements that were recognized in Judaism, his list would have resonated with a Roman audience, where the display of one's honors was commonplace. Indeed, Romans included achievements by birth alongside acquired achievements (Hellerman 2005, 123). While the details of Paul's list of achievements would have been unfamiliar to a Roman audience, the style would have been familiar. "The order in which Paul presents his Jewish status corresponds precisely to the typical structure of honor inscriptions found in the colony. In Phil. 3:5, as in the honor inscriptions, ascribed honor precedes acquired honor" (Hellerman 2005, 125). The elite class in Philippi present their birth status before they present their achievements. Thus Paul does not present an argument against the dogs, evil workers, and mutilators but presents an example of "confidence in the flesh" (3:4) and the quest for honor. Thus "confidence in the flesh" is not only a reference to circumcision, but to all human achievements that function as a basis for status. The comment "if anyone else has a reason for confidence in the flesh, I have more" is reminiscent of Paul's decision to engage in foolish boasting (2 Cor. 11:16–12:10) in response to others who boasted of their achievements. In both instances, Paul is apparently engaged in *synkrisis* on the grounds for boasting (S. Ryan 2012, 76). While those

Synkrisis

Synkrisis is a rhetorical device that takes persons, objects, or abstract concepts that are comparable in order to demonstrate either their equality or the superiority of one over the other. It was included in the *progymnasmata*, the exercises in composition practiced in grammar schools.

who insist on circumcision are only a potential threat, the boasting in one's achievements is pervasive in Philippi and a consistent threat to community cohesiveness.

Philippians 3, therefore, is not a polemic against a heresy but a rhetorical exemplum that Paul uses as a model for the Philippians to follow (Smit 2014, 353). His focus on his past achievements, the athletic imagery, and his current striving correspond to the way in which moral philosophers encouraged their students to imitate them. The reference to counterexamples in Phil. 3:2, 18–19 is also a common rhetorical device.

As 3:7–11 indicates, Paul's conversion marked a radical break in his narrative that would not have resonated with a Roman audience. In saying "whatever gains I had, these I come to regard as loss for the sake of Christ," he speaks of his conversion, applying commercial terminology of profit (*kerdos*) and loss (*zēmia*). The literal sense of *zēmia* appears in Acts 27:10, 21 for the loss of property incurred in the shipwreck on Paul's way to Rome. *Kerdos* ("gain, profit," BDAG 541) and *zēmia* ("damage," "disadvantage," "loss," BDAG 428) are commonly used as antonyms, especially in the context of accounting (cf. Plato, *Leg.* 8.835b). Aristotle, in describing the equality that is necessary in order to maintain justice, suggests that inequality is removed only when those who have a surplus of things lose and those who have a deficit gain. He adds, "The terms 'loss' (*zēmia*) and 'gain' (*kerdos*) in these cases are borrowed from the operations of voluntary exchange. There, to have more than one's own is called gaining, and to have less than one had at the outset is called

---

A List of Achievements

This inscription honors Lucius Decimius:

> *L(ucio) Decimio L(uci) f(ilio)*
> *Vol(tinia), q(uaestor), II vir(o)*

Translation:"For Lucius Decimius, son of Lucius, of the tribe Voltinia, quaestor, duumvir" (Pilhofer 2000, 232)

This inscription honors Publius Marius Valens:

> *P(ublius) Marius P(ubli) f(ilius) Vol(tinia) Valens or(namentis)*
> *dec(urionatus) hon(oratus), aed(ilis), id(em) Philipp(is),*
> *decurio, flamen divi Antonini Pii, IIvir, mun(erarius).*

Translation: "Publius Marius Valens, son of Publius, from the tribe Voltinia, honored with the decorations of a decurion, aedile, also Decurion of Philippi, priest of the divine Antoninus Pius, duumvir, sponsor of games" (Pilhofer 2000, 397, trans. Hellerman 2005, 97)

losing, as for instance in buying and selling" (*Eth. nic.* 5.4.1133b). One may compare the comment of Epictetus: "When a vase that is not broken and is still useful is discarded, whoever finds it carries it off and considers it a gain [*kerdos hēgēsetai*], but with you, everyone will consider it a pure loss [*pas zēmia*]" (*Diatr.* 3.26.25). Josephus (*Ant.* 4.274) speaks of profit and loss when he says, "They consider it immoral to profit from the loss of another." This accounting metaphor is evident in Jesus's statement, "What will it profit them to gain [*kerdēsē*] the whole world and forfeit [*zēmiōthē*] their life?" (Matt. 16:26).

In the statement "I have come to regard as loss" (*hēgoumai*),

Figure 9. Artist's depiction of Paul's encounter on the road to Damascus

Paul employs the perfect tense to describe a point in the past that remains the reality in his life. Paul indicates that "not only were the profits wiped out; they became losses" (*TLNT* 2:159). One may compare the references to his conversion in Gal. 1:13–24 and 2 Cor. 4:5–6.

The imagery of profit and loss also appears in rabbinic literature, where it is applied to the observant Jewish life: one should balance the loss incurred by keeping the commandments by the greater profit that it entails (*m. 'Abot* 2.1; cited in Bockmuehl 1998, 205). Thus perhaps the image was known to Paul before his conversion.

In 3:12–16 Paul turns from commercial imagery to the imagery of the runner in pursuit of a goal. The phrase "I press on [*diōkō*] that I might lay hold of [*ei kai katalabō*, lit. "if I may grasp"]" (3:12) has no object in Greek; thus it is a generic description of a pursuit, with a special emphasis on the intense effort involved. *Diōkō* ("I press on," "I pursue") can be used either in the negative sense of "persecute" (Matt. 5:10–12; 10:23; 1 Cor. 4:12; 2 Cor. 4:9) or in the positive sense of pursuing a worthy goal (cf. Rom. 12:13; 14:19; 1 Cor. 14:1), with the emphasis on running or chasing after a person or an object (A. Oepke, *TDNT* 2:230). The word is frequently used with forms of *katalambanō* ("to make something one's own, win, attain, grasp," BDAG 519). Together the two verbs suggest the intensity of the pursuit in order to reach the goal. One may contrast Paul's statement "I pursue that I might lay hold of" with the contrast between gentiles who did not pursue (*diōkonta*) righteousness but received (*katelaben*) it, and the Jews who pursued (*diōkōn*) the law of righteousness and did not attain it (Rom. 9:30–31). Paul's singular focus is the opposite of that mentioned in Sir. 11:10, which describes the person who is preoccupied with many matters: "If you pursue [*diōkēs*], you will not overtake [*katalabēs*]" (NRSV).

While Paul does not supply an object in 3:12, he introduces an object in 3:13–14, indicating that the pursuit is toward the finish line in a race. Like the runner who does not look back, he aims toward the goal of the prize (*brabeion*), the victory wreath that was given to the winner. Paul employs similar imagery in 1 Cor. 9:24 to describe the prize (*brabeion*) that goes to the winner of the race. In both instances, the prize is not the laurel wreath but the resurrection (cf. 3:11).

In 3:20–21 Paul contrasts the majority (3:18) with the believing community, moving from the third-person plural to the first-person plural—from the "many" (*polloi*) who will be destroyed to the believing community that says, "As for us, our citizenship [*politeuma*] is in heaven" (3:20). While their end (*telos*) is destruction, "we wait for a Savior." The emphatic *hēmōn* ("our"), placed first in the sentence emphasizes the contrast between the church and the majority population (see comments on 1:27 for further discussion of *politeuma* among Jews and Romans), which takes pride in its Roman citizenship.

Ernst Lohmeyer notes that 3:20–21 is a carefully crafted sentence in Greek, written in a rhythmic style that stands out from the preceding argument, concluding that it is a pre-Pauline hymn (Lohmeyer 1953, 156–57). The main clause, "our citizenship is in heaven" (3:20a), is followed by two subordinate and parallel clauses (3:20b; 3:21a) introduced by the relative pronoun *ex hou* (NRSV "from there") and *hos* ("who," NRSV "he"), followed by the claim of divine power (3:21b). Lohmeyer also observed the unusual vocabulary in this statement: *politeuma* ("citizenship"), *en ouranois* (lit. "in the heavens"), *sōtēr* ("savior"), *metaschēmatisei* ("he will transform"), and *sōma tēs tapeinōseōs hēmōn* ("body of our humiliation"). This unusual vocabulary, as Lohmeyer

---

Emperors Honored as Savior

"[Julius Caesar is] the God made manifest, offspring of Ares and Aphrodite and common saviour of human life." (*SIG* 760, cited in Deissmann 2004, 344)

"Providence . . . created . . . the most perfect good for our lives . . . filling him [Augustus] with virtue for the benefit of mankind, sending us and those after us a savior who put an end to war and established all things . . . and whereas the birthday of the god marked for the world the beginning of good tidings through his coming [tōn di' autōn euangeliōn]." (*OGIS* 458, cited in Oakes 2001, 139)

notes, has points of contact with the poetic narrative in 2:6–11 (see above). The evidence offered by Lohmeyer is not sufficient, however, to determine that 3:20–21 is a hymn, for it lacks many of the characteristics of a hymn.

The passage confronts us with Paul's relationship with Roman power, a theme that he introduced in the first two chapters. "Our citizenship [*politeuma*] is in heaven" has a special significance in Philippi, where Roman citizenship was highly prized. Inscriptions attest the significance of citizenship in Philippi (Schinkel 2007, 103). Over against the high evaluation of citizenship and striving for it in Philippi, Paul points to citizenship in heaven. Believers in Philippi are like colonists in a foreign land (cf. Pilhofer 1995, 127). For this community, Roman citizenship loses its relevance (Wojtkowiak 2012, 209). Believers are obligated, not to Caesar as Lord, but to Jesus Christ as Lord.

To be a citizen is to accept the mores and values that accompany citizenship. Paul suggests that the church and the Philippian society, with its values of competition for honor, are two incompatible states. While Roman society is oriented toward earthly things, the believers are oriented toward their heavenly citizenship with its mores. This passage coordinates with the instruction in 1:27, "Live out your citizenship [*politeuesthe*] worthily of the gospel." This contrasts the community with the world, as in 2:14–15, and explains the hostility that the church faces (1:28). The church belongs to a *politeuma* that surpasses Rome, for it is *in heaven*.

Whereas Rome looked to Caesar as the one who preserves peace and security, "we await a Savior who comes from heaven" (3:20). Although the verb "to save" (*sōzein*) is commonplace in the NT, Paul is the first to use the word *sōtēr* for Jesus Christ. This claim is in direct conflict with the Roman designation for Caesar. The emperor Claudius was frequently referred to as *sōtēr*. Paul

---

Philippians 3:1–4:1 in the Rhetorical Flow

Exordium: **Thanksgiving and prayer for moral formation (1:1–11)**

Narratio: **The present and future advance of the gospel (1:12–26)**

Propositio: **Citizens united in an alternative commonwealth (1:27–30)**

Probatio: **Examples of faithful living (2:1–4:1)**

> The ultimate example (2:1–11)

> Following the example of Christ (2:12–18)

> The examples of Timothy and Epaphroditus (2:19–30)

▶ **The example of Paul (3:1–4:1)**

> Rejoice in the Lord (3:1)

> Paul's conversion and change of values (3:2–11)

>> The true circumcision (3:2–3)

>> Paul's gains and losses (3:4–7)

>> Paul's participation in the sufferings of Christ (3:8–11)

> From the present to the future (3:12–21)

>> Pressing on to perfection (3:12–14)

>> Acquiring a new mind-set (3:15–16)

>> Good and bad examples (3:17–21)

> Concluding the argument: Stand firm (4:1)

promises that the *sōtēr* comes from heaven, the state to which the believers belong (*ex hou*, "from there," 3:20), to rescue them (Oakes 2001, 139). The imagery suggests the role of the emperor as the military leader of the state who comes to drive out the occupying force. The Philippians could have remembered events two decades earlier when the emperor, represented by his legions, arrived to drive away the Thracians (Oakes 2001, 139). This claim should reassure Philippian believers, who see only the threatening power of Rome (Tellbe 1994, 112).

Tracing the Train of Thought

Rejoice in the Lord (3:1)

3:1. Although Phil. 3 is not, as many scholars have maintained, a separate letter written on a different occasion from the other chapters, it is nevertheless a defined rhetorical unit. However, the boundaries of the passage are not entirely clear. Since *to loipon* (NRSV **finally**) does not mark the end of the letter, as in 4:8, it should be rendered "as far as the rest is concerned" (cf. BDAG 602), as it introduces the discussion that follows. **Rejoice in the Lord** (3:1a), a refrain that marks the transition between topics in Philippians (cf. 2:18; 4:4), and "stand firm in the Lord" (4:1) form the outer frame of this section, a reminder that the community's entire existence is "in Christ" (1:1; 2:1, 5). Paul offers the basis for these imperatives in 3:2–21.

In both the beginning and the end of this section, Paul speaks in the intimate tones of the family, addressing the readers as **my brothers and sisters** (3:1, *adelphoi mou*, lit. "my brothers") and as "my brothers and sisters, whom I love and long for, my joy and crown" (4:1). The language of the fictive family reflects the relationship that is the basis for the imperatives, especially the call for imitation (3:17). The Philippians are not only Paul's partners (1:5, 7) but also his "brothers and sisters" and "beloved" (see 1:12; 2:12; 3:1, 13, 17; 4:1, 8). In his care for the church, he also takes a paternal role as the basis for his authority (Still 2012, 63).

Because Paul writes with no conjunctions in 3:1–2, interpreters have debated the relationship between the three sentences, two of which are imperatives. "Rejoice in the Lord" (3:1) is a refrain (cf. 2:18; 4:4) that marks the transition from 2:19–30 to the autobiographical section in 3:2–21. Because of the impending arrival of Timothy, Paul, and Epaphroditus, the Philippians may now rejoice in the Lord (cf. Reed 1996, 82). The relationship between 3:1a ("rejoice in the Lord") and 3:1b **to write the same things is not a matter of hesitation** (*oknēron*, NRSV "troublesome") **for me, and for you is trustworthy** (*asphalē*, NRSV "safeguard") is unclear (cf. Reed 1996, 77). Jeffrey T. Reed (1996, 77) maintains that the phrase is a hesitation formula, a common literary convention. Similarly, the relationship between 3:1b and the imperative in 3:2 ("beware of the dogs . . .") is unclear. Some have interpreted the same things (*ta auta*) as a reference to 3:1a ("rejoice in the Lord"), while others interpret it as a reference to 3:2–21. Paul's indication that he is repeating himself in 3:1b forms an *inclusio* with the statement in 3:18 that he had warned the Philippians many times about the dangers. Thus "to write the same things" is probably to repeat what Paul had said on his earlier visit. Much of the content of his previous instruction is probably present in 3:2–21. Thus the warning and exhortation in 3:2–21 are trustworthy (*asphales*) for the readers.

To rejoice in the Lord (3:1) is to imitate Paul, who rejoices in the context of his imprisonment (1:4, 18; 2:18) and challenges the readers to rejoice with him (2:18). Their rejoicing, like Paul's, is in the context of the anxieties facing the church in its present situation. Paul invites the readers to recognize, with OT writers, that the faithful rejoice in God as their strength (cf. Neh. 8:10). Mount Zion is the joy of all the earth because God is Israel's defense (Ps. 48:2–3). As the remainder of chapter 3 suggests, believers rejoice in the Lord when they look beyond the present duress and recall their participation in a heavenly calling (3:14, 20–21).

Paul's Conversion and Change of Values (3:2–11)

The section 3:2–21 is a carefully structured unit framed by the parallel in 3:2–4 and 3:17–21. This unit contains (a) a warning against opposition (3:2, "beware the dogs, the evil workers, the mutilation") and against the enemies of the cross of Christ whose god is the belly (3:18–19), (b) the first-person plural identifying the church (3:3, "we are the circumcision"; 3:20, "our citizenship is in heaven"), and (c) Paul's first-person reference (3:4, "I have reason for confidence in the flesh"; 3:17, "be my imitators"). At the center of the discussion, as 3:4b–16 indicates, is the Pauline autobiography. Thus the opponents function as the foil for the primary focus on Paul, who is a model for the church.

3:2–3. *The true circumcision.* The opening warning in 3:2 has a strong rhetorical effect. The threefold **beware** (*blepete*) heightens the rhetorical impact. The imperative *blepete*, which can be translated either as "beware" or "observe" is parallel to the imperative "observe" (*skopeite*) in 3:17. Because Paul is pointing to threatening forces in 3:2, the meaning "beware" is probably intended. Thus at the beginning and end of the chapter, Paul challenges the readers to beware of negative models (3:2) and observe (3:17) those who follow his example.

The rhetorical power of Paul's warning is also evident in the alliteration with which he names the opposition: the *kynas* (**dogs**), the *kakous ergatas* (**evil workers**), and the *katatomē* (**those who mutilate**). Because the three terms, like the reference in 3:18–19, are more invective than description, one cannot draw a profile of the opposition. Because of Paul's frequent encounter with those who insist on circumcision, *katatomē* is evidently a word that he has coined to refer to the *peritomē* (circumcision). Since the letter lacks any other reference to the demand for circumcision, the gentile church at Philippi is probably not confronted with this immediate danger. For Paul, they are examples of what he describes as **confidence in the flesh** (3:4).

The emphatic **we**—not "they"—distinguishes the Philippian church from others (3:3). Paul uses the first-person plural for the first time, identifying himself with the church. **We are the circumcision** (3:3) and "our commonwealth is in heaven" (3:20) are parallel claims, contrasting the church with the opposition (Schenk 1984, 254). "We are the circumcision" is a statement of the collective identity of the community and an affirmation that this minority group has an honored place and history. It is not those who insist on circumcision (the mutilation) who are the circumcision, but "we," the community composed of Jews and gentiles, who are. The term indicates that this gentile community not only participates in Israel's story, but is the culmination of that story.

Paul alludes to the metaphorical use of circumcision that described the renewed Israel after the return from exile. Moses commands Israel, "Circumcise the foreskin of your hearts" (Deut. 10:16). Israel looks forward to the time when "God will circumcise the foreskin of [their] hearts" (Deut. 30:6). In Romans Paul reverses the categories of circumcision and uncircumcision, insisting that a Jew is one inwardly, and real circumcision is a matter of the heart—it is spiritual and not literal (Rom. 2:28). The image continues in Colossians, according to which believers "were circumcised with a spiritual circumcision" (Col. 2:11 NRSV).

Paul elaborates on the identity of the church, using three participial phrases to describe those who are the circumcision. They are the ones **worshiping in the Spirit and boasting in the Lord Jesus Christ and having no confidence in the flesh.** As people who already possess the fellowship of the Spirit (2:1, NRSV "sharing in the Spirit"), they have received the promised gift for the renewed people of God. Ezekiel spoke of the time when God would place the Spirit within the people (Ezek. 11:19; 36:26–27). Paul's letters consistently affirm that the Spirit is the divine power that enables believers to do God's will (Rom. 8:1–11; 1 Cor. 12:1–14:40; Gal. 5:16–25; 1 Thess. 4:8). In describing believers as those who worship (*latreuontes*) in the Spirit, Paul employs a verb that was commonly used in the OT for cultic observances (cf. Exod. 4:23; Deut. 10:12; Josh. 22:27; 1 Macc. 2:19; cf. Heb. 9:1–6). In Rom. 12:1 all of Christian conduct is "spiritual worship" (*latreia*). Thus to worship in the Spirit is the equivalent of walking in the Spirit (Gal. 5:16) or being led by the Spirit (Gal. 5:18). The Spirit dwells in the community, God's temple (1 Cor. 3:16), which responds by worshiping in the Spirit. Thus in sending gifts through Epaphroditus, they have sent a sweet-smelling sacrifice (Phil. 4:18).

From Jeremiah, Paul knows the difference between arrogant boasting and boasting in God. Jeremiah condemned boasting in one's wisdom, might, or wealth but challenged his listeners to boast in the fact that God is the Lord (9:23–24). Similarly, Paul cautions against boasting about one's works of the law (cf. Rom. 3:27; 4:2), human leaders (1 Cor. 3:21), or achievements (cf. 2 Cor.

11:12, 16, 18), for all such boasting is "confidence in the flesh" (Phil. 3:4; cf. 2 Cor. 11:18). He probably echoes Jeremiah when he indicates that legitimate boasting is "in the Lord" (1 Cor. 1:31; 2 Cor. 10:17) or "in the cross" (Gal. 6:14). Indeed, because of the saving work of Christ, the community can now boast in hope (Rom. 5:2) and even boast in its sufferings (Rom. 5:3), for boasting is "in God through our Lord Jesus Christ" (Rom. 5:11). Because God is at work, Paul will boast about the Philippian church at the day of Christ (Phil. 2:16; cf. 2 Cor. 1:14; 1 Thess. 2:19). Thus Paul further describes the community as those "boasting in the Lord Jesus Christ" (Phil. 3:3).

Paul emphasizes the exclusive nature of the boast: to boast in Christ Jesus is to deny all other objects of devotion. Thus by identifying the church as those who do not have confidence in the flesh (Phil. 3:3–4), Paul contrasts those who worship in the Spirit and boast in the Lord Jesus Christ with those who have confidence in the flesh. The contrast between worshiping in the Spirit and confidence in the flesh recalls Paul's frequent contrast between flesh and Spirit, the two contrasting powers. The phrase can refer to those who insist on circumcision (cf. Gal. 3:3) or to those who live without the Spirit of God (cf. Rom. 8:1–11; Gal. 5:16–25). In Phil. 3:3–4 Paul contrasts the confidence in the flesh with the worship in the Spirit. Confidence in the flesh is confidence in one's own achievements.

3:4–7. *Paul's gains and losses.* The identification of the church as those who do not put their confidence in the flesh introduces the transition from the description of the church to Paul, whose autobiographical reflections extend from 3:4–17. Paul is a model for the church (3:17) as he looks back over his radical change of values. He responds, **Although I have confidence even in the flesh** (3:4, NRSV "have reason for confidence in the flesh") and adds, **If anyone thinks that he has reason to have confidence in the flesh, I have more**, introducing the list of achievements in 3:5–6. Paul thus engages in a *synkrisis* with any who have confidence in the flesh. This *synkrisis* is parallel to 2 Cor. 11:21, "But whatever anyone dares to boast of . . . I also dare to boast of that," and the list of achievements that follows. Paul is probably comparing himself to many in the city of Philippi who boast of their achievements.

Paul announces the radical change in values in 3:7 with the image of profit and loss, which he develops in 3:7–11. Although some manuscripts add the conjunction *all'* (NRSV "yet") to provide a transition from Paul's gains (3:4b–6) to his change of values in 3:7–11, the best early manuscripts omit the conjunction. Paul gives a thesis statement in 3:7 and then elaborates on the profit and loss. Verses 8–11 are one sentence in Greek that describes the radical change in values:

> Whatever gains [I had] I have come to regard as loss because of Christ.
> Indeed, all things I regard as loss because of the surpassing knowledge
>   of Christ Jesus my Lord,

> for whose sake I regarded all things as loss,
> and [all things] I regard as rubbish in order that I may gain Christ.
> (3:7–8)

All of the achievements of 3:5–6 are the gains (*kerdē*) that Paul now considers loss (*zēmia*). The use of the perfect tense "I have come to regard" (*hēgoumai*) points to an event in the past that is a continuing reality. The verb (from *hēgeomai*) suggests a parallel to the preexistent Christ who did not count (*hēgēsato*) equality with God a thing to be grasped (2:6), and the transference of gain to loss recalls the self-emptying of Christ (2:7). This radical change of values took place "because of Christ." As Paul indicates in Gal. 2:19, he "died to the law" in order to "live for God." While the law continues to be a source of moral instruction (cf. Gal. 5:14; 6:2), Christ is now the source of his righteousness. Although Paul could compare his achievements with those given by the elite citizens of Philippi, he has rejected the values of the dominant society.

3:8–11. *Paul's participation in the sufferings of Christ.* In 3:8–11, which is one sentence in Greek, Paul elaborates on his claim, beginning with the emphatic **more than that** (*alla menounge kai*), a remarkable sequence of particles that are difficult to translate but that in Greek mark the shift from the perfect tense "I counted" (*hēgēmai*, 3:7) to the present tense "I count" (*hēgoumai*, 3:8; Hawthorne 2004, 189). Instead of "whatever gains" (*hatina . . . kerdē*) that he counted as loss (3:7), Paul counts **all things** (*ta panta*) as loss (3:8). The emphasis on "all things" indicates that it is not only the Jewish heritage that he considers a loss but every claim to achievement. He adds the aorist tense **I lost all things** and concludes with the present tense **I count** (*hēgoumai*) **all things as rubbish** (*skybala*) **in order that I might gain Christ.** *Skybala* can mean either the refuse that is thrown to the dogs or the excrement from the dog. Paul employs the strongest language to describe the inversion of values. This is a radical means of describing Paul's participation in the story of Christ's self-emptying. What Paul counts as loss is neither his past in Judaism nor his blameless keeping of the law, but these achievements as examples of confidence in the flesh. Even those things that are highly beneficial lose their value in comparison to Christ (cf. Campbell 2011, 50).

Paul expresses the goal of this new "profit and loss" statement with two verbs: that "I may gain [*kerdēsō*] Christ" (3:8) **and be found** (*heurethō*) **in him** (3:9). Paul has inverted his old values; what were once in the profit column become losses when he gains Christ. To be "found in him" is parallel to the situation of Jesus, who had emptied himself, "being found" (*heuretheis*) as a man (2:7). The second clause explains what it means to gain Christ. Paul expresses this goal in a chiastic structure that contrasts two kinds of righteousness (see O'Brien 1991, 394). The ultimate goal will occur at the end-time, but Paul already experiences this transformation (cf. Fee 1995, 320).

> **Not having** (*mē echōn*)
>> **my own** (*emēn*)
>>> **righteousness** (*dikaiosynēn*)
>>>> **that comes from the law** (*ek nomou*)
>>>> **but through faith in Christ** (*pisteōs Christou*)
>>>> **that comes from God** (*ek theou*)
>>> **righteousness**
>> **by faith.** (3:9)

Paul speaks in the antitheses that are common in Galatians and Romans: his own righteousness in which he was blameless (3:6) and the righteousness by faith (3:9); righteousness from the law and the righteousness of God. He has discovered that the alternative to the righteousness by which he was once blameless (3:6) is the righteousness that comes from faith in Christ (*pisteōs Christou*), stating succinctly here what he develops in Galatians and Romans, where he frequently speaks in the stark alternatives between law and faith (Gal. 3:12), Christ and the law (Gal. 2:19–20), and one's own righteousness and the righteousness of God (Rom. 10:1–4). Thus to gain Christ is to count as loss the quest for his own righteousness.

Interpreters debate the meaning of *pistis Christou* as the alternative to the righteousness based on law. The phrase appears also in Galatians and Romans as the alternative of works of the law (e.g., Rom. 3:22, 26; Gal. 2:16). Most translations render this genitive phrase "faith in Christ" (objective genitive), although the phrase may be also rendered "faithfulness of Christ" (subjective genitive). Indeed, the most common rendering of *pistis* followed by the genitive of the person refers to the faithfulness of the individual rather than faith in an individual (O'Brien 1991, 398; cf. Rom. 3:3, faithfulness [*pistis*] of God; 4:16, faithfulness [*pistis*] of Abraham). However, the numerous times that Paul uses *pistis* without an object (cf. Rom. 1:5, 8, 12, 17; 3:28–30; 5:1; 2 Cor. 5:7) or speaks of believing in Christ (Rom. 10:10–11; Gal. 2:16) or God (Rom. 4:3, 5) suggest that faith is the human response to God's grace. The parallel between *pistis Christou* and *pistis* in Phil. 3:9 indicates that the alternative to righteousness from the law is faith in Christ, the human response to God's gift. This faith is not, however, a virtue, but a gift—as Paul has declared already in Philippians (1:28)—that brings great joy (1:25). Thus Paul has made a radical turn from the confidence in the flesh to faith in Christ. Neither in describing his previous gains as loss nor in his abandonment of his own righteousness does he deny the continuing importance of the Torah in his life. What he has counted as loss is the confidence in the flesh. This radical break is a challenge not only to those who boast of achievements under the law but to all who have confidence in the flesh.

Paul elaborates on this new balance sheet in 3:10 with the infinitive phrase **to know him** (NRSV "I want to know Christ"), which is evidently the equivalent of "the knowledge of Christ" (3:8) that he gained when he counted his achievements as loss. Paul once knew Christ "in a worldly way" (*kata sarka*, 2 Cor. 5:16), but he has come to know him in a new way. The phrase, expressing purpose, elaborates on Paul's earlier purpose statement, "in order that I may gain Christ and be found in him . . ." (3:8–9). "To know him," a phrase that recalls the OT theme of knowing God (cf. Jer. 31:34; Hosea 2:20; Wis. 15:3), is an alternative way of describing faith in Christ (3:9). To know him is not to have a body of information about Christ but to enter into a relationship with him.

The relationship between "to know him" and **the power of his resurrection and the sharing of his sufferings** (3:10) is unclear. Most translations render the *kai*s (and) as parallel, indicating that "to know" has a threefold object: him (Christ), the power of his resurrection, and the sharing of his sufferings. A more likely reading is to interpret the first *kai* as epexegetic; that is, the power of his resurrection and the sharing in his sufferings indicate what it means to know him. Thus the appropriate translation is "to know him, that is, the power of his resurrection and the sharing of his sufferings" (Fee 1995, 328).

Paul expresses the meaning of knowing Christ in a chiasm (3:10–11):

A **Both the power** (*dynamin*) **of his resurrection** (*anastaseōs*)

B **And the sharing** (*koinōnian*) **of his sufferings** (*pathēmatōn*)

B′ **Being conformed** (*symmorphizomenos*) **to his death**

A′ **If somehow I will attain to the resurrection of the dead.**

In contrast to the old existence, to know Christ is to experience God's power (cf. Rom. 1:16; 15:13; 1 Cor. 1:18, 24; 2:4; 4:19–20; Gal. 3:5). As the juxtaposition of "the power of his resurrection" and "the sharing of his sufferings" indicates, this power is present for those who share in his sufferings, as Paul indicates in the other letters. Believers "suffer with him" and will be glorified with him (Rom. 8:17). The sufferings of Christ overflow in Paul's life (2 Cor. 1:5), and other believers share in his sufferings for Christ (2 Cor. 1:7). God's power is present in Paul's own weakness (2 Cor. 4:7; 12:9) as he carries around the dying of Jesus in his body (2 Cor. 4:10). Paul has already mentioned the suffering of the Philippians (1:29), indicating that they are involved in the same struggle that he faces (1:30). Thus God's power is especially present in the sharing of the sufferings, which Paul models for his readers.

Parallel to the sharing of his sufferings is "being conformed to [*symmorphizomenos*, NRSV "becoming like him"] his death." Just as Jesus, though being in the form (*morphē*) of God, became obedient to death, to know Christ is to be conformed (*symmorphizō*) to his death, which is the prelude to being conformed (*symmorphon*) to the body of his glory (3:21). Paul's present sufferings, therefore, are not unexpected events that call into question the legitimacy of his ministry but are instead participation in the narrative of Jesus (2:6–11).

Indeed, Paul may be anticipating that his imprisonment will result in death. Thus if the Philippians now suffer with Paul (cf. 1:30), they are following in the path of Jesus.

This path leads ultimately to resurrection, as Paul indicates, saying, "if somehow [*ei pōs*] I might attain [*katantēsō*] the resurrection from the dead." "If somehow" expresses not doubt about the outcome of Paul's sufferings but the reality that being conformed to his death is the necessary prelude to the resurrection. As Paul says in Romans, "If we suffer with him, we shall be glorified with him" (8:17). *Katantaō* ("attain") suggests the journey toward a destination (cf. BDAG 523), the resurrection from the dead. Thus Paul stands between the radical break in his life and its ultimate outcome, the resurrection.

From the Present to the Future (3:12–21)

3:12–14. *Pressing on to perfection.* This journey is incomplete, however, for the final act in the drama awaits him. Although Paul has shared with Jesus the self-emptying of Christ, he remains on the path to the ultimate goal. Anticipating a misunderstanding, he adds, **not that** (*ouch hoti*) **I received** (*elabon*, NRSV "obtained this") **or have been made perfect** (*teteleiōmai*, NRSV "have reached the goal"), **but I press on** (*diōkō*) **to make it my own** (*ei kai katalabō*) (3:12). In Greek, neither "received" (*elabon*) nor "press on" (*diōkō*) has a direct object, but the referent is apparently the resurrection mentioned in verse 11. To be "made perfect," therefore, is to reach the ultimate goal, the resurrection, which Paul then describes with the imagery in 3:13–14.

The images suggested by "press on" (*diōkō*) and "make it my own" (*katalambanō*) were probably familiar to the ancient audience. Paul was once a "persecutor [*diōkōn*] of the church" (3:6), but now he claims, "I press on" (*diōkō*), suggesting the intense effort that he makes in order to reach the goal. *Katalambanō* ("lay hold of") is an intensified form of "receive" (*lambanō*) and means "win," "catch up with," or "grasp" (BDAG 520; G. Delling, *TDNT* 4:9). The two words are frequently used together in Greek literature. Extending the image of grasping, Paul adds the reason for his pursuit: **because** (*eph hō*) **I have been grasped** (*katelēmphthēn*) **by Christ Jesus.** That is, Paul hopes to grasp the goal because he has been "grasped" by Christ. He counted all things as loss at his conversion and was also grasped by Christ at that moment.

Paul elaborates on the images of pursuing and reaching the goal in verses 13–14, speaking in intimate terms and addressing the readers once more as siblings (*adelphoi*, 3:13). The negative statement **I do not consider that I have made it my own** (*kateilēphenai*) reiterates the claim that he has not yet been made perfect. Instead, in **forgetting what lies behind and straining forward to what lies ahead,** he is like a runner. In forgetting what lies behind, he recalls the achievements he mentions in 3:5–6, which he counted as "loss." In straining forward to what lies ahead, he indicates the intense labor that is involved in the pursuit of the goal, using the image of the runner who exhausts himself.

Figure 10. Greek vase depicting runners at the Panathenaic Games, ca. 530 BCE

In 3:14 Paul elaborates on the earlier statement (3:12), now explicitly indicating the object of the pursuit. He presses on **toward the goal** (*kata skopon*) of the **prize** (*brabeion*). *Skopos* is an image commonly used for the target in archery. In combination with *diōkō*, it suggests the runner looking at the finish line. Paul uses a similar image in 1 Cor. 9:24 for the prize that the runner wins in the contest. In this instance the prize is **the heavenly** (*anō*, lit. "upward") **calling in Christ Jesus**. The genitive is probably a genitive of apposition, indicating that the prize is the upward calling. Paul envisions the Christian life as a calling. He has been called to be an apostle (Rom. 1:1; 1 Cor. 1:1), and his converts have also been called into the fellowship of Christ (Rom. 1:6, 7; 8:28; 1 Cor. 1:26; 7:17–24; 1 Thess. 2:12; 4:7). This call is "upward" to the resurrection (3:11), the "perfection" (3:12) that he has not yet received, and the ultimate destiny of those who are conformed to the death of the Son.

For anyone who is disoriented by the present suffering, Paul demonstrates from his own life that the struggle is the prelude to the ultimate triumph. The higher calling indicates that the Philippians who share Paul's suffering anticipate participation in the glory of Jesus (3:20–21).

3:15–16. *Acquiring a new mind-set.* Paul turns from autobiography to exhortation in 3:15–21, stating the implications of his autobiography for the readers. This section has a chiastic structure, as Paul proceeds from *A* (the hortatory appeal in first-person plural, 3:15–16) to *B* (the negative examples,

3:18–19) and again to *A'* (the first-person plural, 3:20–21; cf. Willis 2007, 187). **As many of us who are mature** (*teleios*, 3:15) forms an *inclusio* with Paul's personal claim (3:12), "Not that I have become perfect" (*teteleiōmai*). The contrast between Paul's statement that he has not been perfected (NRSV "reached the goal") and "as many of us who are mature" (*teleios*) has suggested to numerous scholars that Paul is being ironic in speaking of those who are *teleios* in 3:15. However, since Paul includes himself, he is probably not using the word in an ironic sense (cf. Bockmuehl 1998, 226), but is using *teleioō/ teleios* in two different ways. The NRSV rendering "mature" is appropriate in 3:15. *Teleios* is used in the Septuagint for those who wholeheartedly follow God's ways (cf. Gen. 6:9; 1 Kings 8:61; 11:4). Those "of us who are mature" are the people who recognize, with Paul, that they have not yet reached the goal but are striving to reach it.

The exhortation **let us have this mind** (NRSV "be of the same mind") is an appropriate conclusion to the autobiography. Paul introduced the Christ hymn (2:6–11) with the imperative "Have this mind among you" (*touto phroneite*, 2:5) and concludes his autobiography with the same injunction, "Have this mind" (*touto phronōmen*), which he contrasts with anyone who **thinks differently**. Thus in conforming his life to that of Christ, he exemplifies the moral reasoning (*phronēsis*) that he hopes to instill among the readers. The Roman emphasis on honor and selfish ambition is to be put away, and the mind of Christ is to be adopted.

Paul contrasts those who have the same mind (*touto phronōmen*) with those who think differently (*heterōs phroneite*, 3:15b). He is probably envisioning not opponents among those who think differently but believers who differ on anything that remains unresolved (cf. O'Brien 1991, 438). He assures them that God **will reveal** (*apokalypsei*) to the readers where their thinking has gone wrong, but he does not say when this occasion will take place. Both the verb *apokalypsei* and the noun *apokalypsis* refer to divine communication that occurs in the gospel (see Rom. 1:17; 1 Cor. 2:10; Gal. 1:12, 16), in prophetic disclosures or ecstatic visions (see 1 Cor. 14:6, 26, 30; 2 Cor. 12:1, 7; Gal. 2:2), and at the eschaton (Bockmuehl 1998, 227). Paul probably envisions the continuing revelation in the community, as in 1 Cor. 14:6–30.

Having indicated that we have not reached the destination, Paul concludes the image of the runner pursuing the goal, encouraging the Philippians, **let us hold fast** (*stoichein*) **to what we have attained** (*ephthasamen*). Thus while we have not reached the resurrection (3:11) or the prize (3:14), we have reached a stage along the way. One may compare Paul's statement that Israel, while pursuing (*diōkōn*) righteousness by the law, did not attain (*ephthasen*) it (Rom. 9:31). The opposite is the case, according to Phil. 3:16. Believers have attained the righteousness of faith (cf. Phil. 3:9), and the task of the community is to hold fast (*stoichein*) to it. *Stoichein*, which has the literal meaning of "be in line with a person or thing considered to be a model of conduct" (BDAG 946), is a term that can mean "to follow in someone's footsteps" (Rom. 4:12) or conform to a rule (Gal. 6:16). This exhortation is parallel to the earlier exhortation to conduct oneself worthily of the gospel (Phil. 1:27). The examples of Jesus and Paul provide the standard for the Philippians.

3:17–21. *Good and bad examples.* Paul draws his autobiography to a close in 3:17, addressing the Philippians as siblings and challenging the readers, **join together in imitating me** (*symmimētai mou ginesthe*). While he encourages the Corinthians, "Be my imitators" (*mimētai mou ginesthe*, 1 Cor. 4:16; 11:1; cf. 1 Thess. 1:6; Eph. 5:1), the compound verb *symmimētai* emphasizes the solidarity of the community as the members join together in imitating Paul, who frequently indicates the solidarity of the community with the prefix *syn-* (cf. *synathlountes*, "struggle together," 1:27; 4:3; *synchairete*, "rejoice together," 2:18). Paul is probably referring to the coordinated efforts to imitate his way of life as he imitates the path of Jesus from descent to ultimate glory. When Paul adds **observe** (*skopeite*) **those who live according to the example** (*typos*) **that you have of us**, he changes the pronoun from singular to plural but probably refers to himself, Timothy, and Epaphroditus (2:19–30) as the primary examples.

While he encourages the readers to "beware" of the negative examples (3:2), he challenges them to observe (*skopeite*) the positive examples. As the example (*typos*) for the Philippians, Paul stands in sharp contrast to the negative examples in 3:18–19, which describe the majority culture—**the many,** who are **enemies of the cross of Christ.** The fact that Paul told them this **many times** suggests that his message had encountered resistance during his founding visit. As he indicates to the Corinthians, the cross is an offense to Jews and foolishness to the Greeks (1:23). In Philippi especially, with its values of honor, the majority were the adversaries (1:28) and would have been enemies of the cross of Christ. These dominant views were probably a constant temptation for Philippian believers, who were now alienated from the larger society by the message of the cross. Thus the enemies of the cross could have been both outsiders as well as believers who wished to avoid the message of the cross. As Paul indicates in 1 Cor. 1:18–2:17, all who trust in human wisdom are enemies of the cross of Christ. Paul's insistence that Jesus humbled himself to death, even death on a cross (2:8), and his own statement that he is a participant in the suffering and death of Christ (3:10) were a challenge to any who maintained the values of Philippian society. The enemies of the cross of Christ are the negative examples who stand in contrast to Paul's own life of participating in the cross.

Paul gives a fourfold description of the enemies of the cross of Christ. His concern is not their teaching but their moral conduct. In contrast to believers, whose goal is the "prize of the high calling" (3:14), their **end** (*telos*) **is destruction** (*apōleia*, 3:19). As in 1:28, Paul distinguishes between those who are destined for salvation and those who are destined for destruction. As he told the Corinthians, the word of the cross is foolishness to "those who are perishing" (*apollymenois*, 2 Cor. 2:15). The telos of a life of sin is death (Rom. 6:21–22; 2 Cor. 11:15, "their *telos* is according to their deeds").

In contrast to believers, **their god is the belly** (*koilia*). Paul is referring neither to libertines, as some (e.g., Bockmuehl 1998, 231–32) have maintained, nor to those who insist on circumcision (cf. 3:2), as others (e.g., K. Barth 2002, 118) have argued. He is referring to all who do not look to the ultimate goal. *Koilia* is metonymy for the earthly and transitory aspect of human existence. One may compare the description of apostates in 3 Macc. 7:11, who have abandoned the commandments "for the sake of the belly."

Parallel to "their god is the belly" is **the glory** (*doxa*) **is in their shame** (*aischynē*). While believers anticipate the time when they will "be conformed to the body of his glory" in the future (3:21), the majority culture finds glory in their shame. Shame (*aischynē*) can refer to a variety of unregenerate types of behavior, including sexual debauchery (cf. Rom. 1:27). Paul summarizes their situation with the words **setting their minds** (*phronountes*) **on earthly things** (3:19). Paul has set before the Philippians two alternative ways of thinking. One takes on the mind of Christ (2:5; cf. 3:15) while the majority culture sets its mind on earthly things.

In sharp contrast to those who have their minds on earthly things is the believing community, whose **citizenship is in heaven**. The emphatic "our citizenship" at the beginning of 3:20 highlights the distinction between the church and the majority culture (BDF 284; cf. Sumney 2007, 94). Although the translations (NRSV, NIV) render the conjunction *gar* as **but**, Paul is actually establishing a logical reason for his call to imitation (Bockmuehl 1998, 233). This emphatic claim strengthens the identity of those who are a minority in a hostile community (cf. 1:28). The first-person plural in 3:20 corresponds to the earlier claim that "we are the circumcision" (3:3) in contrast to others. The church that is alienated from the local society and its government is composed of the citizens of a state that is in heaven, thus mightier than Rome. Rather than have their minds on earthly glory and honor in the present, they wait for a Savior from heaven who is greater than the earthly savior, the emperor, who comes from Rome. As Paul indicates in 1:27, this *politeuma* has its own standards of conduct and claim for total allegiance. While Roman citizenship is either the status or the goal of the majority population, believers hold citizenship in a mightier state. For them, Roman citizenship has lost its relevance (Wojtkowiak 2012, 209). Heavenly citizenship precludes the longing for status and honor on earth.

The assurance in 3:20–21 continues the narrative of the Christ hymn in 2:6–11. The one whom God "highly exalted" (2:9) is **in heaven, and it is from there that we await** (*apechdechometha*) **a Savior** (*sōtēr*)**, Jesus Christ the Lord** (*kyrios*). The imagery evokes memories of the coming of the emperor from Rome to rescue the people from the Thracians. The alternative *politeuma* has its own Savior and Lord. Thus, contrary to the official claims of the Roman Empire, the real Savior (*sōtēr*) and Lord (*kyrios*) is the one whom God highly exalted, not the emperor. A visit from the Roman emperor is insignificant in comparison with the coming of the Lord and Savior.

In the present, however, the community awaits the Savior as it lives in the midst of the visible power of Rome. Paul frequently speaks of the church as a waiting community. While it suffers persecution in the present (cf. 1 Thess. 3:2–3), it waits for the Son from heaven, who will deliver the church from the wrath of God (1 Thess. 1:9–10). Despite present sufferings (cf. Rom. 8:18), both the creation and the community wait for the end (Rom. 8:19, 23). Thus the whole community, like Paul himself, presses on toward a goal that it has not yet reached.

Echoes of Phil. 2:6–11 shape Paul's description of the outcome of the Savior's coming. The Savior who once appeared in a human form (*schēma*), took on the form (*morphē*) of a slave, and humbled (*etapeinōsen*) himself by dying on the cross (2:7–8) will **transform** (*metaschēmatisei*) **the body of our humiliation** (*tapeinōseōs*) so that it **will be conformed** (*symmorphon*) into the **body of his glory** (3:21). That is, he shared the human form (*morphē*, 2:7), a body that was subject to death. Paul is an example for others insofar as he desires to share the sufferings of Christ, being "conformed" (*symmorphomenos*) to the death of Christ. Believers will ultimately be conformed (*symmorphon*) to the body of his glory. The language corresponds to the declaration in Rom. 8:29 that believers who share the destiny of Christ in their present suffering (Rom. 5:2–5; 8:18) will be conformed (*symmorphon*) to the image of the Son. Paul elaborates on this assurance in 1 Cor. 15:50–55: "We will all be changed" (15:51) and take on an incorruptible body (15:52–54).

The exalted Lord will transform believers **in accordance with** (*kata*) **the power** (*energeia*) **that enables him to make all things subject to himself.** Contrary to many translations (ESV, RSV, NRSV, NIV), *kata* is best rendered "in accordance with" or "because" rather than "by." Thus the transformation is "in accordance with" the power (*energeia*) of the exalted one. *Energeia* (lit. "working, operation, action,") is used in the NT exclusively for the action of divine beings (BDAG 335). According to Ephesians and Colossians, by this *energeia* God raised Jesus from the dead (Eph. 1:19), called Paul to be an apostle (Eph. 3:7; cf. Col. 1:29), and equips the church for growth (Eph. 4:16). Paul uses the verb *energein* in Philippians to describe the God who is at work (*energōn*) among (2:13; cf. 1 Cor. 12:6) believers. This power that is at work among believers is the one who makes all things subject to himself.

The description of Christ as the one who "makes all things subject [*hypotaxai*] to himself" corresponds to the portrayal in 1 Corinthians of the exalted Christ, who will "destroy every ruler and every authority and power" and reign until all enemies are defeated (15:24–25), leaving all enemies subjected (*hypetaxen*) to him (15:27). Similarly, in the Christ hymn all cosmic powers will acknowledge the sovereignty of Jesus as Lord. Thus Paul points his anxious readers to the ultimate power that will transform their lives. The ultimate power is not Caesar but Jesus, the one who triumphed over death.

Concluding the Argument: Stand Firm (4:1)

4:1. Paul's model (3:4–17) and the reassurance that the ultimate power will save the community are the foundation for the conclusion in 4:1. As **therefore** (*hōste*) in 4:1 indicates, the exhortation **to stand firm in the Lord** is the conclusion to the argument (*probatio*) of the letter (chaps. 2–3) and the transition to the imperatives that follow. Before Paul commands, however, he reassures the readers of his deep emotional concern for them, using a lengthy series of appellatives that indicate his love for them. They are his **beloved** (*agapētoi*) and **longed for** (*epipothētoi*) **brothers** [**and sisters**], his **joy** (*chara*) **and crown** (*stephanos*). While Paul frequently prefaces his commands by addressing his readers as beloved (see Rom. 12:19; 1 Cor. 10:14; Phil. 2:12), the series of affectionate terms appears nowhere else in his writings. He frequently indicates that he longs to be united with his readers (Rom. 1:11; 15:23; Phil. 1:8; cf. 2:26) and that they long to see him (1 Thess. 3:6; cf. 2 Cor. 7:7, 11), but only here does he describe his readers as "longed for." As one who hopes that they will be his grounds for boasting at the end (2:16; cf. 2 Cor. 1:14; 11:1–4; 1 Thess. 2:19), he employs the tender language of a parent, encouraging them to "stand firm [*stēkete*] in the Lord." The crown, the laurel wreath given to the winner in a race, is the metaphor for the successful completion of Paul's pastoral work. This exhortation forms an *inclusio* with the earlier exhortation, "stand firm in one spirit" (1:27). The presence of a hostile populace (1:28) undoubtedly is a constant temptation for the readers to return to the comfort of the previous existence. The examples of both Jesus and Paul provide the motivation for the readers "to stand firm in the Lord." Believers "stand firm in the Lord" because Jesus Christ, not the Caesar, is the Lord and Savior who comes to rescue the beleaguered community (3:20–21).

Theological Issues

Paul's Conversion and Change of Values

Paul offers himself as an example a second time (see also 1:12–26) as a foundation for the exhortation "stand firm in the Lord" (4:1; cf. 1:27). Having reminded believers that they stand in the middle between the beginning and the end of their existence in Christ (1:6), he presents his own autobiography, placing himself in the middle between his upbringing (3:4–7) and his ultimate destination (cf. 3:12, 14), contrasting himself sharply with alternatives that may tempt the Philippians (3:2, 18–19). Indeed, his speech is filled with sharp dichotomies—between the believing community that boasts in Christ and those who have confidence in the flesh (3:3), profit and loss (3:7–8), human achievements and Christ (3:7–8), his own righteousness (3:6) and the righteousness from God (3:9). In the downward spiral of his life that he describes in 3:4–7, he exemplifies choices between two alternatives and the moral reasoning, or *phronēsis*, that he commends for the readers (Kraftchick 2008, 250–51).

The real issue is the choice between confidence in the flesh and boasting in Christ. Paul speaks in sharp dichotomies because he sees no middle ground. While confidence in the flesh may be manifested in religious achievement, as it was with Paul, it may also be present in other achievements, as with the Philippian society. For our culture, confidence in the flesh may be present in single-minded pursuit of economic or political success, or even in religious self-righteousness.

The images of profit and loss vividly depict the alternatives faced by the believer. All sources of confidence have become a loss because of Christ (3:7) in order that Paul may know Christ (3:8), gain Christ (3:8), and be found in him (3:9). The sharp dichotomies indicate that boasting in Christ is not the casual commitment that is common in Christendom—an item to add to a list of achievements—but the exclusive claim of Christ on the lives of believers.

According to the popular interpretation of Paul that was dominant before the emergence of the "new perspective on Paul" in the 1970s, Paul had struggled to find a gracious God before he discovered God's grace. While this was the experience of Martin Luther, who discovered God's grace while reading Paul, it was not Paul's experience. He was blameless with respect to righteousness (3:6), but he discovered that he had no righteousness of his own when he experienced the righteousness from God (3:9). Only as Paul looks back on his achievements does he recognize that righteousness was not his own achievement but the work of God's act in Jesus Christ.

Paul elaborates on what it means to know Christ in 3:9–10, offering in summary form in 3:9 the message that he develops at length in Galatians and Romans. The claim that righteousness (*dikaiosynē*) is from God on the basis of faith (*pistis*) reiterates Paul's affirmation that God's righteousness has been revealed for all who believe (Rom. 3:22, 26; cf. 5:1; Gal. 2:16). Many interpreters understand the parallel phrases "righteousness . . . through the faith of Christ" (*pistis Christou*) and "righteousness by faith" (*dikaiosynēn epi tē pistei*) in 3:9 as references to the divine initiative (faith[fulness] of Christ) and the human response (faith), maintaining that *pistis Christou* refers to the faithful obedience of Christ. While the traditional reading of *pistis Christou* as "faith in Christ" is probably correct, Paul nevertheless speaks of divine initiative and human response. As he demonstrates in Galatians and Romans, righteousness is a divine gift to which one responds with faithfulness.

Faith is not a passive assent to the divine initiative, as Paul indicates in 3:10. In contrast to modern usage, in which it may be used for positive thinking or basic trust, Paul indicates that it involves the partnership in the sufferings of

Christ and even being conformed to his death. Paul does not speak here of suffering as the basic human condition, but the self-denial that Jesus demonstrated in his incarnation and death (2:7–8). Paul mentions this cruciform existence in several instances. As he says to the Corinthians, "One died for all; therefore all died. He died for all that they may no longer live for themselves" (2 Cor. 5:14–15). Paul has been "crucified with Christ" (Gal. 2:19), and he reminds believers that they have "died with him" (Rom. 6:2). Indeed, the cruciform life is *"the all-encompassing, integrative reality of Paul's life and thought, expressed in every dimension of his being"* (Gorman 2001, 371, emphasis original). As Dietrich Bonhoeffer wrote, "When Christ calls a man, he bids him come and die" (Bonhoeffer 1963, 89). Thus faith involves a cruciform existence. In many instances, this existence involves imprisonment and death, while in other instances it involves a life of looking out for the interests of others (cf. 2:3–4).

Because the cruciform existence was not welcome in Philippian society, its avoidance was probably a temptation to the Philippian church. It has a similar challenge for the contemporary church (Gorman 2001, 368). Some reject the cruciform life, regarding it as the acceptance of abuse or persecution without self-defense. Those who regard the church as the place for meeting needs may maintain the cross as a visible symbol, but find little place for the cross as the integrative center of their lives. Similarly, a gospel of success is incompatible with the cruciform life. The omission of the cruciform life is the denial of the foundation of the Christian faith. Susan Wood has correctly said, "Either the entire Christian community follows the model that Jesus sets for us, or we are doomed to struggle for positions of honor and elitism, domination and power" (Wood 1997, 183; I am indebted to Gorman 2001, 381, for this quotation).

From the Present to the Future

Paul's narrative does not end with his loss of all things for the sake of his partnership in the sufferings of Christ. His ultimate destiny, as he indicates in 3:11, is the resurrection of the dead. Thus he exemplifies the experience of the community, which also stands in the middle between their conversion and their ultimate destiny (1:6). To live in the middle, as Paul frequently demonstrates, is to live between the times. Believers have entered the new age (cf. Rom. 6:1–11; 2 Cor. 5:17; Gal. 1:4), but they still await the final triumph. Like other believers, Paul experiences the power of the resurrection in the context of his sufferings as he hopes to attain the resurrection of the dead, his ultimate destiny (3:11). As he participates in the sufferings of Jesus, he has shared in the downward spiral of Jesus (cf. 2:6–8), but he has not shared in the triumph of Jesus (2:9–11). As his call for imitation (3:17) and the transition to the first-person plural (3:20–21) indicate, his experience is paradigmatic for the entire believing community.

The end of the narrative is the resurrection of the dead (3:11), to be made perfect (3:12), to receive the prize (3:14), the coming of the Savior and the transformation of our body of lowliness to be conformed to the body of his glory (3:20–21). Just as Christ took on the form of a slave, the believing community will share in the form of the resurrection body of Christ. Such expectation is countercultural. While the many place their minds on earthly things (3:18–19), the church has seen the future in the triumph of Christ. Thus when Paul says "have this mind" (3:15), he contrasts the church with a culture that looked only to the present. Paul is thus the earliest Christian theologian of hope (Migliore 2014, 151).

The contemporary church also lives in a culture that, like ancient society, is "without hope" (cf. 1 Thess. 4:13). However, because hope is largely marginalized or distorted among believers, the church rarely exhibits the alternative mind-set that Paul commends in 3:15. Hope may be reduced to a vague optimism about the future, a mere wishing, or an individual desire to escape from the troubles of this life by a "rapture" of true believers (Migliore 2014, 151). For Paul, however, hope is not an escape from this world but an orientation that shapes our conduct in the present. The athletic images of pursuing, focusing on the mark, and straining forward (3:12–14) indicate the intensity of human effort that hope evokes. Christian belief, therefore, is an exhausting journey toward the finish line (cf. Lively 2010, 42). Ernst Käsemann spoke of the community that is perpetually moving toward the goal, distinguishing it from conventional church membership, declaring that "we achieve evangelical freedom only by setting out on the never-ending wandering of the people of God. According to Paul's word in Phil. 3:13, we must forget what lies behind and strain toward what is daily held before us as the goal of our calling. But this is what middle-class morality resists" (2010, 315). Eschatology gives urgency to our ethical commitments (cf. 1 Thess. 5:1–11) and places all other commitments in perspective (cf. 1 Cor. 7:29–31). Only a community that is hopeful for God's ultimate triumph can stand firm (4:1).

A missing dimension in current reflections about the end is the corporate nature of eschatology. When Paul says "let us have this mind" (3:15), he speaks to the whole church. The affirmation "our citizenship is in heaven" indicates the collective identity of the whole church, which waits for a Savior and the ultimate transformation into his image (3:20–21). God's work among them will be complete when the whole church reaches the day of Christ as transformed people (cf. 1:6; 2:16).

PART 5

Philippians 4:2–23

Peroratio: *Summarizing the Case*

Introductory Matters

The argument (*probatio*) of Philippians ends with the admonition introduced by "therefore" (*hōste*) in 4:1. Because of the hope for the Savior who will transform the people into the body of his glory (3:20–21), the community may now "stand firm" (*stēkete*) in the Lord who has subjected all things to himself. This admonition forms an *inclusio* with the exhortation "that you stand firm [*stēkete*] in one spirit" in the *propositio* of the letter (1:27). Thus the argument (*probatio*) in chapters 2–3 has laid the foundation for the concluding exhortation.

The final chapter of Philippians contains features that are commonplace in the concluding chapter of each of Paul's letters. Paul encourages the readers to "stand in the Lord" at the conclusion of other letters (1 Cor. 16:13; cf. Gal. 5:1; 1 Thess. 3:8). Exhortations introduced with the polite request *parakalō* ("I urge, appeal to") and *erōtō* ("I ask") frequently appear near the end of Paul's letters to draw out the practical consequences of the preceding argument (see Rom. 12:1; 15:30; 16:17; 2 Cor. 10:1; 1 Thess. 4:1; 5:12, 14; Philem. 9–10; cf. Eph. 4:1). The staccato group of imperatives in Phil. 4:4–9 is similar to those at the end of other letters (see 1 Cor. 16:13–14; 2 Cor. 13:11; 1 Thess. 5:14–22).

The adverbial use of *loipon* (finally, 4:8) is commonplace at the conclusion of Pauline letters (2 Cor. 13:11; Gal. 6:17). Even the imperative *to auto phronein* (be of the same mind) appears at the conclusion of other Pauline letters (Rom. 12:16; 15:5; 2 Cor. 13:11). Indeed, the exhortation to rejoice (*chairete*, 4:4) is one of the common features of the concluding exhortation (cf. 2 Cor. 13:11; 1 Thess. 5:16), as is a reference to Paul's own rejoicing (Rom. 16:19; 1 Cor. 16:17; cf. Weima 2010, 320–22). Because the exhortations at the conclusion of Pauline letters share numerous common elements, interpreters have debated the extent to which they develop the argument of the specific letters. The relevance of these instructions to Philippians will be treated under "Tracing the Train of Thought."

Philippians 4:21–23 contains the customary ending of Paul's letters. The imperative "greet every saint in Christ Jesus" (4:21) conforms to the usual greetings at the close of the letters and to the conclusion that was common among ancient Greek letters. Paul never uses the first person to extend his own greetings but employs the imperative *aspasasthe*, which challenges the readers to greet the others in the assembly (see Rom. 16:3–16; 1 Cor. 16:20; 2 Cor. 13:12; 1 Thess. 5:26). This form is both a surrogate for Paul's own greeting (Weima 2010, 328) and a call for the assembled community to extend greetings to others. In contrast to the other letters, however, Philippians does not have the customary "Greet [*aspasasthe*] one another with a holy kiss" (cf. Rom. 16:16; 1 Cor. 16:20; 2 Cor. 13:12; 1 Thess. 5:26; cf. Col. 4:15).

The greeting from others, "The brothers and sisters [NRSV "friends"] who are with me greet you" and "all the saints greet you" (4:21–22) also conforms to the ending of Paul's other letters (see Rom. 16:16, 21, 23; 1 Cor. 16:19–20; 2 Cor. 13:12; Philem. 23). In contrast to other letters, however, Paul mentions neither the names of those who send greetings (cf. Rom. 16:16–23; 1 Cor. 16:19; Philem. 23) nor the location of those who send greetings (cf. 1 Cor. 16:19). The distinctive feature in Philippians is the sending of greetings from the emperor's household (4:22). As Paul has indicated earlier in the letter, he is in prison (1:7, 13–14, 17), and his message has become known to the praetorian guard (1:13).

In contrast to the secular letters of Paul's day, which ended with the farewell wish "be strong" (*errhōso*) or "prosper" (*eutychei*), all of the Pauline letters conclude with a grace benediction (Weima 2010, 340) that is either identical or closely similar to Paul's concluding words, "The grace of the Lord Jesus Christ be with your spirit" (4:23). This benediction, which normally includes the wish ("grace" or "grace and peace"), the source ("our Lord Jesus Christ"), and the recipient (e.g., "with you" [plural]), forms an *inclusio* with the opening of the letter, "Grace to you and peace" (Phil. 1:2). Thus whereas secular letters expressed the wish for the prosperity and physical strength of the recipients, Paul's letters begin and end with a prayer that the community will be empowered by Christ.

While the concluding chapter of Philippians shares common features with the other Pauline letters, it contains significant differences that have puzzled interpreters during the past century. The appeal to Euodia and Syntyche (4:2–3), the specific ethical advice (4:4–9), and the expression of thanks (4:10–20) are distinctive.

Paul's Appeal to Euodia and Syntyche

While the exhortation introduced by "I appeal to you" (*parakalō*) is common, Paul names specific individuals only in Philippians (4:2). Euodia and Syntyche appear nowhere else in the Pauline correspondence but are common names in antiquity, as ancient inscriptions indicate (BDAG 409, 976). Euodia means "pleasant journey" and Syntyche, a name derived from the goddess of fortune, Tyche, means "good luck." As their names suggest, they are gentiles and apparently members of the Philippian church. Paul's application of the earlier exhortation to the whole church (2:2) to "be of the same mind" (*to auto phronein*) to these two women suggests that they have been engaged in a quarrel. While Paul does not indicate the nature of the quarrel, the contrast between *to auto phronein* and selfish ambition in 2:2–4 suggests the presence of some form of rivalry that has a destructive impact on the whole church. Paul's constant focus on living in harmony (1:27–30; 2:1–4; 2:13–16) may also be a response to the quarrel between Euodia and Syntyche. The extent to which Paul's previous exhortations to harmony have been laying the foundation for addressing Euodia and Syntyche is a matter of debate. David Garland has suggested, for example, that Paul finally addresses the issue openly in 4:2–3 that he has been alluding to throughout the letter (Garland 1985, 173). Other issues have probably also played a role in the focus on harmony. As Paul indicates in the letter's *propositio*, hostility from the surrounding culture made the unity of the community especially critical.

The description of Euodia and Syntyche as people who "have struggled beside me [*synēthlēsan moi*] in the gospel" indicates their leading role in the Philippian church. This work involved activity in the midst of opposition and required bravery, as *synēthlēsan* indicates. This term, which Paul has applied to the whole church in 1:27, is an athletic metaphor that was frequently used for those who suffer for Christ (cf. 1:30). The metaphor can suggest a fight with adversaries such as wrestling or boxing. Thus believers are like athletes who train and exercise strict discipline, even if it causes pain, in order to advance the gospel (Dahl 1995, 6). Paul emphasizes the bravery of these women, who were on the front lines in the battle along with Clement and the rest. This could be the event in Philippi when Paul was abused (see 1 Thess. 2:2). These women have done in the past what Paul encouraged the readers to do in the *propositio*: fight together side by side (1:27).

The description of Euodia and Syntyche offers significant evidence of the role of women in the Pauline churches. The two women joined Clement, who is also otherwise unknown, and the other fellow workers (*synergoi*) in spreading the gospel. *Synergoi* is a term that is frequently used for those who are involved in evangelistic work in the Pauline literature. Numerous people are identified as fellow workers, including Prisca and Aquila (cf. Rom. 16:3), Urbanus (Rom. 16:9), Timothy (Rom. 16:21; 1 Thess. 3:2), Apollos (1 Cor. 3:5), Titus (2 Cor. 8:23), Epaphroditus (Phil. 2:26), and Philemon (1). Indeed, Paul himself is a "fellow worker of God" (1 Cor. 3:5, 9; 2 Cor. 1:24) on behalf of his churches. Fellow workers were missionary colleagues who accepted the toil, struggle, and renunciation involved in advancing the gospel (W.-H. Ollrog, *EDNT* 3:304).

In a letter addressed to the whole church, the request to an individual member is unprecedented. The appeal to an unnamed individual is particularly unusual. The identity of the "loyal companion" (*gnēsie syzyge*, lit. "true yokefellow," 4:3) whom Paul asks to "help" (*syllambanou*) is also uncommon. Some (e.g., Gnilka 1968, 166; K. Barth 2002, 119) have suggested that "Syzygus" is a proper name. However, no records exist of this as a proper name. Some have suggested that the "true yokefellow" is Epaphroditus (Lightfoot 1888, 158), who delivered the gift to the Philippians (4:18). Other names that have been suggested include Silas (G. Delling, *TDNT* 7:749–50), Timothy (Collange 1979, 143), and Luke (Fee 1995, 394–95; Bockmuehl 1998, 241). The "true yokefellow" is likely a traveling companion of Paul who acts on Paul's behalf, but the identity of the person is unknown.

The word "yokefellow" (*syzygos*) appears nowhere else in the NT, but the verb "yoke together" is used for marriage (Matt. 19:6 par.), and the opposite, "unequally yoked" (*heterozygō*), is used for inappropriate relationships (see 2 Cor. 6:14). The word was also used for soldiers standing in one rank (Polybius, *Hist.* 10.23.7, cited in Reumann 2008, 609), a wife (Euripides, *Alc.* 314), lovers (Plutarch, *Amat.* 770c), and friends (Plutarch, *Amic. mult.* 93e, cited in Fitgerald 1996, 149). According to Cicero, "That friendship is sweetest which is yoked together with [*coniugaivit*] congeniality of character" (*Off.* 1.58, cited in Fitzgerald 1996, 149). It is reminiscent of the numerous *syn-* words that Paul applies to his fellow workers. Indeed, it is closely related to the description of Euodia and Syntyche, who "struggled beside" (*synēthlēsan*, BDAG 954, "fought at my side") Paul in the gospel; to Epaphroditus (Phil. 2:25), the fellow worker (*synergos*) and fellow soldier (*systratiōtēs*); and to the fellow workers (*synergoi*) mentioned by Paul (4:3).

The names of Euodia, Syntyche, Clement, and all the rest are enrolled in "the book of life." The idea of a heavenly book that includes the names of the saints is suggested in Exod. 32:32 and Ps. 69:28 and appears frequently in both apocalyptic literature (cf. Dan. 12:1; *1 En.* 47.3; 1QM 12.3) and the NT. Jesus speaks of those whose names are written in heaven (Luke 10:20; cf. Heb. 12:23). This language is employed several times in Revelation to describe believers (3:5; 13:8; 17:8). Those whose names are written in the "book of life" are believers who belong to the heavenly commonwealth and wait for the Savior (3:20–21). Just as the citizens of Philippi are enrolled in the Roman commonwealth, believers are enrolled in the book of life (Dahl 1995, 8).

Paul's Ethical Advice

The repeated "rejoice in the Lord" (4:4; cf. 2:18; 3:1) is both a familiar refrain in Philippians and a common feature at the conclusion of Paul's letters (e.g., 2 Cor. 13:11; 1 Thess. 5:16). Along with the other imperatives in 4:4–7, it has a special significance for a community confronted by hostility from the local populace (cf. 1:28). The Greek adjective for "gentleness" (*epieikēs*, 4:5) does not appear elsewhere in Paul, but the noun form (*epieikeia*) is used for the "gentleness of Christ" (2 Cor. 10:1). The exhortation "do not worry about anything" (*mēden merimnate*, 4:6) recalls the words of Jesus, "Do not worry [*mē merimnate*] about your life" (Matt. 6:25), suggesting that Paul may be familiar with the Jesus tradition, although the injunction appears nowhere else in the Pauline letters. Indeed, he assumes that some worries are natural. He speaks of his own anxiety for the churches (2 Cor. 11:28). Together, these instructions have a particular significance for the Philippian situation. Paul encourages the readers not to worry, despite the situation at the present, just as he had earlier encouraged them not to be intimidated by adversaries (1:28). Rejoicing in his imprisonment, he challenges the readers to "rejoice in the Lord" in the context of their own struggles. They respond to a hostile society with gentleness that is "known to everyone." These commands are supported by the assurances "The Lord is near" (4:5) and "the peace of God will guard your lives in Christ Jesus" (4:7).

In 4:8–9 Paul offers ethical guidance on what the Philippians should "think about" (*logizesthe*) and "continue to do" (*prassete*). He lists six moral qualities in adjectival form, each introduced by "whatever is" (*hosa*), instructing the readers, "if there is any virtue [*aretē*, NRSV "excellence"] and anything worthy of praise [*ei tis epainos*], think about these things" (*tauta logizesthe*). While Paul's ethical instruction frequently includes lists, a literary device also in common use among moral philosophers, the six qualities listed in 4:8 are atypical in Paul (cf. Willis 2012, 65). Of the six qualities, two (*prosphilē*, NRSV "pleasing"; *euphēma*, NRSV "commendable") appear only here in the NT. One (*semnos*, NRSV "honorable") appears elsewhere only in the Pastoral Epistles (1 Tim. 3:8, 11; Titus 2:2). Two (*alēthē*, NRSV "true"; *dikaia*, NRSV "just") are used with a connotation that is uncommon in Paul (Willis 2012, 68). The term *virtue* (*aretē*, NRSV "excellence") appears in the NT only here and in 2 Pet. 1:3.

While this combination of the words is not attested in Greek sources, the terms do appear in various combinations elsewhere. Three of the words—*aretē*, *dikaia*, and *euphēma*—appear on the Stone of Miletopolis, an inscription containing moral aphorisms discovered near Delphi (full list in Hasluck 1907, 63). All of the individual terms play a role in Greek moral instruction. The search for what "is true" (*alēthēs*) was a major concern of Greek philosophers, who searched for truth as the opposite of opinion, falsehood, or mere appearance (cf. Diogenes Laertius, *Vit.* 7.42, 73, 81; 9.22). According to Plutarch, "To arrive at the Truth, and especially the truth about the gods, is a longing for the divine" (*Is. Os.* 351e, trans. F. C. Babbitt, LCL; cf. *TLNT* 1:66–67, for other texts). *Semnos* (NRSV "honorable") was frequently used to describe those who were respectable, serious, or dignified (cf. *TLNT* 3:244). Ancient epitaphs honored those who possessed this quality (see texts in *TLNT* 3:248). The word appears frequently in the Pastoral Epistles to describe the quality expected of old men (Titus 2:2) and deacons (1 Tim. 3:8, 11).

From the time of Homer, *hagna* ("pure"), which is fourth in Paul's list of six, designated the absence of impurity. It was first used for cultic matters, but then came to mean everything that was morally blameless (H. Balz, *EDNT* 1:22). It also appears in Hellenistic texts (Diogenes Laertius, *Vit.* 7.119) to describe moral character. *Dikaia* ("just") is the only one of the Greek cardinal virtues mentioned here. The word is used in classical texts for one who conforms to the law and practices fairness toward others (*Eth. nic.* 5.2.8; cf. Aeschylus, *Ag.* 1604). This common usage is also evident in the NT on the lips of pagans (e.g., Matt. 27:19, 24; Luke 23:47). *Prosphilē* (NRSV "pleasing"; NIV "lovely") does not appear elsewhere in the NT or in any ancient ethical lists. It describes that which calls forth love from others. *Euphēma* (NRSV "commendable") is literally "well-sounding" and probably has the sense of "a good reputation." The Delphic commands at Melitopolis include "Be *euphēmos*, practice *euphēmia*" (Wibbing 1959, 102). The word often has the sense of a good reputation (LSJ 737).

All of these qualities would have resonated in Greco-Roman society. Martin Dibelius maintained that the list is drawn from Greek moral philosophy. Numerous interpreters have maintained that Paul says nothing in 4:8 that could not have been a part of contemporary moral exhortation (see Dibelius 1937, 95; Gnilka 1968, 221; Bockmuehl 1998, 250). J. B. Lightfoot paraphrases Paul as saying "whatever value may reside in your old heathen conception of virtue, whatever consideration is due to the praise of men; as if the Apostle were anxious not to omit any possible ground of appeal" (1888, 162). Consequently, interpreters have concluded that Paul affirms all of the virtues that are intrinsically good in society and that benefit others (cf. Bockmuehl 1998, 250; O'Brien 1991, 503). Thus according to one common interpretation, Paul, having maintained the sharp distinction between the behavior of believers in their alternative commonwealth and that of their neighbors, now seeks common ground with the best in ancient society.

Although the six attributes listed by Paul are well attested among Hellenistic writers, they are not especially Stoic (cf. Lohmeyer 1953, 174–75). If Paul had intended to affirm ancient morality, he would have probably appealed to the well-known cardinal virtues (wisdom, courage, self-control, justice; cf. Plato, *Phaed.* 69c; *Resp.* 427d–e; *Leg.* 631c; 963a) as well as other words that appear most frequently in Hellenistic moral instruction, including the beautiful (*kalos*) and the good (*agathos*; for common Greek virtues, see Thompson 2011, 91; cf. also Wojtkowiak 2012, 262). Of the cardinal virtues, only *dikaia* ("just") appears in both Paul and Greek lists. As Engberg-Pedersen has shown, while Paul employs Stoic terminology in Philippians (see especially 1:10; 4:11 and my comments on these verses), the attributes in 4:8 are commonplace terms in popular morality (Engberg-Pedersen 1995, 256–90). Indeed, most of the words appear in the Septuagint, where they take on a significance that is different from that of Hellenistic moral philosophy (cf. Thompson 2011, 108). "Whatever is true" (*alēthē*) is the concern, not only of Greek philosophy, but also of the biblical faith. For Paul, the truth is the revelation of God (Rom. 1:17–18, 25), the gospel (2 Cor. 4:2; 6:7; 11:10; 13:8; Gal. 2:5; cf. Col. 1:5). *Semnos* ("honorable") appears in Proverbs (8:6; 15:26 LXX), the Maccabean literature (e.g., 4 Macc. 7:15; 17:5), and 139 times in Philo. In the Septuagint the word is used for those who are faithful in following the divine will. Similarly, *dikaios* ("just") is used in Jewish literature for those who are faithful in keeping the law (Gen. 6:9; 4 Macc. 16:21; cf. Josephus, *Ant.* 6.165; 9.33). Indeed, Paul speaks of himself as "blameless" with respect to righteousness (*dikaiosynē*, Phil. 3:6). *Hagna* ("pure") is employed in the Septuagint for the words and ways of God (Ps. 11:7 [12:6 Eng.]; Prov. 21:8), the moral purity of faithful people (Prov. 20:9; 4 Macc. 18:7–8), and for ritual cleanness (2 Chron. 29:16; 30:19). Elsewhere in Paul the word is used for ethical purity (cf. 2 Cor. 11:3), as it is in Phil. 4:8. *Prosphilē* ("pleasing") appears in Sirach (4:7; 20:13) to describe those who conform to the will of God. Except for *euphēma* (NRSV "commendable"), all of the ethical qualities listed in 4:8 appear in the Septuagint. Thus while the language would resonate with the Greek audience, the terms had already been incorporated into the literature of Hellenistic Judaism to signify the Jewish ideals that were defined by the will of God. Similarly, Paul did not employ the six attributes to affirm compatibility between Hellenistic popular morality and the conduct of believers in the heavenly commonwealth but followed the Jewish tradition in appropriating Greek categories into an alternative worldview.

Since the six adjectives are not comprehensive, Paul adds the conditional sentence, "If there is any virtue [*aretē*], if there is any praise, consider these things." *Aretē*, commonly translated "virtue," is the central category in Greek ethics. Although in early Classical Greek it simply meant "excellence" and could be applied to humans, animals, and things, from the time of Socrates it meant moral excellence (Willis 2012, 70). The four cardinal virtues became the topic for discussion for Aristotle and the Stoics, all of whom maintained that the good life is determined by virtue (*aretē*). Although Paul shares with the philosophic tradition a concern for moral development, he employs the term *aretē* only here, where it is parallel with praise (*epainos*). Paul does not indicate whether the praise is from God (as in Rom. 2:29; 1 Cor. 4:5; 1 Pet. 1:7 in reference to the final judgment) or from others. Praise can come from a congregation (2 Cor. 8:18), from Paul himself (1 Cor. 11:2, 17, 22), and from authorities appointed by God (Rom. 13:3–4; 1 Pet. 2:14; O'Brien 1991, 507). In this instance Paul probably refers to praise from others.

Paul's "Thankless Thanks" and the God Who Supplies Our Needs

The most distinctive feature in the final chapter of Philippians is the acknowledgment of the financial support from the Philippians in 4:10–20. Although Paul's statement "I rejoiced" (*echarēn*) is parallel to expressions of the apostle's joy at the conclusion of other letters (cf. Rom. 16:19; 1 Cor. 16:17; 2 Cor. 13:9), the extended reflection in 4:10–20 is without parallel at the close of a Pauline letter. Paul's statement "I rejoiced greatly that now at last you have revived your care for me" (4:10) is an acknowledgment of the Philippians' gift to him. He reiterates the acknowledgment in the comments "You did well [*kalōs epoiēsate*] to share my affliction" (*synkoinōnēsantes mou tē thlipsei*, 4:14) and "I have been paid in full" (*apechō de panta*, 4:18). Because of the absence of an explicit expression of gratitude, interpreters have commonly referred to 4:10–20 as a "thankless thanks."

The acknowledgment of the gift in 4:10–20 raises two primary questions that have puzzled interpreters. First, why does Paul wait until the end of the letter to acknowledge the gift? Second, why is Paul oblique in expressing gratitude? Numerous interpreters (e.g., Reumann 2008, 676–78; H. Koester, *IDBSup* 666; Collange 1979, 8–10) have accounted for the anomaly of a thank-you note at the end of the letter with the suggestion that 4:10–20 is part of an earlier letter that Paul wrote shortly after receiving the gift from Epaphroditus (cf. 2:25–30; 4:18). As a self-contained unit, it would conform to the ancient letter of gratitude, which was one of the twenty-one types of letters catalogued by Demetrius.

The absence of an explicit expression of thanks in Phil. 4:10–20 is not unusual in antiquity, as G. W. Peterman has demonstrated. Of the twenty-six ancient papyrus letters he examined, only four contained an expression of thanks (Peterman 1997, 78). Seneca indicated that the reception of a gift obligates the receiver to show gratitude. While one may express gratitude verbally (Seneca, *Ben.* 2.24.4), the primary way of expressing gratitude was by repayment (Peterman 1997, 70). The recipient frequently responded with an expression of endearment but did not normally give a verbal expression of thanks (Peterman 1997, 82). Thus to assume that the thank-you note should come at the beginning of the letter is to superimpose modern conventions on the ancient text. Indeed, 4:10–20 is not only a thank-you note but also an affirmation of Paul's relationship to the Philippians and a summary of the argument of the letter (see under "Tracing the Train of Thought"). Paul's task is not only to acknowledge the gift but also to ensure that the Philippians do not misinterpret it according to their own social conventions. The oblique acknowledgment and the repeated "not that" (4:11, 17) indicate his desire to avoid misunderstanding. He devotes as much space to the explanation that he neither needed nor sought the gift as to the expression of gratitude (Berry 1996, 108).

Paul's statement that the Philippians "now at last" (*ēdē pote*) have revived their concern for him has been taken as a mild rebuke. As ancient correspondence demonstrates, a reference to the delay of one's response is not uncommon. Seneca reflects on the proper timing for returning a benefit. One should not return a benefit too promptly. "He who hastens at all odds to make a return shows the feeling, not of a person that is grateful, but of a debtor. And, to put it briefly, he who is too eager to pay his debt is unwilling to be indebted, and he who is unwilling to be indebted is ungrateful" (*Ben.* 4.40.5, cited in Malherbe 1996, 129). At the same time, one should not delay in returning a benefit. Seneca declares, "No gratitude is felt for a benefit when it has lingered long in the hands of him who gives it. . . . Even though some delay should intervene, let us avoid in every way the appearance of having deliberately delayed; hesitation is the next thing to refusing, and gains no gratitude" (*Ben.* 2.1.2; cited in Malherbe 1996, 129).

Paul does not explain why the Philippians "had no opportunity" (*ēkaireisthe*) to send gifts earlier. His comment may be illuminated by P.Enteux 45 (222 BCE), in which the writer pleads with King Ptolemy for a redress of grievances against Apollonius and Philotida, who refuse to repay a loan, claiming to be hindered (*akairein*), apparently because of their inability to pay (Peterman 1997, 133). Similarly, the Macedonians' poverty, which Paul mentions in 2 Cor. 8:1–3, may be the reason for their delay in sending Paul the most recent gift.

Paul has faced the problem of receiving financial support before. At Corinth his refusal to accept financial support resulted in strained relationships among some of the members (see 1 Cor. 9:1–18; 2 Cor. 11:7–11; 12:14–15). Indeed, the distrust in Corinth was exacerbated by the fact that Paul had accepted support from the Macedonians, who undoubtedly included the Philippians (2 Cor. 11:9), while refusing the support of the Corinthians. Thus because of the social conventions commonly associated with the giving and receiving of gifts, the Philippians' gift required an explanation.

Seneca's essay *De beneficiis* indicates the centrality of the exchange of gifts in ancient society. The essay begins with the statement, "Among the numerous faults of those who pass their lives recklessly and without due reflexion, my good friend Liberalis, I should say that there is hardly anything so hurtful to society as this, that we neither know how to bestow or how to receive a benefit" (1.1). He adds, "What we need is a discussion of benefits and the rules for a practice that constitutes the chief bond of human society" (1.4.2). In the remainder of the essay, Seneca offers collected wisdom from antiquity on the expectations of giving and receiving. A gift (*beneficium*), according to

Seneca, is freely given (3.19.1) and for the benefit of the recipient. Ingratitude for a gift is contemptible behavior and evidence of poor character (2.26.1–2).

The concentration of terms that were commonplace in ancient conversations about the giving and receiving of gifts in 4:10–20 suggests that Paul is now engaging in a discussion that was common in antiquity. The "matter of giving and receiving" (*eis logon doseōs kai lēmpseōs*) in 4:15 is a phrase that can be rendered "in settlement of a mutual account" (BDAG 601) or "debit and credit" (BDAG 259). The commercial image extends to the description of the gift as the "profit [*karpos*, lit. "fruit"] that accumulates to your account" (*ton pleonazonta eis logon hymōn*, 4:17) and to Paul's acknowledgment (4:18), "I have been paid in full" (*apechō . . . panta*), a commercial term for a receipt for services (BDAG 102). *Karpos* (lit. "fruit") was a common word for profit, and *pleonazein* ("accumulate") suggests compound interest (P. Marshall 1987, 159). Finally, *koinōnia* (4:15, NRSV "shared") was sometimes used for a joint business venture (Ogereau 2014, 366–67).

Although these terms refer to literal financial transactions, they were also commonly used with the extended meaning of the relationship between friends (Peterman 1997, 65). While Greeks and Romans detested a purely utilitarian understanding of friendship that reduced relationships to a financial transaction, "giving and receiving"—the mutual exchange of gifts and services—was regarded as essential (P. Marshall 1987, 160). The giver should not give only in order to receive something in return, but the recipient was nevertheless obligated to express gratitude by reciprocating a gift of equal or greater value than the gift that was received (Aristotle, *Eth. nic.* 8.14.1; 9.1.8–9; 9.7.1).

Paul alludes to ancient expectations of reciprocal benefits in describing the collection elsewhere. He explains the collection from gentile churches for the Jerusalem church to the Romans, declaring that the gentile churches "were pleased" to share their resources (*koinōnein*) and were obligated to do so (Rom. 15:26–27), for those who had shared (*ekoinōnēsan*) spiritual blessings from Jerusalem owe physical blessings in return (cf. 2 Cor. 8:12–15). His refusal to accept payment from the Corinthians (see 1 Cor. 9:1–12; 2 Cor. 11:9; 12:13–15) was probably interpreted as a refusal of friendship (P. Marshall 1987, 257).

Paul twice clarifies the significance of the Philippians' gift with explanations introduced by "not that" (*ouch hoti*, 4:11, 17) in order to correct misunderstandings that the Philippians associated with their gifts. Readers shaped by the dominant social conventions of Greco-Roman society would have interpreted their gifts either as patronage or as part of the "giving and receiving" among friends. Since the reciprocity among friends involved status, obligation, and power, Paul treats the acknowledgment of the Philippians' gift with care (Fowl 2002, 49) because he does not want to conform to the expectations that the Philippians had about their relationship to him.

Paul first qualifies his expression of gratitude, explaining, "not that I am referring to being in need" (*kath' hysterēsin*). Although he speaks elsewhere

---

On the Cynics and Epicureans

The Cynics *"hold that we should live simply, eating only enough food [autarkesi sitiois] and wearing a single garment, and they despise wealth, fame, and noble birth."* (Diogenes Laertius, *Vit.* 6.105)

From the Epicureans: *"We regard independence of outward things as a great good, not so in all cases to use little, but so as to be contented with little if we have not much, being honestly persuaded that they have the sweetest enjoyment of luxury who stand least in need of it."* (Diogenes Laertius, *Vit.* 10.131)

---

of his financial need (*hysterētheis*, 2 Cor. 11:9), here he denies that he refers to being in need because he emphasizes he has "learned to be content" (*autarkēs*). Paul's readers would have recognized *autarkēs* as the term describing the ideal Cynic and Stoic. Contentment (*autarkeia*) was the goal of human existence. For Diogenes the Cynic, *autarkeia* meant two things: "on the physical plane, contentment with the bare necessities of life; and on the spiritual level, complete detachment from the world and worldly value" (Rich 1956, 23). All that he required for his physical existence was food, shelter, and clothing of the simplest kind. Everything else was an unnecessary luxury (cf. Malherbe 1996, 132). The Cynic prays

> that I may not need bedclothes any more than the lions, nor expensive fare than the dogs. But may I be *autarkēs* in having for my bed the whole earth; may I consider the universe my house, and choose for food that which is easiest to procure. Gold and silver I do not need, neither I nor any of my friends. (Pseudo-Lucian, *Cynicus* 15)

Teles wrote the tractate *Peri autarkeias* in which he is primarily concerned with the wise man's attitude toward poverty. He develops the theme that the wise man adapts himself to circumstances and that he is not really in want of things since he has learned to be satisfied with what is at hand (Malherbe 1996, 134). According to Seneca (*Ben.* 6.2), "The happy man is content with his present lot, no matter what it is, and reconciled to his own circumstances" (Fowl 2002, 51). Thus Edward N. O'Neil says of the text in Philippians, "These words of Paul could just as easily have been uttered by Antisthenes, Diogenes, Crates, or even Teles" (O'Neil 1978, 312).

Overtones of the philosophical discussion appear elsewhere in the NT. According to 1 Tim. 6:6 (NRSV), "There is great gain in godliness combined with contentment [*autarkeia*]." According to Hebrews, one should avoid the love of money and be content with what one has (13:5). Although these statements contain the vocabulary of Stoicism, the assumptions underlying this language are different. For the Stoics, contentment was found in virtue alone, and virtue was found in oneself alone, independent of others (Fowl 2002, 32).

Paul's declaration that he was not "in need" corresponds to the Stoic insistence that friendships are not based on need. According to Cicero, "It is far from being true that friendship is cultivated because of need [*indigentiam*]; rather it is cultivated by those who are most abundantly blessed with wealth and power and especially with virtue, which is man's best defense; by those least in need of another's help; and by those most generous and most given to acts of kindness" (*Amic.* 51, cited in Malherbe 1996, 136). However, Paul departs from Stoic reflection when he reveals the source of his contentment, the God who strengthens him (4:13).

Paul's second clarification, that he did not seek the gift (4:17), suggests that he had no desire to enter into the reciprocity that defined ancient friendship. His concern was not the establishment of the reciprocity between friends, but the well-being of the Philippian church. Thus while the terminology of giving and receiving is common in ancient discussions of friendship, Paul redefines the concept to avoid misunderstandings by the Philippians. With his attempts to define the nature of the gift, he ensures that the Philippians not understand their relationship according to Greco-Roman expectations. He does not mention the obligation of reciprocity. All mention of repayment is omitted (Peterman 1997, 149).

Tracing the Train of Thought

The conclusion of a deliberative speech, the *peroratio*, has two main functions: to refresh the memory and to appeal to the emotions (Lausberg 1998, §431; cf. Quintilian, *Inst. or.* 6.1.1). The speaker refreshes the memory by repeating statements made in the argument (*probatio*) and appeals to the emotions by arguing from pathos, gaining the goodwill of the hearers (Thompson 2007,

302). The speaker may remind the readers of the good that he has done for them and describe the bond of affection that unites him with the audience (Watson 1988, 76). The *peroratio* may correspond to the *exordium*, introducing the speech (Quintilian, *Inst. or.* 6.1.9–12; Lausberg 1998 §432).

Although interpreters disagree over the place where the *peroratio* of Philippians begins, many recognize that either part or all of chapter 4 reiterates the argument of the letter and concludes with a statement establishing the emotional bonds between Paul and the Philippians. Duane Watson (1988, 77) has observed the reiteration of the basic points of the letter in the exhortation in 4:1–9 and the emotional appeal in 4:10–20, designating the former as *repetitio* and the latter as the *adfectus.*

Concluding Instructions: United in Moral Behavior (4:2–9)

4:2–3. *The "same mind" for Euodia and Syntyche.* No conjunction links the imperative "stand firm in the Lord" with the appeal to Euodia and Syntyche **to be of the same mind** (*to auto phronein*). While Paul speaks with the imperative in the ethical instructions in 4:1, 4–9, he introduces the request in 4:2 with *parakalō* (NRSV "urge"; NIV "plead"), a verb he frequently uses to introduce moral instruction (cf. Rom. 12:1; 1 Cor. 1:10; 4:16; 2 Cor. 2:8; 1 Thess. 4:1, 10). It is the term for a polite request (2 Cor. 8:6; 9:5; Philem. 9), encouragement of those who are disheartened (cf. 1 Cor. 4:13; 1 Thess. 3:2), and comforting of those who are bereaved (1 Thess. 4:18; 5:11; Thompson 2011, 60). Paul distinguishes *parakalō* ("urge," "encourage") from *diatassō* ("command," Philem. 8–10), and he suggests that the participle *parakalountes* is a paternal word for the father who urges his children to live appropriately (1 Thess. 2:11–13). In Philippians Paul repeats *parakalō*, addressing each woman individually, as if he were speaking to them separately face to face (O'Brien 1991, 478).

In urging the women "to be of the same mind" (*to auto phronein*), he repeats the instructions that he had given to the whole church (2:2). The advice recalls the earlier exhortations to stand firm "in one spirit" and "of one mind" (1:27) and "be in full accord [*sympsychoi*] and of one mind [*to hen phronountes*]" (2:2). As Paul indicates in 1:27–30, the presence of hostility in the wider community demands the unity of believers. Thus with the appeal to the two women "to be of the same mind," Paul summarizes the consistent challenge to the community (1:27–30; 2:1–4, 12–18).

Paul inculcates a common mind-set (*phronēsis*) that unites the community and distinguishes it from the surrounding culture. At the center of the letter is the imperative "Have this mind [*touto phroneite*] which you have in Christ Jesus" (2:5), which indicates that the *phronēsis* is determined by the narrative of Christ (2:6–11). The challenge to Euodia and Syntyche suggests that they lack this common *phronēsis* based on the story of Christ. The rupture in their relationship will have a disastrous effect on the community. This terminology, drawn from ancient expressions of friendship, is thus a summary of the major focus of the letter.

This mind-set (*phronēsis*) is only **in the Lord** (*en kyriō*). What unites them and demarcates them from the surrounding culture is their incorporation in Christ. They are the saints "in Christ" (1:1), experience encouragement in Christ (2:1), have a mind-set in Christ (2:5), stand firm in the Lord (4:1), and rejoice in the Lord (3:1; 4:4). That is, Christ is the sphere in which they live and the bond that unites them.

Because of the effects of the quarrel between the two women, Paul makes an additional request, **Yes** (*nai*), **I ask you** (*erōtō*), **my loyal companion, help these women**, giving it special emphasis with the particle *nai* ("yes"). Whereas Paul made his request to the two women, using the familiar *parakalō*, he entreats the loyal companion with the verb *erōtō*, which he uses only in the letters to the Philippians and Thessalonians (1 Thess. 4:1; 5:12; cf. 2 Thess. 2:1). O'Brien suggests that the change of verbs of request reflects Paul's different relationship to those who are addressed (O'Brien 1991, 479), maintaining that *erōtō*, a polite request, is addressed to an equal, while *parakalō* is addressed to subordinates. The juxtaposition of the two verbs in 1 Thess. 4:1 suggests, however, that there is little difference between the two verbs.

The crisis created by the quarrel of the two women is so great that Paul appeals to the unnamed loyal companion (*gnēsie syzyge*, lit. "true yokefellow"), "help [*syllambanou*] these women." While the true yokefellow remains unnamed, he is identified only by his task. The *syzygos* is a comrade in arms, a friend, and a coworker (see under "Introductory Matters"). Because of his role as *syzygos* in Paul's ministry, the apostle requests that he help the women. *Syllambanou*, a word that can mean "conceive" (Luke 1:24) or "seize" (Matt. 26:55 par.), also means "to help." It is used in this sense when the partners helped bring in the fish (Luke 5:7), and it is used in Phil. 4:3 in directing the loyal companion to help the women find harmony.

Paul motivates the loyal companion to help the women **because** (*haitines*, NRSV "for") **they struggled together** (*synēthlēsan*) beside him **with Clement and the other fellow workers** (*synergōn*). In contrast to the ESV, which renders *haitines* as a relative pronoun identifying the two women ("who"), the NRSV appropriately renders the word as "for," indicating the reason for helping the women. Paul recalls that the women have done in the past what he now challenges the whole church to do (1:27): to "struggle together" in spreading the gospel. This task involves a joint struggle against adversaries.

The combination of *syn-* words indicates the joint effort that is required for the spread of the gospel. Paul asks the *syzygos* (comrade in arms) to help (*syllambanou*) women who had struggled together (*synēthlēsan*) with Clement and the other fellow workers (*synergoi*). Both *syzygos* and *synēthlēsan* have overtones of gladiatorial contests and suggest the bravery and hard struggle that was involved in spreading the gospel. Euodia and Syntyche are among the group **whose names are enrolled in the book of life.**

4:4–9. *Final ethical advice.* No conjunction links the imperatives in 4:4–7 to the preceding request in 4:2–3. Similarly, the series of imperatives that appear in a staccato style are grammatically independent of each other, and the relationship between the imperatives and the declarative statements

> ## Asyndeton
>
> Asyndeton is a rhetorical term for the intentional omission of connective particles or conjunctions between words, sentences, or paragraphs.

in 4:5b ("the Lord is near") and 4:7 ("the peace of God . . . will rule your hearts") is not explicit. Thus, through the use of asyndeton each command takes on individual importance and becomes emphatic (O'Brien 1991, 485).

The command **rejoice in the Lord** repeats the refrain that is a distinctive feature of the letter (see 2:18; 3:1). The repetition **again I say rejoice** gives special force. Paul has been a model of rejoicing in the midst of deprivation. He rejoices in his bonds (1:4, 18), and he rejoices in the progress of his community (2:2). He speaks of their joy of faith (1:25) and invites the church to rejoice with him (2:18). He anticipates that the readers will rejoice when they again see Epaphroditus, who risked his life for the gospel (2:28–30). Citizens of the heavenly commonwealth (*politeuma*), despite the dangers that threaten them, rejoice because of the coming triumph of the Lord (3:20–21). They have been formed to see beyond the crisis they face and now have powers of perception that are contrary to ordinary ways of seeing (Fowl 2005, 182). This is neither the rejoicing that accompanies celebration of significant events in one's life (cf. H. Conzelmann, *TDNT* 9:369–70) nor that which occurs when one is oblivious to threatening forces, but rejoicing "in the Lord" in the context of deprivation. As Paul has repeatedly said, the community's entire existence is in the Lord (2:19, 24; 3:1; 4:1) or "in Christ" (1:1; 2:1, 5; 3:3). To rejoice **always** is to maintain the same spirit of hope in all circumstances.

The call to rejoice is deeply rooted in Israelite faith. The prophets challenge Israel to rejoice because of God's coming triumph (Joel 2:21, 23; Zech. 9:9). It has a significant place in Paul's letters. The kingdom of God is not eating and drinking but righteousness, joy, and peace in the Holy Spirit (Rom. 14:17). Paul prays that the Romans will be filled "with all joy and peace in believing" (Rom. 15:13 NRSV). His converts received his preaching in persecution "with the joy of the Holy Spirit" (1 Thess. 1:6). He lists joy second in the fruit of the Spirit (Gal. 5:22), and he consistently describes his churches as his joy (Phil. 4:1; 1 Thess. 2:19). He rejoices in their progress, even in the midst of his own distress (2 Cor. 2:3; 7:7, 9; 1 Thess. 3:9).

Without transition, Paul adds the second imperative, **Let your gentleness** (*epieikēs*) **be known to everyone** (4:5). *Epieikēs* (= Latin *clementia*), a word used nowhere else in the moral instructions in the undisputed Pauline letters, is a quality that is admired both by Greco-Roman moralists and biblical writers.

Roman writers spoke of the *clementia* of Caesar (Cicero, *Marcell.* 11; *Lig.* 6.19.15; *Deiot.* 34; Plutarch, *Caes.* 57.4; Cassius Dio 44.6.4). In the Septuagint the adjective *epieikēs* and the noun *epieikeia* are used for the gentleness and forbearance of God (1 Sam. 12:22; Ps. 85:5 [86:5 Eng.]; Wis. 12:18; Bar. 2:27; Dan. 3:42; 4:27; 3 Macc. 3:15; 7:6), connoting judgment combined with mercy. The word appears elsewhere in the undisputed letters only in 2 Corinthians, when Paul makes his appeal through the "meekness [*prautētos*] and gentleness [*epieikeia*]" of Christ (2 Cor. 10:1). In the Pastoral Epistles *epieikeia* is a qualification for church leaders (1 Tim. 3:3; Titus 3:2) and is used as the opposite of quarrelsome. In Wisdom 2:19 *epieikeia* is used for the patient firmness of the righteous one who is scorned by the godless and accepts mistreatment by relying on God (cf. H. Giessen, *EDNT* 2:26). Just as the instruction to rejoice in the Lord is a call for the believers' response to outward hostility, the gentleness that he requests is probably also a response to hostility after the model of the "meekness and gentleness of Christ" (cf. Fowl 2005, 182).

Paul not only applies to the community a word that was commonly used in reference to the Caesar but urges the community to let their "gentleness be known to everyone" (4:5). Just as Paul's message is known to the whole praetorian guard (1:12–13), he urges the community to let their gentleness be known to everyone. As he indicates earlier, as they are surrounded by a hostile environment, they shine as lights in the world (2:15). The church does not live in isolation but bears witness to its countercultural existence to the surrounding world (1 Thess. 5:15). The community accepts suffering, knowing that believers will ultimately triumph, while the oppressors will face destruction (cf. 1:28). Paul develops this advice more fully in the exhortation to respond to evil by doing good (cf. Rom. 12:17–20; Wojtkowiak 2012, 254).

Also without conjunction is the declaration **the Lord is near** (4:5), an assurance to a community surrounded by reminders that the Lord Caesar is near. That is, the one who is near is the Lord who humbled himself and will be acknowledged as Lord by the whole world (2:11). The Lord is Jesus Christ, whom the community awaits (3:20). Paul does not indicate whether "the Lord is near" is a reference to the imminent return of Christ or a statement of the proximity of the Lord in daily life. As a spatial image, Paul's assurance recalls the psalmist's confidence that the "Lord is near those who call on him" (145:18; see also 119:151). As a temporal statement, Paul's assurance recalls the announcement in the Gospels that "the kingdom of God has drawn near" (Mark 1:15; cf. Matt. 3:2; Mark 13:28–29 par.) and his statement that "salvation is nearer [*engyteron*] to us now than when we first became believers" (Rom. 13:11). One does not need to choose between the spatial and temporal meaning, for the focus is on the Lord who is exalted and will not abandon them.

Nowhere else in the Pauline correspondence does he instruct the community, **Do not worry** (*mēden merimnate*) **about anything**. In fact, he assumes the natural worries of family members for each other (1 Cor. 7:32), and he recalls that Timothy is genuinely concerned about others (*merimnēsei*, Phil. 2:20). He also acknowledges his own "anxiety" (*merimna*) for his churches (2 Cor. 11:28). Paul's instruction, which recalls Jesus's words (Matt. 6:25), involves corporate anxiety over the church's vulnerable situation. It recalls the earlier instruction not to be intimidated by the adversaries (1:28).

The alternative to corporate anxiety is prayer. **In everything** (*en panti*, 4:6) is parallel to "in nothing" (NRSV "Do not worry about anything"), indicating the totality of the community's trust. Paul offers a comprehensive view of **prayer**. *Proseuchē*, the general word for prayer, includes both **supplication** (*deēsis*) and **thanksgiving** (*eucharistia*). Paul has been a model of prayer (1:3–11), having given thanks (cf. *eucharistō*, 1:3) in every petition (cf. *deēsei*, 1:4). He prays (cf. *proseuchomai*, 1:9) for the spiritual progress of the community, and he hopes that through their prayers (*deēseōs*) recent events will result in salvation (1:19). Having instructed the readers to "let their gentleness be known [*gnōsthētō*] to everyone" (4:5), he urges the readers to **let their requests** (*aitēmata*) **be known** (*gnōrizesthō*) **to God**. As the alternative to corporate anxiety, their requests grow out of the living conditions in which they find themselves (Popkes 2004, 252).

Kai (**and**) in 4:7 probably introduces the result of making requests to God. The **peace of God** is the peace that comes from God (genitive of source), about which Paul prays at the beginning and end of his letters. The peace of God is a common theme in the OT, the equivalent of God's steadfast love and mercy (Jer. 16:5). God is the source of peace (Num. 6:26; Ps. 29:11; Job 25:2). Because the message of eschatological salvation is a proclamation of peace (Isa. 9:6; 52:7), Paul describes the believers' new status as "peace with God" (Rom. 5:1), and he frequently reminds his churches that peace is the reality of the new existence. Indeed, joy and peace appear together in his descriptions of existence in Christ (Rom. 14:17; 15:13; Gal. 5:22). The superlative **which surpasses** (*hyperechousa*) **all power of thought** (*nous*, BDAG 680) may be a comparison to lesser forms of peace, that is, the peace that is known by the majority culture. The superlative *hyperechousa* recalls the earlier reference to the "surpassing value" (*hyperechousa*) of the knowledge of Christ (3:8). The *nous*, the faculty of intellectual perception (BDAG 680), can be turned away from God (Rom. 1:28) but renewed in Christ (Rom. 12:2). While unredeemed people do not know the mind (*nous*) of the Lord (Rom. 11:34; 1 Cor. 2:16), believers have the mind (*nous*) of Christ (1 Cor. 2:16). In response to the community's prayers, this peace will **guard** (*phrourēsei*) their **hearts and thoughts** (*noēmata*, NRSV "minds") in Christ Jesus. The phrase "hearts and minds" refers to the whole of Christian existence. The heart (*kardia*) is the center of the inner life with its thinking, feeling, and volition (BDAG 508), involving both the affections (cf. Rom. 9:1; 2 Cor. 2:4; Phil. 1:7) and the intellectual process. Among unredeemed people, both the hearts and minds are alienated from God (cf. Rom. 1:21, 24, 28; 2:5; Eph. 4:17), but in Christ the Spirit is written on the hearts (2 Cor. 3:3), and the mind is being renewed (Rom. 12:2) while all thoughts (*noēmata*) are taken captive to Christ (2 Cor. 10:5). Paul evokes the image of the night watchman who guards the city (cf. 2 Cor. 11:32; Jdt. 3:6; Josephus, *J.W.* 3.12) to describe the activity of the peace of God. The answer to the community's anxiety, therefore, is the peace of God that functions like a night watchman protecting vulnerable believers. This promise reaffirms the earlier assurances that, despite appearances, God is at work to bring the community to completion (cf. 1:6; 2:13).

The reference to the hearts and thoughts in 4:7 provides the transition to the final exhortation in 4:8–9, which indicates what believers should **consider** (*logizesthe*, 4:8) and **continue to do** (*prassete*, 4:9). **Finally** (*to loipon*), **brothers** (and sisters; *adelphoi*, 4:8) marks the conclusion of instructions about life in the alternative commonwealth. *To loipon*, used earlier to mean "furthermore" (3:1), here means "in conclusion." The imperatives that follow are based on a relationship, as Paul indicates with the vocative *adelphoi* (brothers and sisters), which he has employed earlier in the letter (1:12; 3:1; 4:1). The focus on thought and action, a popular theme in Hellenistic moral philosophy (Willis 2012, 73), is an appropriate summary of the letter, inasmuch as a major focus of Philippians is the development of an appropriate way of thinking and doing. Paul prays that the community will increase in love with full knowledge (1:9), and he consistently urges the readers either to think the same thing (*to auto phronein*) or have this mind (*touto phronein*). *Logizesthe* ("think about") is parallel to *phroneite* (Willis 2012, 72).

The numerous exhortations (1:27–2:18) and Paul's own example (1:12–26; 3:4–17) have indicated what the apostle expects the readers "to continue to do." Thus Paul begins the letter with the prayer for the community's moral formation (1:9–11) and returns to the same theme here in the *peroratio*.

The parallel sentences in 4:8–9 indicate the significance of thought and action. Verse 8 contains a series of six ethical qualities introduced by **whatever** (*hosa*) and concluding with the imperative "think about these things" (*tauta logizesthe*), while 4:9 (in Greek) has four items describing what the Philippians have been taught, introduced by **what** (*ha*) and concluding with "continue to do these things" (*tauta prassete*) and a benediction. The rhythmic structure (cf. Lohmeyer 1953, 175) is enhanced by the repetition of "whatever" (*hosa*) before each ethical quality (4:8) and by **and** (*kai*) before each verb in 4:9. The parallel structure of 4:8–9 indicates that these two verses should not be interpreted independently of each other.

The six moral qualities introduced by "whatever" stand in sharp contrast to the similarly structured list of behavioral moral qualities introduced by "if there is any" in 2:1. Here the mind of Christ was defined by love, fellowship, mercy, and compassion—qualities that would have been contrary to the values of the society (Bockmuehl 1998, 250), while the adjectives listed in 4:8 would have resonated with the ancient society. However, while the terms **true, honorable, just, holy, lovely, and of good report** (4:8) may correspond at some level with Hellenistic morality, the meaning of the terms depends on the context in which they appear. Having argued throughout the letter that conduct in the heavenly commonwealth is shaped by the narrative of the one who emptied himself and humbled himself (2:6–11), Paul does not conclude the letter with the commendation of Greek moral philosophy or a recognition of whatever "there is in the world's treasury of wisdom that can be reckoned morally excellent and praiseworthy" (cf. Furnish 2005, 72). While he employs the vocabulary of popular philosophy (cf. 1:10; 4:11), he chooses terms that reflect a concern for the community's reputation to the larger society. The terms honorable (*semna*), just (*dikaia*), lovely (*prosphilē*), and good report (*euphēma*) focus on the community's reputation among outsiders (Wojtkowiak 2012, 257). These values may correspond in some cases to the values of Philippian society, but Paul reinterprets them in light of the cross, calling for a communal *phronēsis* determined by the Christ event (cf. Fowl 2005, 185–86).

Paul has provided the model for the qualities that he lists in 4:8, as he indicates in 4:9. His appeal to his own example is not a contrast to the qualities listed in 4:8 but the embodiment of the moral formation that he has commended. The appeal to his own example is an appropriate conclusion to a letter that is filled with autobiography (1:12–26; 3:4–16) and the call for imitation (3:17). He employs the rabbinic terminology of the passing on of a tradition when he speaks of what the readers have **learned** (*emathete*) and **received** (*parelabete*), which includes the moral instruction he gave after their baptism (cf. 1 Cor. 11:2, 23; 15:3; 1 Thess. 4:1). What they have **seen** and **heard** in him is the example that he has described in the letter—his selfless conduct and willingness to suffer for Christ. Having appealed to his example earlier in the letter (1:12–26; 3:4–17), he concludes the ethical instruction, urging the community to continue to follow his model of moral conduct and participate in his struggle (cf. 1:30).

Just as Paul concludes the imperatives in 4:4–7 with the promise that "the peace of God will guard [their] hearts and minds," he concludes the imperatives in 4:8–9 with the promise, **the God of peace will be with you.** Paul speaks of the "God of peace" elsewhere (Rom. 15:33; 2 Cor. 13:11; 1 Thess. 5:23; cf. 2 Thess. 3:16; Heb. 13:20), especially in the context of real or potential conflict (1 Cor. 14:33; Rom. 16:20). In contrast to passages that refer to the God of peace in petitions (Rom. 15:33; 1 Thess. 5:23), in both Phil. 4:9 and 2 Cor. 13:11 the phrase "the peace of God will be with you" is a promise to those whose lives are determined by their heavenly citizenship and a reaffirmation that God is at work among them (cf. 1:6; 2:13; 4:7).

The "Thankless Thanks" (4:10–20)

4:10–20. As part of the *peroratio*, 4:10 continues to summarize themes from the earlier part of the letter, turning from direct exhortation to a reiteration of the partnership between Paul and the Philippians. The untranslated *de* signals the transition to a new topic. These final words correspond especially to the *exordium* in 1:3–11. Indeed, the *exordium* (1:3–11) and the concluding part of the *peroratio* comprise a "well-crafted frame" for the letter (Fowl 2002, 49).

1:3–11	4:10–20
"I give thanks . . . with joy" (1:3–4)	"I rejoiced" (4:10)
"I am concerned about you" (1:7)	"You are concerned about me" (4:10)
"your partnership" (*koinōnia*; 1:5)	"No one partnered [*ekoinōnēsen*] except you" (4:15)
"my partners" (*synkoinōnoi*; 1:7)	"your partnering" (*synkoinōnēsantes*; 4:14)
"God began a good work" (1:6)	"at the beginning of the gospel" (4:15)

As the *peroratio*, 4:10–20 returns to other themes introduced in earlier parts of the letter. Epaphroditus, first mentioned in 2:25–29, reappears (4:18). Paul's humble circumstances (4:11) correspond to the humility he commends to the church (2:3–4; cf. 2:8). The theme of the empowerment of God (1:6; 2:13) for a marginalized community again appears in this section (4:13). Thus 4:10–20 is not merely a thank-you note but a reaffirmation of the divine promise for those who live according to the norms of the alternative commonwealth. While the appearance of the thank-you note in 4:10–20 is unusual among Paul's letters, the structure of the letter suggests that it is a fitting conclusion to the argument (Holloway 2001, 27–28).

The structure of the passage reflects the sensitivity of the topic of finances, for Paul's acknowledgment of the gift is accompanied by two disclaimers (cf. Snyman 2007, 172).

> Acknowledgment of the gift (4:10)
>   Disclaimer (4:11)
>   God's response (4:13)
> Acknowledgment of the gift (4:14–16)
>   Disclaimer (4:17)
> Acknowledgment (4:18)
>   God's response (4:19–20)

Paul first acknowledges the gift, declaring **I rejoiced** (*echarēn*) **greatly that now at last you have revived your concern for me** (4:10). Contrary to the ASV, RSV, and NRSV, which render *echarēn* as an epistolary aorist ("I rejoice"), Paul recalls the moment when he rejoiced at the Philippians' expression of concern for him. He employs the present tense elsewhere to indicate that he gives thanks for the Philippians "with joy" (1:4) and describes his rejoicing in the midst of imprisonment (1:18). Because the Philippians' transformed behavior "makes [his] joy complete" (2:2), he rejoiced (4:10) at their response to him. He does not mention their gift specifically but speaks of how they revived their concern for him. *To hyper emou phronein* ("your concern for me") corresponds to Paul's expression of his concern for them in 1:7 (*emoi touto phronein hyper pantōn*). The phrase *phronein hyper* with the genitive is the language of friendship (cf. Reumann 2008, 648), indicating the Philippians' concern for him (cf. Berry 1996, 111).

The phrase "now at last" (*ēdē pote*) indicates a delay in the sending of the gift. This is not a mild rebuke of the Philippians' delay but a reflection of Paul's anxiety for the community. The imperfect tense in the two verbs **you were concerned** (*ephroneite*), but **you had no opportunity** (*ēkaireisthe*) indicates the Philippians' continuing concern for Paul, even if they have only recently sent the gift. He uses a botanical image to indicate that their concern has recently "revived" (*anethalete*, lit. "it blossomed" or "sprang up"; BDAG 63), using imagery that indicates that their active partnership was like a plant that has bloomed again after being dormant for a period of time.

Because the topic of funds was a sensitive matter, Paul offers disclaimers in 4:11, 17 introduced by "not that" (*ouch hoti*). The rhetorical theorists called the disclaimer a correction, a qualifying statement intended to prevent a misunderstanding. He introduces the first disclaimer, **not that I speak because of need** (*kath' hysterēsin*), indicating his independence. While *hysterēsis* can refer to the lack of faith (1 Thess. 3:10), lack of spiritual gifts (1 Cor. 1:7), or humans who "fall short" of the glory of God (Rom. 3:23), Paul refers in Phil. 4:11 to physical poverty (cf. BDAG 1044), which is a persistent reality for him. Indeed, he responds to his refusal to accept financial support from the Corinthians, recalling that he was "in need" when he was with them (2 Cor. 11:9). In his catalog of trials that he had endured, he mentions that he was at that moment "hungry and thirsty, poorly clothed, beaten and homeless" (1 Cor. 4:11; cf. 2 Cor. 6:5). Despite these conditions, which have been exacerbated by his imprisonment, Paul maintains to the Philippians that he is not speaking of being in need.

Paul explains how he could speak of not being in need, despite his circumstances, in 4:11b–13 in a rhythmic sequence of phrases introduced by verbs of cognition: **I have learned** (*emathon*, 4:11), **I know** (*oida*, 4:12a) . . . **I know** (*oida*, 4:12b) . . . **I have learned the secret** (*memyēmai*, 4:12c). The statement "I have learned" to **be content** (*autarkēs*) **with everything** introduces the circumstances in which Paul has found contentment, using language reminiscent of his catalogs of deprivation in other letters (cf. 1 Cor. 4:9–12; 2 Cor. 4:7–15; 6:4–10; 11:23–30). The chiastic pattern and the repetition of **and** (*kai*) articulates the circumstances with special effect. He knows how **to have little** (*tapeinousthai*) and **to have much** (*perisseuein*), and he has "learned the secret" **of being filled** (*chortazesthai*) and being **hungry** (*peinan*). Both *tapeinousthai* (lit. "to be brought low" or "to be humbled") and *perisseuein* (lit. "abound") have a wide range of meanings. The statement recalls that Jesus "humbled himself" (*etapeinōsen heauton*) by dying on the cross (2:8). Forms of *tapeinoō* also have financial overtones, as Paul indicates when, in refusing financial support, he asks the Corinthians, "Did I commit a sin by humbling myself [*emauton tapeinōn*] so that you might be exalted?" (2 Cor. 11:7 NRSV). Similarly, *perisseuein* ("abound," "have plenty") can refer to physical resources (cf. 2 Cor. 9:8) but also describes an abundance of other things. The statement "I have learned the secret" employs a verb (*memuēmai*) borrowed from the mystery religions and can be rendered "I have been initiated." The secret is "to be filled and to be hungry." Paul speaks of his hunger in the other references to his sufferings (cf. 1 Cor. 4:11).

While Paul's statement in 4:11–13 could have been made by a Stoic, his reason for contentment is decidedly different, as he concludes, **I can do all things through Christ who strengthens me** (4:13). While the Stoic seeks inner peace, Paul is empowered by Christ. The statement is reminiscent of his focus on divine power in the context of his weakness. When the Corinthians criticize his weakness, he concludes his list of sufferings, "Whenever I am weak, then I am strong" (2 Cor. 12:10 NRSV). As he participates in the sufferings of Jesus, he also experiences resurrection power (Phil. 3:10). He has indicated that God is at work (1:6; 2:13) among believers.

After the disclaimer in 4:11–13, Paul again acknowledges the Philippians' gift, declaring, **Nevertheless you did well** (NRSV "it was kind of you") **to share my distress** (*synkoinōnēsantes mou tē thlipsei*). He elaborates in 4:15 that no other church **shared** (*ekoinōnēsen*) **in the matter of giving and receiving.** This memory corresponds to the beginning of the letter when Paul expresses gratitude for the Philippians' sharing (*koinōnia*) because they are "sharers" (*synkoinōnoi*) in God's grace (1:7). *Koinōnia*, a term that was widely used for friends who were committed to the reciprocity of giving and receiving, is inseparable in the Pauline literature from the larger context of sharing. Paul speaks of his sharing (*koinōnia*) in the sufferings of Christ (Phil. 3:10) and of all believers who now experience the *koinōnia* of the Son (1 Cor. 1:9), the *koinōnia* in the Spirit (Phil. 2:1), and the *koinōnia* of believers in the body and blood of Christ (1 Cor. 10:16). He does not separate the *koinōnia* in Christ from the concrete realities of the sharing of resources. As he indicates to the Romans, those who have shared (*ekoinōnēsan*) spiritual blessings ought to share material things (15:27); thus the collection for the poor saints in Jerusalem is a *koinōnia* (2 Cor. 8:4; 9:13) among the churches. By sharing their resources with Paul, the Philippians have "shared in his distress" (4:14). Having earlier urged the Philippians to engage with him in a struggle against adversaries (1:27–30), he recalls that their *koinōnia* with him was also a participation in his sufferings (cf. 3:10). They have placed themselves at risk in identifying themselves with him.

Although Paul indicates that he does not speak from need (4:11), he acknowledges that the Philippians sent to his **need** (*chreia*) **once and twice** (4:16), using an idiom that means "more than once." The readers had established a pattern of supporting Paul in his early ministry in Thessalonica, demonstrating their partnership (*koinōnia*, 4:15), which has now "blossomed" again.

Having acknowledged the Philippians' gift a second time (4:14–16), Paul offers a second disclaimer in 4:17. He did not **seek the gift,** not wanting to be a burden (cf. 2 Cor. 12:14–16) or to establish the obligation that ancient people connected with giving. What he did seek was **the profit that accumulates to their account.** Paul employs the commercial terminology to indicate that he is more interested in the Philippians' progress than in his own material welfare. *Karpos* (lit. "fruit," NRSV "profit") is an agricultural metaphor commonly used in the NT for the conduct of one's life that leads either to positive or negative results (cf. Rom. 6:21–22; H.-T. Wrege, *EDNT* 2:252). Paul employs the term for ethical formation empowered by the Spirit (cf. Gal. 5:22; Rom. 1:13). In Philippians he uses the financial image to amplify his earlier concern for the Philippians' progress. He prays for the "harvest [*karpos*] of righteousness" (1:11) and anticipates "fruitful labor" (*karpos ergou*)—a successful mission (cf. Rom. 1:13)—if he is reunited with the Philippians (Phil. 1:22). His major concern is the progress and joy of their faith (1:25–26). Thus while *karpos* can refer to a financial transaction (cf. Rom. 15:28), the fruit is the transformation of the community, their capacity for sacrifice. One may compare Paul's comments about the Macedonians as he urges the Corinthians to participate in the collection. The Macedonians had "singleness of heart" (*tēs haplotētos autōn*, 2 Cor. 8:2) and "gave themselves to the Lord" (*heautous edōkan . . . tō kyriō*, 2 Cor. 8:5) when they sacrificed their possessions.

The language of compound interest also elaborates on what Paul says elsewhere. "The profit that accumulates to your account" (4:17) is the progress of the church and its mission. The language of abundance is a thread running through Paul's letters. He prays that the Philippians' love will "overflow [*perisseuē*] more and more with knowledge and full insight" (1:9), and he hopes that their boasting in Christ may abound (*perisseuē*) in him when he returns (1:26). When he urges the Corinthians to participate in the collection for the poor saints in Jerusalem, he encourages those who abound (*perisseuete*) in everything to also abound (*perisseuēte*) in the collection (2 Cor. 8:7). He promises that God will multiply their gift (2 Cor. 9:10), so that the givers will have enough of everything (2 Cor. 9:8) and be enriched (2 Cor. 9:11) while they supply the needs of the saints (2 Cor. 9:12). Their gift will result in many thanksgivings to God (2 Cor. 9:11–12). What "accumulates to the account" of the Philippians, therefore, is the result of the new mind-set that they have demonstrated in sharing in Paul's distress. Paul seeks the demonstration that the Philippians are willing to follow his model of sacrifice, knowing that God is at work in human weakness.

Paul mixes the metaphors in 4:18, acknowledging the Philippians' gift with the commercial phrase **I have been paid in full**, adding redundantly, **I abound** (*perisseuō*) and **I am filled** (*peplērōmai*), and interpreting its significance in language drawn from the sacrificial system of the OT. He has received from Epaphroditus **a fragrant offering** (*osmēn euōdias*), **a sacrifice** (*thysian*) **acceptable and pleasing** (*euareston*) **to God**. The image recalls the sacrifices in the OT that were a "pleasing odor" to God (cf. Gen. 8:21; Exod. 29:18; Lev. 1:9, 13). In 2 Corinthians (2:14–17), Paul describes his own ministry as one of spreading the fragrance (*osmē*) of the knowledge of Christ. He speaks of his own life as a "libation over the sacrifice and the offering of [their] faith" (Phil. 2:17). Now he is filled, not only by the quantity of the gift but also by the demonstration of the Philippians' sacrificial mind-set.

Just as Paul can be content with deprivation because of the Christ who strengthens him (4:13), he is certain that God **will satisfy** the Philippians' **every need according to his riches in glory** (4:19). One may compare his promise to the Corinthians that God will supply the participants in the collection with every blessing so that they would have enough of everything (2 Cor. 9:8). The assurance of God's power is an appropriate conclusion to the letter, with its recurring emphasis on God's power (1:6; 2:13; 4:7, 13) in the midst of communal suffering.

Final Greetings: A Community in God's Grace (4:21–23)

4:21–23. While the final greetings in the Pauline letters exhibit near uniformity and conform largely to Hellenistic letters, they also serve the rhetorical purpose of Paul's correspondence. The appeal to the readers **to greet every saint in Christ Jesus** (4:21) provides the frame for the letter, which began with the address "to all the saints in Christ Jesus" (1:1). This outer frame is the reminder of the community's identity as saints—those who are set apart from the local society and now belong to the heritage of Israel (cf. Lev. 19:2) because they are incorporated in Christ. To greet every saint is to demonstrate solidarity with the others who have separated themselves from the larger society. They greet one another when they gather in the regular assembly.

As in the other letters, Paul extends greetings from believers in other places. The **brothers who are with** him include Timothy and Epaphroditus (cf. 2:19–30) and probably others whom Paul does not name. The passing of greetings from a distant place indicates that followers separated by distance are united in faith. Paul says hyperbolically, **all the saints greet you** (cf. Rom. 16:16), again mentioning no names but demonstrating the international character of the movement. The greeting from **those of Caesar's household** (4:22) offers encouragement to the marginalized believers in Philippi, reinforcing Paul's earlier claim that the gospel is advancing, even among the Romans. The conclusion of the letter, **the grace of the Lord Jesus Christ be with your spirit**, forms an *inclusio* with the opening prayer, "grace to you and peace from God our

Father and the Lord Jesus Christ" (1:2), reminding the listeners that they are not powerless but are partners in God's grace (cf. 1:7; 1:28).

Theological Issues

Maintaining Unity

Because communities that were connected neither by ethnicity nor by social class were unprecedented in antiquity, Paul's constant challenge was to maintain unity among people of diverse backgrounds. Since he has focused on the unity of this house church throughout the letter, the most appropriate conclusion is a challenge to a marginalized group to maintain unity. His appeal to Euodia and Syntyche to "be of the same mind" (4:2) is also a challenge to the whole church (2:2) and a reminder that only a united church stands as a witness to God's reconciling activity.

To "be of the same mind" is not to have uniformity of opinion (cf. Rom. 14:1–7). Nor is it the easy tolerance that arises from the absence of strong convictions. What Paul urges is a community that is countercultural insofar as it puts aside selfish ambition and the desire for power. Undoubtedly Paul knows that a mere request to people who are involved in conflict will not bring reconciliation. Consequently, he has devoted the entire letter to the description of the mind that unites believers. The centerpiece of the letter describes the mind that believers have in Christ (2:5), which Paul has illustrated with his descriptions of Timothy (2:19–24), Epaphroditus (2:25–30), and himself (3:4–17). Believers have the same mind when they are united by the story of the one who did not look to his own interests but to the interests of others. Thus, despite the inevitable differences of opinion, Paul appeals to believers to be united as they tell the story of the one who emptied himself.

The address to Euodia and Syntyche is a reminder that a unified church is not, like the associations of antiquity, limited to men. We know Euodia and Syntyche not only for their disputes but also for their activities in the church. As coworkers they fought side by side. From the beginning of the church, women have been fellow workers with men, often risking their lives alongside the men. In a world that commonly relegated the women to the home, they were on the front lines.

The imperatives in 4:4–7 also express the unity of the church. Paul challenges the whole church to practice a shared ethos. A common mind results in shared habits. Boundaries from the local society are evident. The church is not composed of individuals who establish their own morality. They rejoice together because together they see the ultimate triumph of God. At the same time, they interact with the outside world when they let their forbearance be known to all. Their united morality is a witness to the world.

Scholars have observed that the six ethical qualities listed in 4:8 are compatible with the values of the local society, concluding that Paul offers an affirmation of the culture. That is, Paul would affirm the values of art, music, and ethics of the surrounding culture. While it is probably true that Paul chooses qualities that are attractive to outsiders, he is discriminating in his theology of culture. There is much in culture that he does not mention; indeed, his communities reject much from the local culture. Whatever he takes from culture is filtered through the Christian story. Indeed, Paul's own example (4:9) is an interpretation of the values mentioned in 4:8 (cf. Gräbe 2006, 299).

This is obviously not a comprehensive statement of the life in the alternative commonwealth. Paul may be giving only the commands that are most urgent in Philippi. Nevertheless, he assumes the existence of the church as a cohesive moral community. He anticipates Justin Martyr's description of the church:

> We formerly rejoiced in sexual immorality but now love only chastity. We also used magic arts but have now dedicated ourselves to the good and unbegotten God. We loved resources of money and possessions more than anything, but now we actually share what we have and give to everyone who has need. We hated one another and killed one another and would not share heart and table with those who were not of our tribe, but now, since the manifestation of Christ, we have a common life and pray for our enemies and try to win over those who hate us unjustly. (*1 Apology* 14)

Church Finances

Financial matters in the church are both sensitive and unavoidable, as Paul's expression of gratitude in 4:10–20 indicates. Indeed, the issue of finances is a consistent feature in Paul's letters. When he desires to demonstrate the solidarity of affluent gentile churches with the poor saints of Jerusalem, he initiates a collection project that lasts several years. As his appeals indicate (see Rom. 15:22–29; 2 Cor. 8–9), he does not separate spiritual and financial matters (Rom. 15:25–28; 2 Cor. 8:5). However, while he encourages the Corinthians to contribute to the collection, he incurs their enmity by refusing financial gifts from them while he accepts funds from the Philippians (2 Cor. 11:7–11).

While the Christian mission requires material support, financial matters complicate relationships between donor and recipient who may now be patron and client. The recipient comes under obligation to the donor. Churches with major capital expenditures are sensitive to the wishes of donors. Decisions on the mission of the church become financial issues. Because of the possibility of a misunderstanding, Paul cannot express gratitude to the Philippians without guiding them to think theologically about finances. Contrary to many interpreters, 4:10–20 is not a "thankless thanks" but a theological reflection describing his relationship to the Philippians. His reflections are beneficial to the contemporary church.

In the poetic statement in 4:10–13, he again presents himself as a model, indicating his identification with the Christ who humbled himself. He has learned to be content because of the one who strengthens him to do his ministry (4:13). Just as he now lives by the power of the resurrection even in the midst of his suffering (3:10), so the effectiveness of his ministry depends not on the abundance of his resources but on God. Similarly, he assures the Philippians that God will supply their needs when they give sacrificially (4:19). Thus a countercultural community will reject the acquisitive spirit of modern society. The abundant resources of churches in North America may satisfy the desires of consumers but do not fulfill the Christian mission. The growth of the church in developing countries, despite the lack of financial resources, demonstrates the importance of relying on God to fill our needs.

Financial resources are nevertheless critical, but the giving of money is more than a financial transaction. Paul indicates the theological significance of the gift by describing it as partnership (*koinōnia*). The Philippians were partners in his suffering (4:14). The giving of money was only one dimension of their partnership with him.

Although Paul approaches the subject of finances delicately, he nevertheless acknowledges the importance of the gift. Just as Paul was willing to pour out his life as a sacrifice (2:17), the gift brought by Epaphroditus was a sweet-smelling sacrifice (4:18). The term *sacrifice*, evoking memories of the Israelites who gave their best offerings, is an appropriate term for the contribution of money, for it indicates that the gift is not a gesture from surplus funds but a costly sacrifice.

Philemon

Bruce W. Longenecker

Introduction to Philemon

What Is This Letter About?

Paul's letter to Philemon captures a moment in an ongoing situation that precedes and follows on from this letter. We can make educated guesses about what preceded and prompted the writing of the letter, and we can speculate about what might have transpired as a result of the letter having been sent, but in each instance we are hampered by an inability to be sure about anything.

In fact, we can't even be sure about what the letter was supposed to accomplish. Its author is agonizingly vague when articulating the outcome that the letter was expected to effect in its audience. This adds to the difficulty of understanding the situation with clarity.

One thing, however, is pretty clear (although even this has been challenged on occasion). In this situation we see, up close, a Jesus-follower who was also a slave owner (a situation known to us from Col. 4:1; Eph. 6:9; 1 Tim. 6:2). The twenty-first-century reader will have theological and moral objections to that situation in general. But despite our modern sensitivities to and justified concerns about this issue, slavery was rarely challenged systematically on the basis of Judeo-Christian principles until the last few centuries.

What we have, then, is a window into a past time and an opportunity to see how Paul handled one complex situation in a world very different from our own (for broader studies of this issue, see Fitzgerald 2010a; Huttunen 2009; Glancy 2002; Byron 2003; Wessels 2010). Most moments of this kind have been lost to us; Paul's letter to Philemon captures one of them for us to consider.

Who Wrote the Letter?

Two people are listed as the authors of this letter:

1. Paul, who undertook a controversial ministry as the "apostle to the gentiles" (Rom. 11:13); and

2. Timothy, a close associate of Paul, who is mentioned in ten of the thirteen Pauline letters (except Galatians, Ephesians, and Titus) and who is listed as a coauthor in five others beyond Philemon (see 2 Cor. 1:1; Phil. 1:1; Col. 1:1–2; 1 Thess. 1:1; 2 Thess. 1:1).

If Paul frequently lists coauthors at the beginning of letters, it is usually the case that he himself is the primary author. That this is the case for the letter to Philemon is illustrated by its first-person singular references throughout; after verse 3 almost every verse of the letter contains at least one first-person singular form (except the Greek of vv. 6, 15, and 25).

Although several of the Pauline letters may have been written after Paul's death by others who "borrowed his voice" to address problems that had arisen, the letter to Philemon is not among their number.

Paul seems to have regularly used a secretary to inscribe his letters. Sometimes he picked up the inked stylus himself at the very end of the letter and appended a note (1 Cor. 16:21; 2 Thess. 3:17; Col. 4:18), perhaps to highlight important themes of the letter (as in Gal. 6:11–18). This may have been his intention in Philemon 19 when he mentions writing "with my own hand"—perhaps picking up the stylus at that point in order to emphasize what he promises in that verse ("I will repay you"). But the phrase can also be understood to mean that Paul himself had inscribed the papyrus from start to finish (this point being made explicitly only in verse 19, to emphasize the promise made in that verse).

To Whom Was the Letter Addressed?

The first two verses of the letter offer a glimpse into what was probably a small "house church"—a Jesus-group that met in the house of a householder, together with his family and any slaves he might have had. Jesus-groups probably met in other locations too (for example, small shops and tiny apartments in "tenement blocks"), and this might have been true also for those addressed

Slavery in First-Century Rome

It is commonly estimated that, in the population of first-century Rome, 35 to 40 percent of the city was composed of slaves. With a population of 1 million, the number of slaves in that city alone was roughly 375,000. As N. T. Wright (2013, 32) rightly notes, slavery was "how things got done," being "the electricity of the ancient world; try imagining your home or your town without the ability to plug things in and switch them on, and you will realize how unthinkable it was for them that there should be no slaves."

in this letter. But it seems as if the person addressed was not notably disadvantaged by the temporary loss of one slave, which suggests that other slaves remained available to him in the meantime. Moreover, Paul seems to assume that the person addressed has exercised financial generosity to the extent that allows him to stand out from others (at least with regard to his generosity profile). So although we can't be certain, it seems likely that this group of Jesus-followers met in the home of someone who had at least a modicum of economic resources. In one reconstruction of things, that home may have been located in the Greco-Roman city of Colossae (see "Is the Letter to the Colossians Relevant to the Study of Philemon?" below), or at least its nearby environs.

Three distinct "audiences" can be differentiated in relation to the letter to Philemon.

1. The primary addressee: This is Philemon himself.
2. The secondary addressees: These include the two other recipients named at the outset of the letter—that is, Apphia and Archippus.
3. The wider addressees: These include all the Jesus-followers who worshiped together in the house and who, as listeners to the letter's discourse, observe Philemon in relation to the thicket of rhetorical and theological warrants that Paul articulates.

Although Philemon is the primary addressee, the other addressees must not be left out of the situational picture. This is because their presence when the letter was read is a key dynamic in the rhetorical occasion. As we will see, when Paul addresses Philemon directly, he does so knowing full well that Philemon is being put on the spot in front of the others who are watching him intently to see what he will do. This is not a private letter to a single person; it is public discourse that singles out one person to comply with the wishes of the letter's author.

We know nothing about the wider addressees, although we might imagine them being about two dozen in number—a rough estimate of the size of urban Jesus-groups in general.

Regarding the secondary addressees, we know almost nothing about them. Paul speaks of Archippus as "our fellow soldier" (v. 2). We need not take this descriptor literally. Paul often employs language to function at a metaphorical rather than a literal level (cf. Phil. 2:25, where Paul describes Epaphroditus metaphorically as "my fellow soldier"). With this military metaphor, Paul is highlighting Archippus's role in advancing the gospel, singling him out because of his particular contribution to what unites the senders with the primary and secondary addressees—that is, their mutual concern for the advancement of the gospel. In that joint effort, Archippus had distinguished himself in service, like a single-minded soldier. Having someone like that in the assembly when the letter was read out would help ensure that Philemon would do the right thing, as Paul expected him to do.

Could Archippus have been the householder in whose home the Jesus-followers met (as proposed by Knox 1960)? The possibility cannot be ruled out. When Paul spoke of Jesus-followers meeting in "your house," he used the singular rather than plural pronoun, and Archippus's name is the closest antecedent to the word "your." It seems more likely, however, that Paul was thinking of the house as belonging to Philemon, with the possessive pronoun "your" reaching back to the primary addressee already identified in verse 1.

And what about Apphia? She is sometimes assumed to be the wife of Philemon. But when speaking of the Jesus-followers who meet in the house of the married couple Prisca and Aquila in Rom. 16:3–5 and 1 Cor. 16:19, Paul uses the plural to speak of "their [autōn] house," whereas in Philemon the referent is singular ("your house," v. 2). If Apphia had been Philemon's wife, we might expect Paul to have constructed his greeting differently, permitting a plural personal pronoun to refer to both Philemon and Apphia. Probably Apphia was not Philemon's wife.

Perhaps then Apphia was noted because she had served the community of Jesus-followers well, much like Archippus and Timothy had done. Or perhaps she was among the increasing number of women who adopted a role in the civic arena by acting as a benefactor to associations (see Matthews 2001, 29–50; MacMullen 1980)—and Jesus-groups had many semblances to Greco-Roman associations. We know of other women in Paul's circle who acted as benefactors to Jesus-groups—including Phoebe who is said to have been "the benefactor of many people, including me" (Rom. 16:1–2), and perhaps Lydia (Acts 16:13–15, 40).

How then are we to imagine the situation to which Paul's letter was delivered and in which it was orated? If we answer this question in a certain fashion, we might conceive of a Jesus-group that met in the house of Philemon with one woman and one man being highlighted as excelling in the advancement of the gospel. If we answer them in another fashion, we might conceive of a Jesus-group in which Philemon was a member of a group sponsored by Apphia and meeting in the house of Archippus, who excelled in promoting the gospel. Further still, we might conceive of a Jesus-group meeting in Philemon's house, sponsored by Apphia, among whose members Archippus had taken a noticeable lead in the service of the gospel. There are any number of permutations to these three scenarios, but we really have nothing to gauge which avenue is preferable.

What Was the Situation That the Letter Addressed?

Knowing something about the situation into which a letter is sent informs how that letter is to be understood. But this short letter of 335 Greek words offers very little by way of situational indicators. What we have to work with are the following indicators:

1. Onesimus had served in Philemon's household as a slave (v. 16).
2. Onesimus may have aggrieved Philemon in some fashion (see vv. 18–19, although in those verses Paul may be adding pointedness for rhetorical effect).
3. Philemon may have considered Onesimus to be relatively useless as a slave (v. 11; points 2 and 3 can be reversed in order).
4. Onesimus left Philemon's household (v. 15), although he evidently remained his slave.
5. In some way Onesimus and Paul met while Paul was imprisoned. As a consequence, Onesimus became a Jesus-follower in his own right (v. 10) instead of by association within Philemon's household (as in Acts 16:31–43).
6. Onesimus proved to be useful to Paul during his imprisonment for the gospel (vv. 11, 13).
7. Paul and Philemon already had been associates in some fashion (vv. 1, 17–19).
8. Paul held the view that Onesimus needed to return to his master in order to allow Philemon to decide the next stage in his relationship with his slave. This situation prompted Paul to write a letter to encourage Philemon's best response to Onesimus's situation.

These indicators have been poked and prodded in various ways, resulting in a variety of proposed scenarios lying behind the text, which we can group into four main alternatives.

It has long been held in the traditional scenario that Onesimus had run away after stealing from Philemon, encountered Paul coincidentally during Paul's imprisonment, and became a Jesus-follower as a consequence of that encounter (see Harris 1991; Nordling 1991, 2004). But this scenario has fallen

---

Attitudes toward Slaves

The comments of two ancient philosophers testify to a common perception of slaves. Aristotle (384–322 BCE) proposed that nature had intended "to make the bodies of the freemen and of slaves different—the latter brawny for necessary service, the former erect and unserviceable for such occupations, but serviceable for a life of citizenship" (*Pol.* 1.2). Cicero (106–43 BCE) thought that while a father would care well for his own children, a master should "coerce and break" his slaves with the whip (*De republica* 3.37).

out of fashion, not least because it is hard to believe that Onesimus and Paul met wholly by chance while Paul was imprisoned; the odds of that happening aren't themselves slim (Paul met strangers all the time), but the likelihood of that happening when Paul and Philemon had already known each other for several years is negligible.

In a second scenario, several proposals envisage Onesimus not fleeing from Philemon but having been sent to Paul for some reason—either by his master (see Knox 1960, who thinks his master was Archippus; Schenk 1987, who thinks his master was Philemon) or by local Jesus-followers to assist Paul financially (Winter 1987; Wansink 1996; Elliott 2011). These proposals have not fared well, since it is hard to see why Paul would consider Onesimus's situation to be so fragile if this had been an "authorized" visit, and since it is hard to see why Onesimus would have been entrusted with such a task if he had proved himself to be "useless" (v. 11) and may have done wrong by his master (v. 18) prior to being "birthed" by Paul (v. 10).

In a third scenario, Onesimus has left Philemon not with the intention of deserting him but simply to gain Paul's advocacy in a grievance that had transpired between the slave and the master (see Lampe 1985; Rapske 1991; a variation on this appears in Arzt-Grabner's listed works). As an *amicus domini* ("friend of the master"), Paul would be well placed to arbitrate in a dispute and intercede on Onesimus's behalf (for a situation that has some pertinence, see Pliny the Younger, *Letter* 9.21, 24).

Intercession for Slaves

In the sixth century CE, Justinian compiled a compendium of Roman law that quotes the opinions of various jurists and edicts from earlier centuries (see Scott 1932). Various legal opinions in that work have some pertinence to runaway slaves and friends of their masters interceding on their behalf. Here is one such opinion, voiced by Proculus, a jurist from the first century CE (Justinian, *Digest* 21.1.17.4):

"Proculus, having been interrogated with reference to a slave who had concealed himself in the house of his master for the purpose of finding an opportunity to escape, says that although one who remains in the house cannot be held to have run away, he is, nevertheless, a fugitive. If, however, he concealed himself only for the purpose of waiting until his master's anger had subsided, he is not a fugitive; just as where one whom his master intends to whip betakes himself to a friend in order to induce him to intercede for him. . . . For he says that the opinion held by many unreasoning persons, namely, that he is a fugitive slave who remains away for a night without his master's consent, is not correct; as the offence must be determined by the intention of the slave."

These scenarios all build on the notion that Onesimus was Philemon's slave—a view derived from verse 16. But a fourth scenario reads that same verse in a different fashion (most recently by Callahan 1997; earlier by Barnes 1846). When Paul asks Philemon to receive Onesimus "no longer as a slave," he is not referring to Onesimus's status (i.e., slavery) but is only character-izing Philemon's past treatment of him (i.e., as if he were only as good as a slave). Their real relationship shines through, it is argued, in the second half of the verses: "but as a brother." That is, Onesimus was not Philemon's slave; instead, they are only bickering biological brothers.

While this reading relieves us of one instance in which an early Jesus-follower is also a slave owner and forces us to reconsider an established reading of the text, it is nonetheless a difficult reading to sustain. Not only is the sense of "not only as a slave" in verse 16 stretched too far, but the interpretation fails to do justice to several other features of Paul's letter that resonate perfectly with a slave scenario but not so well if Philemon and Onesimus were simply biologi-cal brothers—such as Paul's talk of Onesimus as Philemon's representative, of Philemon's consent in the matter, and of Philemon's voluntary good deed (vv. 13–14). Accordingly, this interpretation appears more like an exercise in side-stepping uncomfortable features of the text rather than offering a largely compelling reading of the text.

Of these scenarios, then, the most favored explanations are the first and the third, and the truth of the situation probably lies close to at least one of these two scenarios. I say "at least" since the two can also bleed into each other with some ease. Perhaps Onesimus had originally fled from Philemon as a runaway but subsequently rethought his strategy, seeking out Paul (known to be Philemon's friend) to act as a mediator between the slave and his master, facilitating the return of a repentant Onesimus to his master's household (Barclay 1997, 101).

I note, however, that the fourth scenario may also have some merit, although only in a greatly revised form. It is possible that Philemon and Onesimus were, in fact, biologically related as offspring of a single father, with Onesimus also being a slave within the household that was inherited by Philemon from that now-deceased father. (That is, they may have been half-brothers, biologically speaking, even if in social capital they were worlds apart.) In this scenario, Philemon was an offspring of his father's wife, being the legitimate heir of the household; Onesimus, on the other hand, was an offspring of one of his father's slaves, therefore being a slave of Philemon's household despite being biologically related to him. This scenario (common in the ancient world) would add heightened accent to Paul's frequent familial metaphors in this letter—that is, his relatively frequent use of sibling imagery ("brother," "sister") and his claim to have "fathered" Onesimus. Instead of the situation being an either-or (they were either master and slave or biologically related), the reality might have been a both-and.

Caring for Slaves

Caring justly for one's slaves makes good sense, argued Columella (4–70 CE) in his Latin handbook on agriculture, since it "contributes greatly to the increase of his estate" (*De re rustica* 1.8.18). The Jewish scholar Philo of Alexandria (20 BCE–50 CE) argued similarly: "Let so-called masters therefore cease from imposing upon their slaves severe and scarcely endurable orders, which break down the bodies by violent usage and force the soul to collapse before the body. You need not grudge to moderate your orders. The result will be that you yourselves will enjoy proper attention and that your servants will carry out your orders readily and accept their duties" (*Spec. Leg.* 2.90–91). Later he wrote: "It is a praiseworthy action . . . when masters for the sake of benevolence do this [i.e., manumit] for their homebred or purchased slaves" (*Spec. Leg.* 4.15). One first-century inscription from the Appian Way near Rome speaks in highest praise of a man's former master who "often willingly gave me the wealth equivalent to that required for admission to the equestrian order," with many other generous initiatives besides that (see *CIL* 14.2298).

What Did Paul Want to Accomplish with This Letter?

In other letters Paul is not averse to being quite upfront about his expectations for others. But in this letter he takes a different course, choosing to leave unstated his own preference for Philemon's consequent course of action.

The only request that Paul explicitly mentions regarding Onesimus is found in verse 17, where Philemon is encouraged to receive Onesimus in a fashion that replicates how Philemon would receive Paul himself. This scenario piggybacks on what Paul says in verse 16, where he speaks of Philemon receiving Onesimus back as a brother "in the Lord." If Paul could envision several versions of a favorable outcome, the outcome that he sought to avoid involved Onesimus being received by Philemon on unfavorable terms, with Philemon exercising his legal right to treat his slave harshly and maliciously.

Paul subtly directs Philemon's attention to other possible scenarios instead. This is done almost by means of dropping hints about the strategy he would like Philemon to adopt. Paul expects much from Philemon, but he cannot presume to dictate Philemon's course of action. Laying out a specific course of action may only have raised the stakes of honor, thereby backing Philemon into a corner and risking an unfavorable outcome unnecessarily.

In verse 14 Paul talks about not wanting to do anything without Philemon's permission, and in verse 21 Paul emboldens Philemon to "do even more than I'm suggesting." What does Paul envision by this "even more"?

What is "the good deed" that Philemon is to do "voluntarily" that would "delight" Paul and "refresh" his heart (vv. 14, 20)?

The best guess is that Paul wanted Philemon to send Onesimus back to him once again in order to assist him in his apostolic ministry (reading between the lines of verse 13; see J. Ryan 2005). Paul may also have hoped that Philemon would free Onesimus from servitude, but we cannot be too sure about this. Paul may have sat lightly to whether Philemon chose to set Onesimus free. The danger in setting

Figure 11. A mosaic honoring the "Apostle Onesimus"

him free is that, as a free agent, Onesimus (despite his expected loyalty to his former master) might have chosen not to return to Paul. A safer route would have been for Philemon to command Onesimus to return to Paul for service in the gospel—still as Philemon's slave but "on loan" (in a sense) to Paul and his ministry. In that situation, Philemon may also have supported Onesimus financially during his time in his service to Paul. Perhaps Paul was hesitant to propose a strategy since these things were for Philemon to adjudicate. It was up to Philemon to devise a strategy that would take into account not only Paul's desired outcome but also the character of the slave and the best interests of Philemon's own household. (For instance, would giving freedom to a problematic slave have upset stability within Philemon's household by encouraging others to follow Onesimus's example?) Perhaps Paul was simply trusting Philemon to enhance Paul's Christian ministry in a fashion that took account of all the permutations of the situation most satisfactorily.

Although we will never know for sure, it is likely that Paul had various scenarios in mind as part of his tantalizingly obscure reference to the "even more" that he hoped Philemon would do for Onesimus when being "obedient" to Paul's largely unstated request (v. 21). If Onesimus were to return to Paul, either as a slave of Philemon or as a freedman, Paul would likely have apprenticed him with new responsibilities in the service of the gospel.

When Did Paul Write This Letter?

Paul wrote this letter while he was in Roman custody. Paul was in prison at various points in his ministry, and there is some debate as to which of these imprisonments pertains to the writing of Philemon. The main options are as follows:

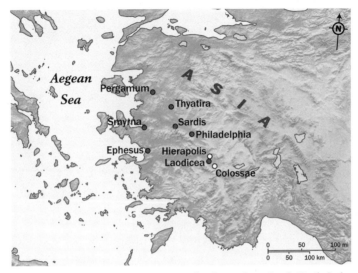

Figure 12. The cities of Ephesus and Colossae are separated by a distance of approximately 110 miles "as the crow flies."

1. Ephesus in the mid-50s (no text refers specifically to Paul being imprisoned in Ephesus, but this can be postulated on the basis of comments in Paul's letters to the Corinthians; see 1 Cor. 15:32; 16:8; 2 Cor. 1:8–9; 6:5; 11:23–24)
2. Caesarea in the late 50s (see Acts 24:27)
3. Rome at some point in the 60s (see Acts 28:16); some think that Paul was a prisoner in Rome on only one occasion in the early 60s, while others think he was imprisoned in Rome on two occasions—the early and late 60s

Of these options, Ephesus and Rome are the two strongest contenders (for Ephesus, see Fitzmyer 2000; for Rome, see Bruce 2000; Cassidy 2001, 68–142). A determination of this matter does not impact the commentary that follows. It only comes into play when reconstructing an outline of Paul's life, an issue that exceeds the bounds of this commentary.

Is the Letter to the Colossians Relevant to the Study of Philemon?

It does not take long to notice a relationship between Paul's letters to Philemon and to the Colossians. Notably, the two letters make mention of the same eight people:

Timothy (Philem. 1; Col. 1:1)
Archippus (Philem. 2; Col. 4:17)

Onesimus (Philem. 10; Col. 4:9)
Epaphras (Philem. 23; Col. 1:7; 4:12)
Mark (Philem. 24; Col. 4:10)
Aristarchus (Philem. 24; Col. 4:10)
Demas (Philem. 24; Col. 4:14)
Luke (Philem. 24; Col. 4:14)

The only people mentioned in Philemon who are not mentioned in Colossians are Philemon (v. 1) and Apphia (v. 2).

For those who think that Colossians was authored by Paul himself, these links testify to the two letters having been written within roughly the same time period. For those who think Colossians was written by one of Paul's followers after Paul's death, these links are taken to be artificially constructed in order to yield a higher level of authenticity to the pseudonymous letter.

If Colossians was authored by Paul, then it would seem that Philemon resided in the city of Colossae, since Paul's letter to the Colossians refers to both Onesimus (Philemon's slave) and Epaphras (Paul's colleague when writing Philemon) as being resident there (Col. 4:9, 12; see also Col. 4:17, where Archippus is mentioned in a fashion that many consider to link him to Colossae). Even if Colossians was not authored by Paul, there is scope for thinking that Philemon was resident in Colossae because linking these people to that city in Colossians was unlikely to have been created out of thin air.

Figure 13. The cities of Rome and Colossae are separated by a distance of approximately 890 miles "as the crow flies."

161

Who Read the Letter to the Community?

Who would have read this letter out loud, in front of Philemon and the rest of the Jesus-followers who had gathered?

Some have thought that Onesimus himself would have read the letter aloud to Philemon. This is unlikely. The letter makes a significant request (albeit largely unspecified) of an aggrieved slave master, encouraging him to make a beneficial decision regarding the fate of his slave, with significant rhetorical pressure being placed upon the master in the process; such a letter is unlikely to have been read to the master by the slave himself. That would have raised the stakes far too high, forcing the situation to become unnecessarily adversarial. As is evidenced throughout the letter, Paul is not averse to pressing Philemon toward a particular course of action, but he is mindful to provide Philemon with an honorable resolution of the situation; having Philemon's slave read the letter would have confused the clarity of "the rhetorical signal" and detracted from the other rhetorical strategies that Paul employed in the letter.

Consequently, we should imagine that Paul made other provisions for the reading of the letter. Perhaps he knew of someone within the local Jesus-group who would be commissioned to read it, allowing Onesimus to slink into the background while the letter was being read, until Philemon had made his decision. Or perhaps funds were provided to enable someone to accompany Onesimus as a fellow traveler (not least to help stave off the dangers of ancient travel, since a single traveler was vulnerable to a variety of threats), with this person acting also as the letter reader.

Moreover, having someone travel with Onesimus to read the letter would not simply have avoided a "showdown" situation but would have added rhetorical advantage to Paul's case. If Philemon were faced with a reader who would soon be returning to Paul with a report about the outcome of the letter, Philemon would be more likely to comply with Paul's wishes, allowing Onesimus to return to Paul with the letter reader. Paul would probably have preferred a situation like this, since his ministry was repeatedly frustrated by miscommunication (sometimes willful miscommunication) among his audiences. With so much emotional investment in the outcome of this situation, sending a letter reader along with Onesimus would have served a number of favorable purposes and decreased the chance of unwanted outcomes (travel dangers, rhetorical ineffectiveness, and miscommunication).

Unfortunately we may never know for sure who that letter reader was. But if the letters known as Philemon and Colossians were sent together, the letter carrier/reader would probably have been Tychicus, since in Col. 4:7 we read, "Tychicus will tell you all the news about me" (NRSV; see further Col. 4:8–9). Other passages might also be read in this light (Eph. 6:21; 2 Tim. 4:12; Titus 3:12), suggesting that Tychicus may have carried several of Paul's letters to

---

An Outline of Philemon

Setting the scene, part 1 (1–3)	**Living up to character (17–22)**
The letter senders (1a)	A request (17)
The letter recipients (1b–2)	A parenthetical promise (18–19)
The grace (3)	An appeal to grant the request (20)
Philemon's character, as illustrated by his past actions (4–7)	An appeal to go beyond the request (21)
Setting the scene, part 2 (8–16)	Incentivizing Philemon (22)
Paul's authority (8–9)	**Final greetings (23–25)**
Onesimus between Philemon and Paul (10–14)	Greetings from those with Paul (23–24)
Onesimus and God's initiative (15–16)	A closing grace (25)

---

their addressees (although all references to Tychicus appear in texts whose authorship is disputed).

What Reception Has the Philemon Letter Had in History?

Although Paul's letter to Philemon has frequently been lauded by theologians, it is only a slight exaggeration to say that few NT texts have had less impact on the course of Christian history than this letter (except perhaps Jude or 2 Peter; an example of moving Philemon from the backseat to the front can be found in Wright 2013, 3–74).

Of course, the Letter to Philemon was preserved within the Pauline corpus, and not all of Paul's letters were. (We lack, for instance, a letter he wrote to the Corinthians [see 1 Cor. 5:9] and apparently another to the Laodiceans [see Col. 4:16]; moreover, it is likely that Paul wrote other letters that have similarly been lost to us.) This fact itself might testify to the letter's early reception as a letter of importance. (Some have imagined that Onesimus himself might have been instrumental in ensuring that the letter was preserved and circulated.)

The reception of the letter in the patristic period is somewhat mixed (see Barth and Blanke 2000, 201–6; Decock 2010; Friedl 2010; Fitzgerald 2010b). It is included in most of the lists drawn up to identify which books should be included within the Christian canon (for example, the Muratorian Canon, probably from the third century), although it was not accepted as canonical by the Syrian church and its theologians. Patristic theologians cited from Philemon with some frequency and wrote commentaries on it, but some also found themselves having to defend its utility as edifying for Christians against voices that expressed dissatisfaction with it.

The letter to Philemon leaves a trace on church history here and there throughout the centuries, but it is only in the nineteenth century, with the American debate concerning the enslavement of African peoples, that this letter took on a prominence it had never previously enjoyed. Both sides in the debate claimed the letter as support for their own positions—forcing further debates about the place of "higher criticism" and the authority of Scripture front and center within the church and society (see, e.g., Harrill 2006; Noel and Williams 2012).

Since that time, not much has changed. Along with other passages in the Pauline corpus where slavery is discussed (see 1 Cor. 7:21–24; Col. 3:22–4:1; Eph. 6:5–9; 1 Tim. 1:10; 6:1–2; Titus 2:9–10), Philemon continues to be a storm center for discussion of Christian theology in relation to corporate ethos and social ethics (see, e.g., Barton 1987; I. H. Marshall 1993, 185–91; Giles 1994; Barclay 1991; Barclay 1997, 119–26; Burtchaell 1998; Osiek 2000, 144–46; Bieberstein 2000; Thompson 2006; du Plessis 2006; Harrill 2006; Cousar 2009, 105–6; Avalos 2011; Wolter 2010; de Villiers 2010). For some, the letter offers a sterling example of how the Christian gospel seeps into situations to offset their inbuilt injustices; for others, it is complicit in the very structures of oppression that the gospel should seek to oppose. Space will not permit much engagement with this issue, except to offer a few signposts at the end of the commentary.

Philemon 1–3

Setting the Scene, Part 1

Introductory Matters

Before starting his primary discourse in verse 4, Paul writes three initial verses that establish the preliminary context of the text—its senders, its recipients, and its theological context (that is, grace). These three verses coincide with the standard introductory sections of most of Paul's letters, with the sender/senders identified first, followed by the recipients (in conformity to letter-writing practices of his day). The recipients of verses 1b–2 are probably all members of a single Jesus-group (in contrast to the various Jesus-groups identified in other letters of Paul; cf. Rom. 16:3–16). Paul usually concludes the introductory sections of his letter with a "grace," as in verse 3, which corresponds exactly with Rom. 1:7; 1 Cor. 1:3; Eph. 1:2; Col. 1:2; and Phil. 1:2.

Tracing the Train of Thought

The Letter Senders (1a)

1a. Of the two people identified as senders of the letter, the first one listed is **Paul** (v. 1). If this much is clear, pinning down the precise nuances of the phrase that Paul uses to identify himself is less obvious. In most Bibles, the phrase is translated simply as "a prisoner of Christ Jesus." This interpretation of the phrase nicely highlights that Paul ultimately imagines himself to be the prisoner not of Rome or of local authorities but of a "higher power"—his master, Christ Jesus.

But the phrase may have other connotations, represented by the words **who is in chains for Christ Jesus** (v. 1). In the rhetorical situation of the letter, Paul

**Philemon 1–3
in the Rhetorical Flow**

▶ **Setting the scene, part 1
(1–3)**

　The letter senders (1a)

　The letter recipients (1b–2)

　The grace (3)

probably wants not simply to identify himself as "a prisoner of Christ Jesus" but, more, to highlight that he is imprisoned for the purposes of spreading the gospel of Christ Jesus. In this way, right from the start of the letter (and in v. 9 where the phrase is used again; see also v. 13) Paul ensures that his unending commitment to the gospel is recognized.

In some rhetorical contexts, this dimension of Paul's self-presentation might simply help to ensure that his ministry in the service of Christ Jesus would not be legitimately questioned. Within the rhetorical context of Philemon, however, it does more than that—in effect raising the bar for Philemon. Wanting Philemon to fall in line with a relatively simple request that Paul will make later in the letter, Paul showcases his own level of commitment from the very start (in chains for Christ Jesus) in the hope that Philemon will seek to emulate Paul's own commitment level.

The second sender of the letter, **Timothy**, is introduced alongside Paul. Timothy is identified as a sibling, although it is left vague as to whose brother he is (there is no possessive pronoun in the Greek). This has the effect of making him simply "brother Timothy," or perhaps one **who is a brother to us all**.

The Letter Recipients (1b–2)

1b–2. The first and main addressee of the letter is **Philemon**, whom Paul addresses as **our beloved and our coworker**. Although Paul will go on to make a request of Philemon later in the letter, he wants that request to be recognized as emerging ultimately from Paul's cherishing of Philemon both as a beloved brother in the Lord and as a coworker or colleague. Philemon is to see that their cherished relationship is not threatened by the request Paul is about to make and to see that Philemon's mutual role in service should incline him to grant Paul's request, which ultimately is intended to foster even greater service.

Paul then identifies others to whom the letter is sent (v. 2). The first is **Apphia, sister to us all**. (Just as Paul referred to Timothy as "brother" without a possessive pronoun, here he refers to Apphia as "sister" without a pronoun.) The second is **Archippus, our fellow soldier**. After mentioning these two people specifically, he then expands the list of addressees to include **the assembly that meets in your house**. For discussion of the interpretive issues surrounding the identity of these addressees, see the introduction of this commentary.

The Grace (3)

3. With the recipients having been identified, a blessing now follows: **Grace to all of you, and peace, from God our Father and the Lord Jesus Christ.**

Although this is a very simple blessing, it accomplishes several things in a short space, as discussed in the "Theological Issues" section of this chapter.

Regarding the phrase "all of you" in the translation of verse 3, the word "all" does not appear in the Greek. It has been added to the translation simply to ensure that the plural Greek pronoun (*hymin*) that appears here is differentiated from other occurrences of the word "you" in the letter. Except for the plural "you" in verses 22 (2×) and 25, and the possible plural "you" in verse 6 (as in some good manuscripts), Paul's references to "you" are always singular in this letter (in Greek this includes verses 4, 6, 7, 8, 10, 11 [2×], 12, 16, 18, 20, 21 [2×], 23), referring to Philemon.

Theological Issues

That Paul regularly incorporates "the grace" within the opening of his letters should not distract us from recognizing its importance within this letter. Verse 3 carries the theological weight of this initial sense unit, even setting up some of the main theological contours upon which Paul builds his request throughout the rest of the letter.

In verse 3 Paul makes theological adjustments to standard letter-writing conventions in order to highlight the theological vision of his letter. In the Greco-Roman world, the standard letter-writing convention was to address recipients with the word *chairein*, "greetings" (see, for instance, James 1:1). But Paul chooses not simply to greet his audience but to bless them, using a word that plays off the standard greeting: *charis*, or "grace." Sounding similar to the standard epistolary greeting, *charis* largely sums up what Paul's ministry was all about, with God's gracious love being "poured into our hearts through the Holy Spirit that has been given to us" (as Paul expresses it in Rom. 5:5 NRSV).

Alongside "grace" Paul adds a reference to "peace" among Jesus-followers. This means much more than calmness (as in "peace and quiet") and probably refers to the traditional Jewish notion of *shalom*—God's righteous peace, in which relationships are properly and justly aligned. This reference to right relationships being established among Jesus-followers is not an afterthought to Paul's blessing, nor is it simply to be elided into the notion of grace. Wanting both notions to be appreciated for their own sake, Paul did not simply write "grace and peace to you"; instead, inserting the pronoun "to you" after "grace," Paul allows the two nouns to have, in a sense, separate spaces of their own. Perhaps the two words enjoy a theological alignment in which Jesus-groups enjoying fellowship with a gracious God also enjoy the establishment of right relationships among themselves as a consequence of that divine grace.

Even if "grace" and "peace" have somewhat distinct connotations, they are yoked together by the fact that they share a common source. But that source itself is comprised of two distinct and yet related referents. The first to be mentioned is "God our Father." Jewish and Greco-Roman traditions are engorged with the conviction that benevolence is a divine gift and that peace transpires by means of divine initiative. But Paul yokes these longstanding traditions to the notion that God is "our Father." Knowing God intimately as "Father" seems to have been at the very heart of the prayer life of the Jew from Nazareth whom Paul proclaimed as Lord. Referring to God as "Father" in his own prayers (e.g., Mark 14:36), Jesus drew his followers into that same intimacy with God, so that with confidence they too were to address God as "Father" in prayer (Matt. 6:9; Luke 11:2; cf. Rom. 8:15; Gal. 4:6).

When the metaphor of "Father" is applied to God, both Jesus and Paul imagined it to refer to one who lovingly seeks to benefit his children. That the all-powerful creator of the universe can be known as an actively beneficent father is surely an astounding notion in any age—especially in our own day when astrophysics and other sciences are awakening to the massive enormity of power that animates and drives the universe. Behind all of those cosmic energies (Paul would tell us today) stands a gracious God whose power not only animates the universe but stirs up right relationships among his followers—a point that has a strong foothold within Paul's letter to Philemon.

What is even more astonishing, however, is that the second source of divine grace and peace is "the Lord Jesus Christ." That Paul can include Jesus Christ with such ease into the territory normally reserved for the God of Israel alone has seemed wholly natural to Christians throughout the centuries, but this should not dull our sensitivities to the astounding magnitude of this in relation to the contours of Jewish monotheism in Paul's own day. Embedding a Jew from Nazareth into the very identity of the eternal and sovereign God of Israel is a radical move that, while more elaborately developed elsewhere in his letters (e.g., 1 Cor. 8:6; Phil. 2:6–11), nonetheless stands behind this dramatic feature of Philemon.

In fact, the theological drivers of Paul's discourse within this brief letter are contained within an *inclusio* at the start and finish of the letter (compare verses 3 and 25)—an *inclusio* that foregrounds the Lord Jesus Christ as the source of divine grace among groups of Jesus-followers.

Philemon 4–7

Philemon's Character, as Illustrated by His Past Actions

Introductory Matters

Having set the scene in the first three verses, Paul now draws out the character of the person who holds the cards in this drama—that is, Philemon. Establishing Philemon's character is a crucial dimension of Paul's strategy, making this an essential and critical section in the letter. Paul's request in later sections of the letter gains force from what he establishes in this section. Paul offers a portrait of Philemon as a person of outstanding service to God, to other Jesus-followers, and to the gospel. It is a sterling reputation that Paul reconstructs here—a reputation that Paul hopes will carry through from the past into the present and future in terms of how Philemon chooses to handle Onesimus's situation.

Tracing the Train of Thought

4–7. It was often Paul's style to begin a letter with the inclusion of a thanksgiving to God on behalf of his readers (see Rom. 1:8; 1 Cor. 1:4; Eph. 1:16; Col. 1:3; 1 Thess. 1:2; 2 Thess. 1:3). The same feature appears toward the beginning of this letter, where Paul gives the following assurance to Philemon (v. 4): **Remembering you in my prayers, I always give thanks to my God.**

It is not wholly clear, however, what it is that Paul gives thanks to God about. In verse 5 Paul highlights two features of Philemon's character that he has heard good reports about, but what those features are and how they are

**Philemon 4–7
in the Rhetorical Flow**

Setting the scene,
part 1 (1–3)

▶Philemon's character,
as illustrated by his
past actions (4–7)

put into practice is open to some interpretation. The first feature Paul mentions is Philemon's **love**, while the second can refer either to Philemon's faith or his faithfulness. The sentence is constructed in such a way that either nuance for the Greek word *pistis* (faith, faithfulness) is possible.

The sentence in which *pistis* occurs reads "your love and *pistis* **which you have toward the Lord Jesus and for the sake of all of Jesus's followers**" (that is, all Jesus-followers in Philemon's local area; lit. the phrase is "all of the saints"). We might be tempted to think of Philemon's love as being for the sake of other Jesus-followers and of his *pistis* as his "faith in the Lord Jesus," as if the two are separate entities with separate referents. This is how the two ideas appear in Eph. 1:15 and Col. 1:4, with faith in Christ and love for others being distinct (although related) features of the addressees' life (i.e., faith toward Christ and love toward others). But the construction of the phrase in Paul's letter to Philemon is somewhat different (and is not chiastic, as some suggest). Philemon's love and his *pistis* are both directed toward the Lord Jesus, and both are for the sake of other Jesus-followers. Perhaps, then, we can do justice to the sense of *pistis* if we take it to include not simply Philemon's "faith" but, more holistically, his **faithfulness**—a faithfulness toward the Lord Jesus and, beneficially for them, toward other Jesus-followers. Philemon is one who has loved and been faithfully, reliably, and loyally devoted to both the Lord Jesus and, as an outworking of that, to other followers devoted to the same Lord Jesus.

While this might seem like a simple gesture of commendation, within the Letter to Philemon this commendation plays a poignant role in setting out the rhetorical context of the letter. It, together with Paul's depiction of Philemon as a cherished "coworker" in verse 1, establishes Philemon's character as one of committed fidelity to the betterment of other Jesus-followers as part of his loyalty to the Lord Jesus. With that track record to Philemon's credit, Paul will expect him to live up to his reputation in relation to Onesimus.

The sixth verse is probably the hardest in Philemon to pin down in terms of what Paul is saying; in 1982 one scholar commented that "there is not the slightest consensus about what Paul really wants to make known to his friend Philemon in this single sentence" (Riesenfeld 1982, 251)—a comment that remains true today.

There is reason for this lack of consensus. Notice, for instance, the possible variants of the first phrase, *hē koinōnia tēs pisteōs sou*, as listed in table 1. In that single phrase, (1) the first word (*koinōnia*) has four possible connotations, (2) its relationship with the second word (*pisteōs*, "faith" or perhaps "faithfulness") is ambiguous, and (3) the final word (*sou*, "your") could modify either of the two nouns that it precedes ("your *koinōnia*," or "your faith," although the latter is more likely). It is possible, moreover, that Paul intended to convey more than one possible meaning. Despite the ambiguities, the one clear thing in that phrase is the personal pronoun "your" being singular and therefore referring exclusively to Philemon.

Table 1. Interpretive Possibilities for the First Clause of Philemon 6

	Sense of *Koinōnia*	Sense of *Pistis*	Sense of the Phrase	Possible Translations (in Order of Probability)
1	fellowship with others	faith is held in common or is the source of fellowship	Philemon has enjoyed fellowship of faith with others	a. "the fellowship of your faith" b. "your fellowship of faith"
2	financial support for others	his faith is the source of his giving	Philemon's faith has led him to share resources with others	a. "the assistance that springs from your faith" b. "your assistance that springs from faith"
3	sharing with others	faith is what he shares with others	Philemon has shared faith or "the faith"	a. "the sharing of your faith" b. "your sharing of the faith"
4	participation	faith is what he participates in	Philemon is a participant in faith	a. "your participation in faith" b. "participation in your faith"

In order to understand how to make our way through the sixth verse, it is helpful initially to frame what Paul says in verse 7 in order then to work backward into verse 6. The Greek link word *gar* ("for"), which is often omitted in translations, connects the two verses, so that what Paul begins in verse 6 flows organically into verse 7. Knowing how Paul ends the flow of thought will help to make interpretive decisions about the more difficult verse 6.

In verse 7 Paul praises Philemon, featuring as the showcase of his praise what Philemon has already done for Jesus-followers. Paul derives **much joy and encouragement** from Philemon's **love** in the Lord—as demonstrated by Philemon's support for others as a **brother** in Christ. Because of his initiatives, **the hearts of Jesus's followers** (lit. "of the saints") **have been refreshed.** The word "hearts" is not the Greek word *kardia*, which occurs fifty-two times in the Pauline corpus, but the word *splanchnon*, which occurs only eight times in the Pauline corpus, three of which are in Philemon (2 Cor. 6:12; 7:15; Phil. 1:8; 2:1; Col. 3:12; Philem. 7, 12, 20). In those occurrences, it usually connotes affection or compassion, referring to the seat of emotions.

If this is where Paul's train of thought ends up in verse 7, we can work back and consider how verse 6 might flow most naturally into verse 7. The key is to pin down the relationship of the words *koinōnia* and "faith." Referring to the table of possible interpretations (table 1), the fourth possibility (where *koinōnia* is understood as "participation") is unlikely, since the personal pronoun "your" likely refers to "faith" and the notion "participation in your faith" is not very Pauline. The third possibility (where *koinōnia* is understood as evangelistic sharing of the gospel) is a Pauline notion but does not fit the context quite as well as the other two options.

Instead, and in view of the emotional dimension of Paul's comments in verse 7, the most likely option is one of the first two, or perhaps a combination of both of them. Probably in verse 6 Paul's prayer regarding Philemon (mentioned in v. 4) highlights what he calls **the fellowship of your faith,** understood as the corporate allegiance that arises within Jesus-groups because of faith—in this case, specifically because of Philemon's faith (or perhaps his "faithfulness"; this connotation of the word has merit to the extent that it was already in play in verse 5 and overspills into verse 6, especially if the definite article *tēn* in verse 6 has an "anaphoric" function, making a gesture to the previous occurrence of the word).

This sense easily bleeds into the second option, since the conceptual membrane between them is thin. That is, Philemon's faith enhances the corporate fellowship with local Jesus-groups precisely because he, as evidently a somewhat wealthier Jesus-follower, supported local Jesus-groups through financial assistance, thereby enhancing their well-being. In verse 7 Paul identifies this as occasioning his own joy and encouragement because Philemon's initiatives have refreshed other Jesus-followers. The fact that Philemon has already enhanced the fellowship of Jesus-followers and willingly absorbed financial loss for greater good is precisely the scenario that Paul hopes to capitalize on later in the letter.

For now, however, he roots Philemon's initiatives in a deeper theological principle. Paul's prayer for Philemon is that "the fellowship of your faith" **may become effective in the realization of every good work that is active among you all, to the glory of Christ.** (Some manuscripts have a first-person plural "us" [*hēmin*] in this phrase, whereas others have the second-person plural "you" [*hymin*]. Although a case can be made for either reading, the better manuscripts favor the second-person plural, translated here as "you all" to differentiate it from Paul's common second-person singulars throughout the letter.)

Theological Issues

In this section, verse 6 provides notable theological resources, particularly with its focus on the "good work" of Jesus-followers (cf. Wright 1988, 168: "the driving force of the whole letter is the prayer of verse 6," although Wright reads the verse differently than I do).

Although Paul does not specifically mention the word "work" in this verse (he simply speaks of "doing the good"), the notion or related concepts would have been supplied to the ancient ear (some Greek manuscripts [F, G] make the point by adding the word explicitly). It is not at all unlike Paul to speak of "good work" being the result of one's faith—as in Gal. 5:6, where he speaks of "faith working practically [*energoumenē*] in love." In Romans Paul speaks twice of "the obedience of faith" (1:5; 16:26), which probably connotes "obedience in life that faith transpires." And in Ephesians Jesus-followers are expected to be doing "good works, which God prepared beforehand to be our way of life" (2:10 NRSV)—a way of life that does not result from doing good works (ironically) but from the gift of God's grace in the lives of Jesus-followers (Eph. 2:8). These examples (and there are more) illustrate that Paul was not averse to thinking that good would flow from Jesus-followers; it was, in fact, a central feature of his theology.

Consequently, when Paul speaks in verse 6 of "every good work" being "in" or "among you" (*en hymin*), he does not mean that Jesus-followers conjure those works up from their own resources. Any good work that is produced "in" or "among" Jesus-followers is not a good work until it is "out of" and "among" them ("faith working practically"), and that happens as divine enablement becomes active in the lives of Jesus-followers, so that they become vehicles for God's initiative.

This explains the phrase "to the glory of Christ" (v. 6), which is an amplification of a more simple Greek phrase *eis Christon*. Some translations understand this to mean "in Christ"—that is, being "in Christ" is the basis for the good work that emerges from the lives of Jesus-followers (KJV, RSV, NET). But while that might be true, the phrase probably does not refer here to the context out of which good work arises in the lives of Jesus-followers. The phrase *eis Christon* refers to the result of that divinely enabled work (with *eis* having a telic sense). That is to say, the result of a benevolent Christian lifestyle is ultimately "for Christ" (NRSV), "for the sake of Christ" (NIV), or (as translated here) "to the glory of Christ" (and is, then, comparable to the *eis*-clause of Rom. 15:7, *eis doxan tou theou*, "to the glory of God"). The phrase *eis Christon*, then, does not suggest that Christian lifestyle leads us "into the Messiah" (contra Wright 2013, 16; 2011, 480). Instead, as Jesus-followers live lives that enhance "the good" through divine enablement, that divinely initiated living is to Christ's own glory (whose grace is upon them; cf. vv. 3, 25), not the glory of Jesus-followers themselves (cf. Eph. 2:9: "so that no one can boast").

This rich theology of working "the good" is probably the primary theological lens through which Paul perceives Philemon's situation. It sets up one of Paul's strongest warrants for Philemon doing "even more" than Paul was explicitly asking in relation to Onesimus. Establishing Philemon's character in verses 4–7 by means of an overview of his efforts for others in the past, Paul will go on in later sections to ask Philemon to continue to live out the character of love that has so characterized his discipleship thus far. In this way, the letter to Philemon is not about slavery, or Onesimus, or Philemon, or anything other than what might be deemed "Christian character." Being a man whose character has shone through repeatedly in the past, Philemon will give consideration to Onesimus's situation in a manner informed (Paul hopes) by his character—a character already shaped by divinely inspired deeds of generous love for others.

For these reasons, these verses not only offer us a glimpse into the heart of Paul's theology in general but also lay out the rich theological soils from which Paul's discourse in this letter draws its essential nutrients.

Philemon 8–16

Setting the Scene, Part 2

Introductory Matters

Having set the scene in its basic outline in verses 1–3 and having drawn up a character reference for Philemon in verses 4–7, Paul now adds further complexity to the situation in verses 8–16—in essence setting the scene further.

In this section Paul initially highlights his own relationship to Onesimus, so that Onesimus's situation is seen in relation to both Philemon's worthy character and Paul's own ministry on behalf of the gospel. It would have been common to analyze Onesimus's situation simply in terms of the master-slave relationship, but Paul complicates the lines of relational consideration by ensuring that the situation is seen to involve not just Philemon and Onesimus but Paul as well, as outlined in verses 10–14.

Paul complicates things even further in verses 15–16, where he introduces yet another consideration into the mix—that is, God's working within Onesimus's life. Although Paul does not articulate it in these terms, there is a sense in which he implies that Philemon should not think that he is the only one who has influence over Onesimus; there is also a higher master to whom even he (Philemon) is responsible. Thus, in this section Paul greatly compounds the relational dynamics surrounding Onesimus.

Tracing the Train of Thought

Paul's Authority (8–9)

8–9. At this point in the letter Paul begins to pivot toward the request that he will make (in one way or another) in verses 17–22. He does so, however, by making a backward gesture toward the theological foundations of the previous section—a gesture encapsulated in the single Greek word *dio*, **for this reason** (v. 8). Although Paul prefers not to articulate his request through complex theological concepts in this letter, the little word *dio* draws attention to the deep theological resources that undergird the request—resources about the enhancement of Jesus-groups through divine enablement, an enablement that overshoots the glorification of individuals and leads instead to the glorification of Christ himself.

In fact, if it is a request that Paul will be making of Philemon, he notes initially that the request could be articulated as a command instead. Paul speaks of the **great confidence** that he has **in Christ** in order **to command you** (Philemon) **to do the appropriate thing** (v. 8). This is a discursive route that Paul prefers not to take, but he dangles the command in the air as a possibility open to him (arising from his apostolic identity). To ask someone to act on the basis of honorable principles (as Paul will soon do) is much different than commanding someone to act (which he notes here that he has the right to do).

In this instance, that Paul will make a request instead of registering a command enables respect for Philemon to be a part of the equation. Paul is convinced that Philemon is of the kind of character that he will do the thing that is most appropriate to his identity as a Jesus-follower, even without compulsion. Avoiding a command also ensures that Philemon is not backed into a rhetorical corner where he either loses face by conforming to the command or stirs up the situation further by refusing to comply and dishonoring Paul.

But Paul adds another reason why he is making a request instead of registering a command. **Rather** than commanding, **I make my request to you because of love** (v. 9). Paul has referenced "love" on three occasions earlier in the letter (and will again in v. 16). In verse 1 Philemon is said to be "our beloved" in Christ. In verse 5 Paul speaks of Philemon's "love for all Jesus-followers." And in verses 6–7 Philemon's initiatives on behalf of other Jesus-followers are virtually equated to his "love" that encourages Paul. Philemon is beloved and has assisted others in love. Consequently, although Paul does not make it clear whether the "love" mentioned here is Philemon's love for others or Paul's love for Philemon (or both), it matters little; Paul has this relationship of giving and receiving love in mind when he speaks baldly of "love."

The one who makes this request now identifies himself in ways not unlike verse 1—**I, Paul, an old man and now also in chains for Christ Jesus** (v. 9). Paul has already identified himself at the very start of the letter as a "prisoner of Christ Jesus"—or more preferably, "in chains for Christ Jesus." He has not always been "in chains," of course, as the little word "now" points out. But neither is this a new situation for him, as we know from other letters (see esp. 2 Cor. 11:23 within the context of 11:23–28). He presents himself, however, as "an old man"—a characterization that was not uncommonly applied to men even in their 40s and 50s (see Barclay 2007). (Some have proposed that the word is not "old man" but, with the change of one letter in the Greek word, "ambassador." The suggestion does not carry much weight; see especially Birdsall 1993.) Here again Paul ups the ante, in a sense; he deserves respect both as a man of seniority (say, at least forty years of age) and as someone in chains for Christ Jesus. Will Philemon (who is probably younger than Paul) refuse to act on the request of a man such as this?

Onesimus between Philemon and Paul (10–14)

10–14. The request that Paul alludes to in verse 9 begins to emerge a bit more clearly in verse 10, not in terms of specifics (for that, the reader waits until v. 17) but in terms of knowing whom the request is about: **I make my request to you concerning my child—Onesimus, whose father I have become during the time of my imprisonment.**

For the first time, Paul mentions the name of the one for whom he is interceding. The name Onesimus is the 145th word of the 335 Greek words in the letter, meaning that 43 percent of Paul's letter has been spent setting up the situation before even getting to the point of mentioning the name of the person he is supporting.

Having laid strong theological and rhetorical foundations before proceeding to his request, Paul now emphasizes the strong bond that exists between himself and Onesimus. In terms of their being in Christ, Paul and Onesimus are as father and son. Paul was the main instrument in the birthing of Onesimus's faith, with that engendering of faith having occurred even while Paul was in chains. Paul is not primarily giving his audience historical information about the occasion of Onesimus's coming to faith; instead, he is establishing a bond of "spiritual kinship" that increases the rhetorical pressure on Philemon. If Philemon has "a claim" on Onesimus, so too does Paul. Judged by first-century canons of honor, if Philemon chooses to disregard Paul's request concerning Onesimus, he will be dishonoring Onesimus's spiritual father, drawing him into a potentially antagonistic relationship. Does he really want to do that?

If, furthermore, Philemon and his slave Onesimus shared a biological paternity (a speculative but possible scenario, as noted in the introduction to this commentary), then Paul's remark concerning his own "spiritual paternity" of Onesimus would carry additional weight in his attempt to diminish the importance of natural relationships while prioritizing relationships in the Lord. (Much the same would apply to Paul's description of Philemon as Paul's own brother in v. 7.)

Paul's Parental Imagery

Paul makes use of father-son imagery elsewhere to describe his relationship to those whose faith he has nurtured (1 Cor. 4:14–15, 17; 2 Cor. 6:13; 12:14–15; Phil. 2:22; 1 Thess. 2:11; 1 Tim. 1:2; 2 Tim. 1:2; Titus 1:4). In Gal. 4:19 he incorporates maternal imagery, comparing himself to a mother giving birth to offspring, and in 1 Thess. 2:7 he compares himself to a nursing mother tenderly caring for her children.

He was useless to you previously, Paul then writes (v. 11). In so doing, he begins a pun that he will complete momentarily. The pun revolves around the name Onesimus, which means "useful." The useful one was previously useless to Philemon. We cannot know the specifics of how Onesimus failed to live up to his name within Philemon's household; perhaps Onesimus had simply been a rather ineffectual slave. Paul, however, offers a different assessment: but now he is useful to you and to me. Paul is not implying that Onesimus, having become a Jesus-follower, is fit to be welcomed back into Philemon's household where he will now be a useful slave. The phrase "useful to you and to me" precludes that meaning, drawing attention to something that both Philemon and Paul have in common. What they have in common is their identity as "coworkers" (v. 1) in the service of the gospel. The phrase "useful to you and to me" intimates that Paul has a vision for how Onesimus can be useful in an arena beyond Philemon's household—a vision that Philemon is to share through the influence of Paul's letter.

There may be yet another dimension at play in Paul's discourse, since the Greek words "useless" (*achrēston*) and "useful" (*euchrēston*) share a lexeme (*chrēstos*) that first-century speakers of Greek probably pronounced in much the same manner as the word "Christ" (*Christos*). If Onesimus was formerly *achrēstos* when he was apart from Christ (*a-Christos*, "without Christ"), he is now *euchrēstos* in Christ (*eu-Christos*, which might suggest that Christ has made him "good"). If Paul had this in mind, he has added a double layer of puns onto his depiction of Onesimus, with the words "useful" and "useless" pivoting around the names Onesimus at one level and Christ on another. Perhaps a few Jesus-followers meeting in Philemon's house would have smiled at this point as the letter was being read out.

If Paul has something in mind for Onesimus, he nonetheless recognizes that Philemon has legal charge of Onesimus. For this reason Paul writes, I have (now) sent him back to you (v. 12). But he immediately qualifies that with another statement of personal affection for Philemon in order to register that Philemon is not the only one who has a stake in the outcome of Onesimus's case. Paul himself has an interest in the matter of Onesimus's fate, describing him as my very heart. This is more than a note of fatherly affection, however; with his sights on what is yet to come in this short letter, Paul here constructs a metaphor that will reemerge with rhetorical significance in the space of eight verses (see v. 20, itself drawing on what Paul says in v. 7 about Philemon having refreshed "the hearts" of others). At this point in Paul's discourse, however, the affective aspect of this metaphor is primarily in play.

Sending Onesimus back to Philemon was not what Paul himself wanted; he makes this point explicitly clear in verse 13, saying **I wanted to keep him with me.** Paul gives Philemon a reason for wanting to retain Onesimus: **so that he, in your stead, could be of service to me while I am in chains for the sake of the gospel.** Paul is letting it be known that Onesimus's assistance was deemed by Paul to be attributable to Philemon himself. It was a popular view that a servant could represent his master, standing in the master's stead. In accordance with this view, Paul suggests that whatever assistance Onesimus had provided Paul in the service of the gospel was, in a sense, an extension of Philemon himself. Even without knowing it, Philemon had been benefiting from Onesimus's association with Paul. The implication is that the same would be true if Philemon agreed to return Onesimus (whether freed or otherwise) to Paul once again—a request that Paul does not make explicitly but strongly hints at.

If Paul's discourse has been revolving around the unstated expectation that Philemon should release Onesimus to Paul's charge, Paul ensures here that this expectation is couched in terms that do nothing to jeopardize Philemon's reputation. Paul does not mind usurping cultural codes of honor when necessary, of course, but in this case he deemed it unnecessary to follow that route; evidently, there was a better prospect of success without overturning the applecart. So he works within those cultural confines in this instance, stating **I did not want to do anything without your agreement** (v. 14).

Philemon's cooperative consent is desirable, says Paul, precisely **so that your good deed might be a voluntary thing rather than something forced upon you** (v. 14). Paul does not want to be seen as coercing Philemon to act along particular lines (which Paul did not have the legal power to do anyway). But if Philemon chose to follow a different course than the one Paul expected, it would have been clear to all that he would not be acting in accordance with Paul's understanding of "the good." Implicit in this is Paul's sense that if Philemon wanted to save face in this situation, the easiest route would be for him to acquiesce to the apostle's expectations and appear to comply voluntarily.

Onesimus and God's Initiative (15–16)

15–16. Having played the "honor" card in verse 14, Paul pivots to look at the situation from yet another angle in verse 15. If Onesimus's original departure from Philemon's household could reflect poorly on Philemon as the householder, Paul suggests a different interpretation of how the situation began in the first place. Instead of interpreting Onesimus's departure in terms of human cause-and-effect relationships, Paul draws back and proposes that the will of God may itself have been primarily in play. When Paul says to Philemon that **it might have been for this reason that he** (Onesimus) **was separated from you for a very short time** (v. 15), the verb "was separated" seems to have God

Abuse of Slaves

Paul's apparent hope that Onesimus will become his helper or apprentice in ministry (either as Philemon's borrowed slave or as a freedman) contrasts sharply with predominant attitudes to slaves in the Greco-Roman world. Being possessions of their masters, slaves (especially low-level slaves) were often pawns to their master's whims, including sexual whims. A (first-century?) inscription found in a basilica (or civic courtroom) of Pompeii reads as follows (*CIL* 4.1863): "Take hold of your servant [for sexual purposes] whenever you want to; it is your right." The Latin poet Martial, who lived from 40 to about 103 CE, praises Linus for his frugality when he (Linus) chose to have sex with his slave's wives (for free) instead of purchasing a prostitute (*Epigrams* 4.66). John Chrysostom testifies to occurrences of sexual abuse of slaves by their masters: "Many [slave owners] have thus compelled their domestics and their slaves. Some have drawn them into marriage against their will, and others have forced them to minister to disgraceful services, to infamous love, to acts of rapine and fraud, and violence" (*Hom. Phil.* 1, trans. Allen 2013).

as its implied subject. Paul is proposing that Philemon and others think of Onesimus's original departure as having been orchestrated by God, thereby subverting blame in relation to Philemon (as a less-than-adequate householder) or Onesimus (as a wayward servant); if Onesimus had left without Philemon's consent, this is ultimately (suggests Paul) because God had desired that to happen. Why would that have been? The phrase "for this reason" refers back to "the good deed" in verse 14, the deed that Philemon is to do voluntarily. If we amplify Paul's innuendo, we arrive at a scenario in which God orchestrated Onesimus's departure from Philemon's household in order that Onesimus, now a follower of Jesus, could be sent to assist Paul more permanently in his ministry on behalf of the gospel.

The imagery of Onesimus having been separated from Philemon at the start of the verse is set against its contrasting imagery at the end of the verse. One result of the scenario Paul is implicitly proposing is that Philemon would **have him** (Onesimus) **back forever** (v. 15). The key to this clause is not the phrase "have him back" but the term "forever," which does not simply mean "until his usefulness as your slave expires." Nor is the term likely to draw on Exod. 21:6 and Deut. 15:17 and mean "embedded within your household for the rest of his life" (a prospect argued for by Wright 2013, 13–15). Instead, while incorporating everyday imagery of having a slave "back," Paul now spins it in a completely different direction through the term "forever." That word alone shifts the imagery from Philemon's household to God's household. In Paul's view, once the frame of reference is expanded to take into account "eternal realities," it becomes clear that Onesimus was only separated from Philemon "for a little while" (lit. "for an hour"), with the result that Onesimus (now a Jesus-follower) is yoked to Philemon in an eternal relationship that transcends their relationship as master and slave.

Paul elaborates this point further in verse 16. Paul wants Philemon to imagine himself as joined now to Onesimus in a relationship "impressed" by the "peace from God our Father and the Lord Jesus Christ" (v. 3) and by "love for and faithfulness to the Lord Jesus Christ and all of Jesus's followers" (v. 5). Consequently, if Philemon has received Onesimus back forever, it is **no longer as a slave but more than a slave, as a beloved brother.**

On three occasions prior to verse 16, Paul has made use of the root word *adelph-* (i.e., "brother" or "sister"), using it to refer to Timothy (v. 1), Apphia (v. 2), and Philemon (v. 7; see also verse 20). Moreover, Paul has made use of the root word *agapē* ("love") on four occasions prior to this verse, using it to refer to Philemon's "love" for others (vv. 5, 7), Philemon's "beloved" character (v. 1), and Paul's request made in love (v. 9). Now Paul brings both of these important terms together and applies them to Onesimus—Philemon's "beloved brother" in Christ (a term that also appears in 1 Cor. 15:58; Eph. 6:21; Phil. 4:1; Col. 4:7). Rather than relating to Onesimus merely in terms of a master-slave relationship, Philemon is encouraged to regard their relationship through the filter of brotherly bonds of kinship—a kinship resulting from the transforming restorative peace that comes from God their Father and the Lord (i.e., the true "master" or *kyrios*) Jesus Christ (v. 3).

This new relational configuration results from nothing other than the fact that they both are **in the Lord** (*en kyriō*). But it is a relationship that Paul also characterizes as being **in the flesh** (*en sarki*). By this phrase Paul might simply be referring to the sphere of life that lies beyond the gathering of Jesus-followers. That is, Philemon and Onesimus are brothers in the Lord not only when Jesus-followers meet together weekly (in Philemon's house) but also beyond that, at other times throughout the week when their relationship is marked out primarily as master and slave. This would be a slightly awkward use of the term, however, since Paul does not usually dichotomize spheres of life in that fashion. If Jesus-followers are to be "in the Lord" in all spheres of life, a distinction between "in the flesh" and "in the Lord" looks somewhat uncharacteristic of Paul's way of thinking.

Perhaps, then, "in the flesh" is a subtle gesture to a biological commonality that Philemon and Onesimus share. As noted in the introduction, Philemon and his slave Onesimus may have been biologically related to a single father through different mothers, with Philemon's mother being the wife of

---

Slave as Brother

Writing after Paul, the Stoic philosopher Epictetus (55–135 CE) proposed that a slave owner should treat his slave as "your own brother, who has Zeus as his progenitor and is, as it were, a son born of the same seed as yourself and of the same sowing from above" (*Diatr.* 1.13.3).

"Humanizing" Slaves

Revelation 18:11–13 lists the commodities of "the merchants of the earth" in order of their value (with the most valuable appearing first and the least valuable appearing last). Read through the list from start to finish and notice where slaves appear on the list. However, notice also how the author of Revelation counters the value system of "the merchants of the earth" by adding a phrase that identifies slaves not as mere chattel for the benefit of merchants and householders but, in fact, as "human lives" (or lit. "human souls").

---

the father and Onesimus's mother being a slave of the household. Against the backdrop of this possible scenario, Paul's depiction of Philemon and Onesimus as brothers in the Lord may be constructed on top of another layer of their identities, one involving a literal kinship (i.e., half-brothers, although that relationship would have held no social import, since one was a slave and the other had been the heir to the householder). Perhaps this goes some way toward explaining Paul's curt and otherwise curious statement that Onesimus is a beloved brother **especially to me but how much more to you** (v. 16). Whereas Paul often frames issues of offspring with the phrase "according to the flesh" (*kata sarka*; e.g., Rom. 1:3; 4:1; 9:3, 5), in this instance he employs the phrase "in the flesh," evidently in order to pair it more closely with the phrase that immediately follows it, "in the Lord." (At times in Paul, the phrase *kata sarka* also suggests ethical depravity [as in Rom. 8:4–5, 12–13], a connotation Paul would have wanted to avoid at this point, thereby prompting him to use the phrase *en sarki*.)

Theological Issues

Social status was a preciously guarded commodity in the Greco-Roman world (just as it is today). Unsurprisingly, the letter to Philemon itself attests to that. In that letter, Paul attempts a difficult balancing act, negotiating the deeply entrenched codes of social honor and the complex registry of social authority.

But if we think of the letter simply in terms of a contest of honor and authority between Paul and Philemon, we miss the arena where Paul wants his audiences to place themselves when thinking through issues that impact their discipleship. The move Paul makes in verses 8 and 9 illustrates the point clearly. In verse 8 Paul intimates that, if the issue needs to be battled out, his own apostolic authority can trump anything Philemon might bring to the table. In verse 9, however, he features one of the select words that bear the theological weight of the letter: "love," which for Paul is less an emotional sentiment than it is the active self-giving for the betterment of others to the glory of God. If Paul prods Philemon a bit, that is simply because of his conviction that divinely bestowed love is the best context in which these issues are to be resolved, with all parties benefitting (even Philemon).

Once in play, divine love completely rewrites the script of honor and worth. Just as Paul shows no cognizance of being disgraced by his imprisonment, so too "in the Lord" he prefers to see beyond people's placement on the ladder of success and to recognize them as beloved members of a family ("my child," "his father," "your beloved brother") who share responsibilities for each other's well-being in the service of the gospel (see Frilingos 2000; Aasgaard 2004). To belong to a family is to prioritize the bonds of family over almost all other bonds of mutuality in service, responsibility, and affection. The perspective of Jesus-followers is less determined by their immediate honor and more determined by the well-being of those in the family, to whom they are "forever" bound.

Within the context of that family of service, people who were once deemed to be "useless" in other contexts become cherished and "useful" contributors. Perhaps behind Onesimus's transformation from useless to useful lie the "gifts of the Spirit" that Paul describes in other letters (Rom. 12:4–8; 1 Cor. 12:4–11; and beyond). Those "in the Lord" are tasked by the Spirit to play essential roles within the body of Jesus-followers; regardless of how those roles appear in relation to the status codes pervading society, in the Lord their role is treasured as enhancing "the body" of those in the service of God. If Onesimus's earthly master had considered him worthless, his divine master does not, and through the empowerment of the Spirit Onesimus is poised for usefulness in the service of the gospel. Paul thinks he has already had a glimpse of what that service might look like and hopes that Philemon will catch the vision too.

Finally, notice that Paul's suggestion that God had already been involved in Onesimus's situation compares notably with the OT story of Joseph and his brothers. Joseph's brothers had maliciously sold him into slavery, but he rose from that situation to become the vizier of all Egypt. Late in the story, when his brothers fear his anger, Joseph recognizes two levels of causation at work when he was handed over to slavery: "You meant to do me harm," he tells his brothers, "but God intended it for a good purpose, in order that the

---

Marks of Slavery

In his letter to Jesus-followers in Galatia, Paul identifies himself as a "slave of Christ" toward the beginning of the letter (1:10; see also Rom. 1:1; Titus 1:1) and notes at the end that on his body he bears the "brandings of Jesus" (6:17)—a reference that recalls the branding of slaves to identify whose property they are. For Paul, the gospel of God's love has rewritten the script of honor.

lives of many people might be saved" (Gen. 50:20). In Philem. 15 Paul, like Joseph, introduces another level of causation into the drama of the story, placing Onesimus's situation within a much larger narrative of divine intention, insinuating that God himself may have been guiding the situation all along. Sometimes individual stories need to be considered in relation to the much bigger purposes of God.

Philemon 17–22

Living Up to Character

Introductory Matters

Having set the scene (vv. 1–3 and 8–16) and focused on Philemon's exemplary character (vv. 4–7), Paul is now ready to get to the point of it all in verses 17–22. The point is spelled out in minimalistic terms. First comes a vaguely articulated request (v. 17). This is followed by an aside about recompense (vv. 18–19), an appeal to grant the request and outperform it (vv. 20–21), and a further request that looks unrelated but, even in that appearance, adds incentive for Philemon to grant the request (v. 22).

Having taken great care to set up the letter's rhetorical and theological dynamics in earlier sections of the letter, this text unit flows smoothly and cleanly in presentation.

Tracing the Train of Thought

A Request (17)

17. Having prioritized Philemon's relationship with Onesimus in the Lord (v. 16), Paul highlights again that Philemon's actions toward Onesimus are to be guided by yet another consideration—Philemon's relationship to Paul (v. 17). Paul writes to Philemon with these words: **If then you regard me as your associate, receive him as you would receive me.** Just as Philemon would not dream of mistreating Paul upon arrival (see v. 22), so he should not mistreat Onesimus upon his return to Philemon. This request is given greater poignancy from Paul's depiction of himself as a (spiritual) father to Onesimus (v. 10), since the way one treats a son reflects how one regards the son's father.

A Parenthetical Promise (18–19)

18–19. It is not clear what Paul means by the word "associate" (*koinōnon*, v. 17). Since the word often has strong economic nuances, it is possible that Paul and Philemon may have shared in a business venture at some point (see Dunn 1996). This would resonate well with what Paul says in verses 18 and 19—verses that read much like a parenthesis in thought, with verse 20 virtually picking up again where verse 17 left off. In the first of these parenthetical verses, Paul registers the fact that **if he** (Onesimus) **has done you** (Philemon) **any injustice or if he owes you anything, charge that to me.** The instruction may not be simply metaphorical (especially if Paul and Philemon had been, and perhaps continued to be, partners in an ongoing business venture of some sort). The same is true when Paul writes in verse 19, **I will repay it.** If these assurances are meant to have economic literalness, they demonstrate the extent to which Paul was willing to "invest" in the situation (see C. J. Martin 1991). To add credibility, Paul adds a note putting his own name to these assurances: **I, Paul, have written this with my own hand** (as discussed in the introduction to the commentary).

But it might also be that Paul's "association" with Philemon is not economically configured but pertains to their mutual partnership in advancing the gospel. They are partners, sharing responsibility in the common goal of enhancing the community to which they both belonged. This would give the accounting imagery a metaphorical sense. Whatever costs Philemon might charge to Paul would be repaid in the currency in which Paul prefers to deal—that is, in prayers of thanksgiving to God for Philemon's initiatives for the sake of the gospel (cf. vv. 4–7). This metaphorical sense of exchange plays directly into Paul's final statement in verse 19, which is yet another highly charged rhetorical moment: **I don't need even to mention to you that you owe me in return—that is, you owe me your own self.** Whereas in verse 8 Paul had no need to command what he commanded, here he has no need to mention what he mentions (see further Wendland 2010).

But what does Paul mean by "you owe me your own self"? Had Paul saved Philemon's life at some point in the past? More likely, Paul is referring to the blessings that Philemon has enjoyed as a result of Paul's ministry. Probably Philemon had become a Jesus-follower through Paul's influence, having gone from spiritual impoverishment to spiritual riches and richness by means of Paul's influence. If Philemon proves to be rather ornery in his attitude toward Onesimus, he will only be making himself look churlish in light of all that Paul has done for him.

An Appeal to Grant the Request (20)

20. Paul's discourse has almost run its course. And so, before registering his concluding comments in verses 23–25, Paul makes it clear that he is asking Philemon to do something significant in relation to Onesimus. So he writes in verse 20, **Yes brother, let me have this delight, in the Lord.** (It is often noticed that the Greek verb *onaimēn*, translated here as "let me have this delight," has strong convergence with the name Onesimus, so that Paul might yet again have constructed a play on words.) That delight will no doubt feed Paul's thanks to God for Philemon (vv. 4–7), owing to the fact that what Philemon is being called to do is an action that derives from his identity "in the Lord"—a phrase that Paul last used in verse 16 when describing Onesimus as a brother "in the Lord."

What is it that Paul is calling on Philemon to do? He says it this way: **Refresh my heart, in Christ.** This is the third time that Paul has used the word "heart" (*splanchna*) in his letter, and it is a word that he uses to great rhetorical effect. In the first instance, Paul praises Philemon for having refreshed the hearts of the holy ones of God (v. 7); in the second instance, Paul identifies Onesimus as his own heart, whom he is sending back to Philemon (v. 12). In verse 20, then, when encouraging Philemon to refresh Paul's heart, Paul is doing two interconnected things:

1. He has established a subtle but appreciable double entendre. Philemon is to act in such a fashion that both Paul and Onesimus (Paul's "own heart") are benefited. The rhetorical pressure is considerable.
2. He is asking Philemon to live up to his established character. Philemon is already well-known for having refreshed the hearts of Jesus-followers; Paul hopes that Philemon will act on that honorable reputation once again, this time in relation to Onesimus.

An Appeal to Go beyond the Request (21)

21. Because this character is lived out in the realm of those "in Christ" rather than in accordance with the standards of "the world," Paul writes in verse 21 of his confidence in Philemon: **I am writing this to you in the confidence that you will be obedient.** At the end of verse 21, Paul articulates not only his full confidence in Philemon's obedience but also his certainty that Philemon **will do even more than I am suggesting.**

This is a key rhetorical moment in the reading of the letter. The wider audience hears of Paul's confidence that Philemon will perform in such a way as to outstrip Paul's implied suggestions. Seeing the pressure that Philemon is coming under, the wider audience also recognizes that if Philemon chooses to act along the lines that Paul has been hinting at, whatever he does should be seen in a positive light, in direct proportion to the extent that he complies with Paul's expectations. As a result, Philemon will not lose face (as might have been the case in the eyes of those beyond this Jesus-group) but will, instead, accumulate honor. In highlighting that Philemon is sure to do even more than Paul articulates, Paul simultaneously heaps up the rhetorical pressure while "envisioning" Philemon (albeit implicitly) with a course of action whereby he will not be dishonored but will, instead, be seen as a critical player in a beneficial move for all involved.

Paul has crafted a way of looking at the situation that fosters a win-win situation for all parties—certainly for Philemon (who gains in honor), for Paul (whose heart is refreshed), and for Onesimus (whose situation is rectified in some fashion).

Incentivizing Philemon (22)

22. Although verse 22 is often linked to the verses that follow it, the way Paul begins the verse suggests that he imagines it linking most strongly to what precedes it. Two simple connectives (*de kai*) appear in conjunction with an adverb denoting temporal simultaneity (*hama*), resulting in a sentence that begins by signaling its dependency on what came previously: **And also at the same time . . .**

This backward link makes perfect sense when the verse is seen not as an outline of Paul's intended travel plans (in which case it might link better with the letter's closure in vv. 23–25) but, instead, as furthering his interest in Onesimus's situation. Paul writes: **prepare a place where I can stay, for I hope that through your prayers I will be restored to you all.** Having already stated his confidence in Philemon's extravagant obedience with regard to Onesimus (v. 21), Paul mentions the prospect of his arrival (his "restoration" among them) as a way of adding urgency to Philemon's decision to comply. Paul implies that, with God's help, he might be arriving among them at any point (a strategy Paul uses also in Phil. 2:24; cf. 1 Tim. 3:14). If Philemon delays in making an acceptable decision in favor of Onesimus, he might have to explain himself to Paul directly, face to face, after Paul's release from prison. This somewhat ominous prospect is not explicitly mentioned, of course; Paul has more tact than that (although he found himself resorting to that strategy in 1 Cor. 4:18–21 and 2 Cor. 13:1–2). But the verse serves as a further incentive for Philemon to undertake his voluntary "good deed" (v. 14) and to do it without delay. As such, it is not so much an outline of Paul's travel plans as it is a rhetorical feature in his case on Onesimus's behalf.

That verse 22 plays a part in Paul's concerns for Onesimus is further evidenced by the use of second-person references in the verse. Paul initially instructs Philemon in the second-person singular ("prepare a place") but then shifts into the second-person plural when speaking of prayers for Paul ("your prayers") and of his return to them ("restored to you"). In this way, Philemon is singled out as having responsibility for organizing hospitality for Paul, and the wider audience is implicitly aligned with Paul as a group that prays for his welcomed return. If Philemon fails to comply with Paul's expectations regarding Onesimus, an eventual visit from Paul would not reap the benefits of joy for the community that it otherwise would. Philemon would, in effect, be letting down all those who are gathered around him. Instead of refreshing the hearts of the people of God, he will have been an impediment. But that is not the Philemon depicted by Paul in this letter—Philemon the "coworker" in the gospel, the one who refreshes the hearts of others, through whom good work flows to others.

The choice is Philemon's to make, of course, but Paul has stacked the rhetorical and theological deck to such an extent that Philemon would simply be foolish to act against Paul's unarticulated yet clear request—foolish, that is, to act in a fashion that undermines his already established character.

Theological Issues

It is intriguing to note the virtual absence of theological themes and argumentation in this text unit of the letter. Paul has engaged theological motifs at every point along the way, with each of the preceding text units being interwoven with theological strands of thought to help Philemon consider the situation with theological clarity. But in this text unit, the big rhetorical moment, Paul's discourse has almost none of that. The request itself is virtually unadorned theologically. Having already established the theological context of the situation, Paul enters the moment of request with theological minimalism marking out his discourse. Even though Paul makes very clear the direction he wants Philemon to take in the matter, there is little theological hand-holding or arm-twisting to guide Philemon in his decision; it is simply decision time for Philemon (cf. Petersen 1985, 73–78).

There are, of course, two notable exceptions to this depiction—that is, the two heavily loaded theological phrases that complement each other in adjoining clauses (v. 20): "in the Lord" and "in Christ." It is as if Paul is saying to Philemon, "Be who you are, and who you are primarily is a person in the Lord, a person in Christ. So, Philemon, act accordingly."

There were various ways in which Philemon could subsequently choose to play the situation, depending on what values he prioritized in the decision-making process. But prioritizing values is done in relation to the character of the person doing the valuing. So the question that ultimately faced Philemon is "Who are you? On what basis will you make your decision? How will the formation of your character in the past impact your decision in the present?" (Or, to quote Steely Dan [2000], what is the "architecture of your soul"?)

This might be why Paul strips his theological discourse down to the two simple phrases that identify Philemon as one who is "in the Lord" and "in Christ." It is Paul's way of framing the ultimate question that Philemon must determine—the question of who he ultimately is. Is he someone whose ultimate concern is to maximize the economic efficiency of his household? Is he someone whose ultimate concern is to protect the honor of his name against potential criticism or mockery, for failing to keep his household affairs in order? Or is he someone whose identity is fundamentally shaped by being "in the Lord" and "in Christ," where values are transformed in conformity with the gospel?

We will never know for sure what Philemon decided to do. Or, better, we will never know for sure *who* Philemon decided he was. We will never know what aspect of his identity informed his decision regarding Onesimus. There is reason for thinking that Philemon may have acted in compliance with Paul's request, since the letter was cherished by early Jesus-followers rather than being lost through embarrassment or contempt (as noted in the introduction), and there is just a chance that the Onesimus who was the bishop of Ephesus a few decades later is the same Onesimus whose case Paul defends in this letter (see Ign. *Eph*. 1.3; this scenario works better if Paul's imprisonment was in Rome sometime in the 60s rather than in Ephesus in the mid-50s).

But it is also worth considering what would have happened if Philemon chose to prioritize economic efficiency or social honor over his identity "in the Lord" and if Paul were then to visit Philemon after that (as proposed in v. 22). In that encounter, perhaps Paul would have interacted with Philemon not so much in confrontation with him or with contempt for him but simply out of concern for him, in the same manner he had already shown for Onesimus.

Philemon 23–25

Final Greetings

Introductory Matters

Believing he has said enough to influence the situation profitably, Paul brings the letter to a quick close. The closing is comprised simply of greetings from five other men (besides Timothy) who were with Paul during the time of his imprisonment, and a final benediction that completes the *inclusio* of "grace" that stands like bookends at the start and finish of the letter (vv. 3, 25).

The five men mentioned in verses 23–24 are all known to us from other texts of the early Jesus movement. If all of the passages about them are taken at face value (see sidebar "Paul's Associates"), then it would seem that each of these five men had an interesting story to tell of their own lives in relation to Paul.

> Aristarchus was a longtime travel companion of Paul (perhaps this was true of Luke as well), who had experienced some persecution with him (according to Acts 19 and Colossians).
>
> Mark was a companion to Paul in his early mission with Barnabas (in the early to mid-40s). Although Paul may have lost confidence in him in the late 40s (if Acts 15 is anything to go by), Mark seems later to have enjoyed Paul's confidence, having also a link to Peter (according to 1 Pet. 5).
>
> Epaphras was a trusted, prominent, and effective leader with Paul among certain Jesus-groups, while Demas had enough stature to be mentioned in the greetings, although he would eventually go on to forsake Paul (if 2 Tim. 4:10 is anything to go by).
>
> Mark and Luke may well have gone on to compose narratives that have nourished the church for millennia (the Gospel of Mark; the Gospel of

---

Paul's Associates

Aristarchus (Col. 4:10; perhaps Acts 19:29; 20:4; 27:2)

Mark (Col. 4:10; 2 Tim. 4:11; 1 Pet. 5:13; Acts 12:12, 25; 15:37–39)

Epaphras (Col. 1:7; 4:12; see also Trainor 2008)

Demas (Col. 4:14; 2 Tim. 4:10)

Luke (Col. 4:14; 2 Tim. 4:11)

Luke and the Acts of the Apostles, although the ascriptions in those Gospels derive from tradition).

Perhaps it would not take much of an inquiring mind to construct an intriguing imaginative narrative about the intersection of these life stories converging at the point where Paul wrote to Philemon.

In verse 25 Paul closes the letter with an invocation of grace upon the recipients of the letter. This is a fairly standard feature of Paul's letters (see also Rom. 16:20; 1 Cor. 16:23; 2 Cor. 13:13; Gal. 6:18; Phil. 4:23; 1 Thess. 5:28). Thus the shortest of Paul's extant letters comes to a close.

Tracing the Train of Thought

Greetings from Those with Paul (23–24)

23–24. Having made his case, Paul closes by sending greetings from others who are with him. The first is **Epaphras,** who is said to be **my fellow prisoner in Christ Jesus.** There may be subtle military imagery in this descriptor, since the Greek term contains nuances of a prisoner of war (cf. the description of Archippus as "our fellow soldier" in v. 2). We cannot tell whether Epaphras's imprisonment is metaphorical or literal. (The Greek word Paul uses of his own imprisonment in verses 1, 9, 10, and 13 [*desm-*] differs from the Greek word used of Epaphras's imprisonment [*synaichmalōtos*], which he also uses of Andronicus and Junia in Rom. 16:7.) But either way, Paul's depiction may imply that Epaphras had been on the battlefield in the cosmic combat that God has won in Christ's death and resurrection (see the battle imagery of 1 Cor. 15:24–25; 2 Cor. 10:3–4, and beyond,

---

Epaphras

Epaphras is probably not (as some have suggested) the Epaphroditus whom Paul mentions in Philippians (2:25; 4:18), with Epaphras simply being the shortened form of his name. Epaphroditus is from the region of Achaia, whereas Epaphras is from the Lycus Valley. They are two different workers for the gospel whose names are variants on the same root name.

---

not least throughout much of Colossians and Ephesians).

The others with Paul are identified both by their names (**Mark, Aristarchus, Demas, and Luke**) and by the descriptor **my coworkers,** which applies also to Epaphras. With this descriptor, Paul is doing more than simply recognizing the importance of these men in his ministry; he also has an eye on Philemon once again. At the very beginning of the letter, Paul referred to Philemon as "our coworker" (v. 1); here he uses the same term to describe people who evidently had a reputation among Jesus-followers as notable leaders. If Philemon chose not to comply with Paul's vision for Onesimus, the term "coworker" would look less appropriate when applied to him—a case of "one of these things is not like the others." In this way, even the final greetings play into the rhetorical force of the letter. Not only do the two authors of verse 1 endorse Paul's request, but so too do the five men of verse 25—resulting in something of a "rhetorical squeeze" between those two verses (see fig. 14).

> ### Philemon 23–25 in the Rhetorical Flow
>
> Setting the scene, part 1 (1–3)
>
> Philemon's character, as illustrated by his past actions (4–7)
>
> Setting the scene, part 2 (8–16)
>
> Living up to character (17–22)
>
> ▶ **Final greetings (23–25)**
>
> > **Greetings from those with Paul (23–24)**
> >
> > **A closing grace (25)**

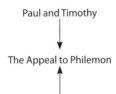

Paul and Timothy

↓

The Appeal to Philemon

↑

Epaphras, Mark, Aristarchus, Demas, and Luke

Figure 14. The "rhetorical squeeze" of Philemon 1 and 25 (based on an illustration in Trainor 2008, 32)

A Closing Grace (25)

25. Paul ends the letter offering what for him is a fairly standard invocation, one that highlights what he and his coworkers were ultimately concerned to foster: **The grace of the Lord Jesus Christ.** It is a grace that Paul prays would **be with your spirit.** Once again, the word "your" is plural. Philemon is not singled out here; the corporate community itself is represented as having a single "spirit" or ethos, through which divine grace is to flow.

All that Paul has to say about the relationship between Philemon and Onesimus is contained within the letter's *inclusio* of grace (vv. 3, 25). That relationship is simply one moment in an ongoing story of the divine grace that was to animate the life of this Jesus-group and of Jesus-groups beyond it.

Theological Issues

With Paul's final mention of "grace" as a foothold, we can now reflect (although only briefly) on the extent to which Paul's letter offers theological resources beyond the small Jesus-group to which Philemon belonged in the first century.

We need to frame our discussion with two caveats. First, more things are said about slavery in the Pauline corpus than what we find in Philemon; our comments here pertain only to Philemon.

Second, it is likely that Paul will not satisfy all of our contemporary expectations about how an issue involving slavery should have been handled. It has not been hard for readers sensitized to the issue of the slave trade of the eighteenth and nineteenth centuries to find weaknesses or faults in Paul's discourse. For instance, the following criticisms have been leveled against Paul's handling of the situation (as in Harrill 2006):

1. Paul speaks for Onesimus; the voice of Onesimus is mute in the letter and Paul did not empower him to articulate things for himself.
2. Paul did not challenge the stereotypical way of thinking about slaves in terms of their usefulness or non-usefulness.
3. Paul failed to address the structural issue of slavery and its injustices.

If we want to spot the ideological weaknesses of Paul's letter in relation to our own sensitivities about justice, then these might be places to start.

Nonetheless, there are also valid replies to these points as well. For instance, allowing Onesimus his own voice would have introduced unacceptable dynamics into the rhetorical situation, increasing the likelihood of an unfavorable result for Onesimus. Or, it is true that Paul's theology of the body does not abandon categories of usefulness and non-usefulness, even when applied to slaves, but in the instance of Onesimus he does at least refocus those categories in terms of service, divinely empowered for the benefit of others.

How Did Paul View Slavery?

Paul's view on slavery (if he had one) is not wholly clear. Paul's comments in 1 Cor. 7:21–22 are difficult to pin down and for that reason do not qualify as a radical statement about Paul's abhorrence of slavery (see Tucker 2011). This is even clearer in the disputed Pauline texts, with their admonition for slaves to obey their masters (Col. 3:22; Eph. 6:5–6; 1 Tim. 6:2; Titus 2:9). In some of these cases, however, Paul does register some resources for recognizing that relationships between slaves and masters are to be transformed "in Christ." When analyzed by twenty-first-century expectations, the full implications of that transformation can be taken further than was the case within Paul's day.

It is true that Paul did not address the structures of power that were deeply ingrained within Greco-Roman culture. Occasionally voices were raised that went some way in that direction, and Paul's was not one of them, at least on this occasion. But we need also to be fair to Paul. After all, the issue of whether slavery is justified or not is not in the mix in Onesimus's situation. Of course, that lacuna might itself leave Paul vulnerable to criticism, if that is what we're after. But it does mean that we first need to analyze Paul's presentation on its own terms before assessing it for what we would have wanted him to say.

There are, however, theological sparks within the letter that, when gently fanned, can ignite a fire in the tinderbox of slavery—

> **World Changers?**
>
> Consider the following statement:
>
> *"How far the Christian Church was from thinking of remolding the world, of adopting an economic or political program, is indicated by its attitude toward property, slavery and the state.... [Since the early Jesus-followers were not in positions of societal power,] such responsibility [for remolding the world] was out of the question."* (Bultmann 1955, 229, 231)

perhaps slaveries of all kinds (Greco-Roman slavery; eighteenth- and nineteenth-century slavery of Africans in Britain and, especially, America; twenty-first-century slavery in the form of human trafficking and exploitation in sex-trade industries; etc.). Changing the metaphor, it has rightly been said that Paul's letter to Philemon "brings us into an atmosphere in which the institution [of slavery] could only wilt and die" (Bruce 2000, 401).

In fact, Paul has put into play key theological motifs that, when expanded upon, can be easily interwoven into a heavy thicket to smother all permutations of enslavement. These include the following:

1. The *inclusio* of divine "grace" or unconditioned favor (against which Jesus-followers are to reassess their own attitudes of entitlement)
2. "Peace," or relationships based on justice
3. "Love," or beneficial self-giving for the betterment of others
4. "Faithfulness," or constancy in serving God and enhancing the lives of others

> **Applying Philemon Today**
>
> Applying the challenge of Philemon to the twenty-first-century context might involve us in supporting efforts to eradicate human trafficking—such as the A21 Campaign, the International Justice Mission, or organizations of that kind.

These ingredients, especially when taken together, are to be the yeast that raises attributes of Christ-likeness within the character of those whose identity is ultimately "in the Lord" and "in Christ." It is there, "in the Lord," that relationships of health are to be awakened—empowered by divine

Slave Trader John Newton

The hymn "Amazing Grace" was written by John Newton (1725–1807) who, as the captain of a ship involved in the slave trade, helped to enslave Africans brought to America. In 1755 he relinquished his ship due to a serious illness. Newton penned the song in 1772 or thereabouts. Although the hymn might resonate with an anti-slavery theme ("Amazing grace . . . saved a wretch like me; . . . was blind but now I see"), it wasn't until 1780 that Newton began making public statements indicating his regrets about participating in the slave trade (although the film *Amazing Grace* has the sequence the other way around). Perhaps his public repudiation of slavery was a delayed reaction to his deep understanding and awareness of divine grace and of who he was in relation to that grace. Sometimes these things take time. Tragically, however, it took centuries for the deep moral values of the Judeo-Christian tradition to take hold, while the lives of untold millions of precious people were destroyed in the meantime.

love, resulting in relationships of "just peace," under a double umbrella of divine grace and effortful faithfulness.

At the center of this lies the transformation of moral character—a transformation that fosters the realignment of relationships. If structures of injustice are founded upon the categories of differentiation (not least, "slave" versus "free"; compare Gal. 3:28; 1 Cor. 12:13; Col. 3:11), those structures of injustice (which permeate cultures of all kinds) are sidelined "in the Lord." It is "in the Lord" that the righteousness of God has come alive to enhance communities of Jesus-followers and to foster within their members patterns of life that reflect something of the glory of the eschatological age, ultimately overspilling for the betterment of society (cf. 1 Thess. 5:15). Little wonder, then, that relationships among Jesus-followers are reconfigured on the basis of their identity as brothers and sisters "forever."

Paul believes in the power of God to shape communities into the character of the self-giving Son of God, enhancing their service to the gospel. Being an essay in the divine transformation of moral character, Paul's letter to Philemon is ultimately a letter of quietly confident hope in the power of God.

Bibliography

Aasgaard, Reidar. 2004. *"My Beloved Brothers and Sisters!": Christian Siblingship in Paul*. Journal for the Study of the New Testament Supplement Series 265. London: T&T Clark.

Adams, Sean A. 2010. "Paul's Letter Opening and Greek Epistolography: A Matter of Relationship." Pages 33–56 in *Paul and the Ancient Letter Form*. Edited by Stanley E. Porter and Sean A. Adams. Leiden: Brill.

Alexander, Loveday. 1989. "Hellenistic Letter Forms and the Structure of Philippians." *Journal for the Study of the New Testament* 37:87–101.

Allen, Pauline, trans. 2013. *John Chrysostom: Homilies on Paul's Letter to the Philippians*. Atlanta: SBL Press.

Arzt, Peter. 1994. "The 'Epistolary Introductory Thanksgiving' in the Papyri and in Paul." *Novum Testamentum* 36:29–46.

Arzt-Grabner, Peter. 2001. "The Case of Onesimos: An Interpretation of Paul's Letter to Philemon Based on Documentary Papyri and Ostraca." *Annali di storia dell'esegesi* 18:589–614.

———. 2003. *Philemon*. Göttingen: Vandenhoeck & Ruprecht.

———. 2004. "Onesimus erro." *Zeitschrift für die neutestamentliche Wissenschaft* 95:131–43.

———. 2010a. "How to Deal with Onesimus? Paul's Solution within the Frame of Ancient Legal and Documentary Sources." Pages 113–42 in *Philemon in Perspective: Interpreting a Pauline Letter*. Edited by D. F. Tolmie. Berlin: de Gruyter.

———. 2010b. "Paul's Letter Thanksgiving." Pages 129–58 in *Paul and the Ancient Letter Form*. Edited by Stanley E. Porter and Sean A. Adams. Leiden: Brill.

Ascough, Richard S. 2003. *Paul's Macedonian Associations: The Social Context of Philippians and 1 Thessalonians*. Wissenschaftliche Untersuchungen zum Neuen Testament 2/161. Tübingen: Mohr Siebeck.

Avalos, Hector. 2011. *Slavery, Abolitionism, and the Ethics of Biblical Scholarship.* Sheffield: Sheffield Phoenix.

Bakirtzis, Charalambdos, and Helmut Koester, eds. 1998. *Philippi at the Time of Paul and after His Death.* Harrisburg, PA: Trinity.

Barclay, John M. G. 1991. "Paul, Philemon and the Dilemma of Christian Slave-Ownership." *New Testament Studies* 37:161–86.

———. 1997. *Colossians and Philemon.* Sheffield: Sheffield Academic Press.

———. 2007. "There Is Neither Old nor Young? Early Christianity and Ancient Ideologies of Age." *New Testament Studies* 53:225–41.

Barnes, Albert. 1846. *An Inquiry into the Scriptural Views of Slavery.* Philadelphia: Perkins & Purves.

Barth, Gerhard. 1996. "Phil. 1,23 und die paulinische Zukunftserwartung (Eschatologie)." Pages 335–40 in *Neutestamentliche Versuche und Beobachtungen.* By Gerhard Barth. Waltrop: Hartmut Spenner.

Barth, Karl. 2002. *Epistle to the Philippians.* 40th anniversary ed. Louisville: Westminster John Knox.

Barth, Markus, and Helmut Blanke. 2000. *The Letter to Philemon: A New Translation with Notes and Commentary.* Eerdmans Critical Commentary. Grand Rapids: Eerdmans.

Barton, Stephen C. 1987. "Paul and Philemon: A Correspondence Continued." *Theology* 90:97–101.

Bauckham, Richard. 1998. "The Worship of Jesus in Philippians 2:9–11." Pages 128–39 in *Where Christology Began.* Edited by Ralph P. Martin and Brian J. Dodd. Louisville: Westminster John Knox.

Berry, Ken L. 1996. "The Function of Friendship Language in Philippians 4:10–20." Pages 107–24 in *Friendship, Flattery, and Frankness of Speech: Studies on Friendship in the New Testament World.* Edited by John T. Fitzgerald. Leiden: Brill.

Bieberstein, Sabine. 2000. "Disrupting the Normal Reality of Slavery: A Feminist Reading of the Letter to Philemon." *Journal for the Study of the New Testament* 79:105–16.

Birdsall, J. N. 1993. "ΠΡΕΣΒΥΤΗΣ in Philemon 9: A Study in Conjectural Emendation." *New Testament Studies* 39 (4): 625–30.

Black, David A. 1985. "Paul and Christian Unity: A Formal Analysis of Philippians 2:1–4." *Journal of the Evangelical Theological Society* 28:299–308.

Bloomquist, L. Gregory. 1993. *The Function of Suffering in Philippians.* Journal for the Study of the New Testament Supplement Series 78. Sheffield: Sheffield Academic.

Bockmuehl, Markus. 1995. "A Commentator's Approach to the 'Effective History' of Philippians." *Journal for the Study of the New Testament* 60:57–88.

———. 1998. *The Epistle to the Philippians.* Black's New Testament Commentaries. Grand Rapids: Baker Academic.

Bonhoeffer, Dietrich. 1954. *Life Together.* New York: Harper & Row.

———. 1963. *The Cost of Discipleship.* Rev. ed. New York: Macmillan.

Bormann, Lukas. 1995. *Philippi: Stadt und Christengemeinde zur Zeit des Paulus*. Supplements to Novum Teastamentum 78. Leiden: Brill.

Böttrich, Christfried. 2004. "Verkündigung aus 'Neid und Rivalität'? Beobachtungen zu Phil. 1,12–18. *Zeitschrift für die neutestamentliche Wissenschaft* 95:84–101.

Bruce, F. F. 2000. *Paul, Apostle of the Heart Set Free*. Grand Rapids: Eerdmans.

Bultmann, Rudolf. 1955. *Theology of the New Testament*, vol. 2. New York: Scribner.

Burtchaell, James. 1998. *Philemon's Problem: A Theology of Grace*. Grand Rapids: Eerdmans.

Byron, John. 2003. *Slavery Metaphors in Early Judaism and Christianity*. Tübingen: Mohr Siebeck.

Callahan, Allen Dwight. 1997. *Embassy of Onesimus: The Letter of Paul to Philemon*. Valley Forge, PA: Trinity.

Campbell, William S. 2011. "'I Rate All Things as Loss': Paul's Puzzling Accounting System; Judaism as Loss or the Re-evaluation of All Things in Christ?" Pages 39–61 in *Celebrating Paul: Festschrift in Honor of Jerome Murphy-O'Connor, O.P., and Joseph A. Fitzmyer, S.J.* Edited by Peter Spitaler. Catholic Biblical Quarterly Monograph Series 48. Washington, DC: Catholic Biblical Association.

Cancik, Hildegard. 1967. *Untersuchungen zu Senecas Epistulae Morales*. Hildesheim: Georg Olms.

Cassidy, Richard. 2001. *Paul in Chains: Roman Imprisonment and the Letters of St. Paul*. New York: Crossroad.

Collange, Jean-François. 1979. *The Epistle of Paul to the Philippians*. London: Epworth.

Cotter, Wendy. 1993. "'Our Politeuma is in Heaven': The Meaning of Phil. 3:17–21." Pages 92–104 in *Origins and Method: Towards a New Understanding of Judaism and Christianity; Essays in Honor of J. C. Hurd*. Edited by Bradley McLean. Sheffield: JSOT Press.

Cousar, Charles B. 2009. *Philippians and Philemon*. Louisville: Westminster John Knox.

Croy, N. Clayton. 2003. "'To Die Is Gain' (Philippians 1:19–26): Does Paul Contemplate Suicide?" *Journal of Biblical Literature* 122:517–31.

Dahl, Nils. 1995. "Euodia and Syntyche, and Paul's Letter to the Philippians." Pages 3–15 in *Social World of the First Christians: Essays in Honor of Wayne A. Meeks*. Edited by L. Michael White and O. Larry Yarbrough. Minneapolis: Fortress.

Dailea, Thomas F. 1990. "To Live or Die: Paul's Eschatological Dilemma in Philippians 1:19–26." *Interpretation* 44:18–28.

Davis, C. W. 1999. *Oral Biblical Criticism: The Influence of the Principles of Orality on the Literary Structure of Paul's Epistle to the Philippians*. Journal for the Study of the New Testament Supplement Series 172. Sheffield: Sheffield Academic Press.

Decock, Paul B. 2010. "The Reception of the Letter to Philemon in the Early Church: Origen, Jerome, Chrysostom, and Augustine." Pages 273–88 in *Philemon in Perspective: Interpreting a Pauline Letter*. Edited by D. F. Tolmie. Berlin: de Gruyter.

Deissmann, Adolf. 2004. *Light from the Ancient East: The New Testament Illustrated by Recently Discovered Texts of the Graeco-Roman World*. New York: Harper, 1922. Repr., Eugene, OR: Wipf & Stock.

deSilva, David A. 1994. "No Confidence in the Flesh: The Meaning and Function of Philippians 3:2–21. *Trinity Journal*, n.s., 15:27–54.

De Villiers, Pieter G. R. 2010. "Love in the Letter to Philemon." Pages 181–204 in *Philemon in Perspective: Interpreting a Pauline Letter*. Edited by D. F. Tolmie. Berlin: de Gruyter.

De Vos, Craig Steven. 1997. *Church and Community Conflicts: The Relationships of the Thessalonian, Corinthian, and Philippian Churches with Their Wider Civic Communities*. Society of Biblical Literature Dissertation Series 168. Atlanta: Scholars Press.

Dibelius, Martin. 1937. *An die Thessalonicher I–II und die Philipper*. 3rd ed. Handbuch zum Neuen Testament 11. Tübingen: Mohr Siebeck.

Donfried, K. P., and I. H. Marshall. 1993. *The Theology of the Shorter Pauline Letters*. New Testament Theology. Cambridge: Cambridge University Press.

Droge, Arthur J. 1988. "*Mori Lucrum*: Paul and Ancient Theories of Suicide." *Novum Testamentum* 30:262–86.

Dunn, James D. G. 1996. *The Epistles to Colossians and to Philemon*. Grand Rapids: Eerdmans.

Du Plessis, Isak J. 2006. "How Christians Can Survive in a Hostile Socio-Economic Environment: Paul's Mind concerning Difficult Social Conditions in the Letter to Philemon." Pages 387–413 in *Identity, Ethics, and Ethos in the New Testament*. Edited by Jan G. van der Watt. Berlin: de Gruyter.

Elliott, Scott S. 2011. "'Thanks, but No Thanks': Tact, Persuasion, and the Negotiation of Power in Paul's Letter to Philemon." *New Testament Studies* 57:51–64.

Engberg-Pedersen, Troels. 1995. "Stoicism in Philippians." Pages 256–90 in *Paul and His Hellenistic Context*. Edited by Troels Engberg-Pedersen. Minneapolis: Fortress.

———. 2003. "Radical Altruism in Philippians 2:4." Pages 197–214 in *Early Christianity and Classical Culture: Comparative Studies in Honor of Abraham J. Malherbe*. Edited by John T. Fitzgerald, Thomas H. Olbricht, and L. Michael White. Supplements to Novum Testamentum 90. Leiden: Brill.

Fee, Gordon D. 1995. *Paul's Letter to the Philippians*. New International Commentary on the New Testament. Grand Rapids: Eerdmans.

Fitzgerald, John T. 1992. "Philippians." Pages 318–26 in vol. 5 of *Anchor Bible Dictionary*. Edited by David Noel Freedman. New York: Doubleday.

———. 1996. "Philippians in the Light of Some Ancient Discussions of Friendship." Pages 141–62 in *Friendship, Flattery, and Frankness of Speech: Studies in Friendship in the Ancient World*. Edited by John T. Fitzgerald. Supplements to Novum Testamentum 82. Leiden: Brill.

———. 2010a. "The Stoics and the Early Christians on the Treatment of Slaves." Pages 141–75 in *Stoicism in Early Christianity*. Edited by Tuomas Rasimus, Troels Engberg-Pedersen, and Ismo Dunderberg. Grand Rapids: Baker Academic.

———. 2010b. "Theodore of Mopseustia on Paul's Letter to Philemon." Pages 333–63 in *Philemon in Perspective: Interpreting a Pauline Letter*. Edited by D. F. Tolmie. Berlin: de Gruyter.

Fitzmyer, Joseph A. 2000. *The Letter to Philemon*. New York: Doubleday.

Fowl, Stephen E. 2002. "Know Your Context: Giving and Receiving Money in Philippians." *Interpretation* 56:45–58.

———. 2003. "Philippians 1:28b, One More Time." Pages 167–79 in *New Testament Greek and Exegesis: Essays in Honor of Gerald F. Hawthorne*. Edited by Amy M. Donaldson. Grand Rapids: Eerdmans.

———. 2005. *Philippians*. Two Horizons New Testament Commentary. Grand Rapids: Eerdmans.

Friedl, Alfred. 2010. "St. Jerome's Dissertation on the Letter to Philemon." Pages 289–316 in *Philemon in Perspective: Interpreting a Pauline Letter*. Edited by D. F. Tolmie. Berlin: de Gruyter.

Frilingos, Chris. 2000. "'For My Child, Onesimus': Paul and Domestic Power in Philemon." *Journal of Biblical Literature* 119:91–104.

Furnish, Victor P. 2005. "Uncommon Love and the Common Good: Christians as Citizens in the Letters of Paul." Pages 48–85 in *In Search of the Common Good*. Edited by Dennis P. McCann and Patrick D. Miller. London: T&T Clark.

Garland, David E. 1985. "The Composition and Unity of Philippians: Some Neglected Literary Factors." *Novum Testamentum* 27:141–73.

Gaventa, Beverly. 1986. "Galatians 1 and 2: Autobiography as Paradigm." *Novum Testamentum* 28:309–26.

Geoffrion, T. C. 1999. *The Rhetorical Purpose and the Political and Military Character of Philippians: A Call to Stand Firm*. Lewiston, NY: Mellen Biblical Press.

Giessen, Heinz. 2006. "Eschatology in Philippians." Pages 217–82 in *Paul and His Theology*. Edited by Stanley E. Porter. Leiden: Brill.

Giles, Kevin. 1994. "The Biblical Argument for Slavery: Can the Bible Mislead? A Case Study in Hermeneutics." *Evangelical Quarterly* 66:3–17.

Glancy, Jennifer. 2002. *Slavery in Early Christianity*. Oxford: Oxford University Press.

Gnilka, Joachim. 1968. *Der Philipperbrief*. Herders theologischer Kommentar zum Neuen Testament. Freiburg: Herder.

Gorman, Michael J. 2001. *Cruciformity: Paul's Narrative Spirituality of the Cross*. Grand Rapids: Eerdmans.

Gräbe, Petrus J. 2006. ". . . As Citizens of Heaven Live in a Manner Worthy of the Gospel of Christ . . ." Pages 289–302 in *Identity, Ethics and Ethos in the New Testament*. Edited by J. G. van der Watt. Berlin: de Gruyter.

Grieb, A. Katherine. 2007. "Philippians and the Politics of God." *Interpretation* 61:261–69.

Gupta, Nijay. 2008. "'I Will Not Be Put to Shame': Paul, the Philippians, and the Honourable Wish for Death." *Neotestamentica* 42:253–67.

Harrill, J. Albert. 2006. *Slaves in the New Testament: Literary, Social, and Moral Dimensions*. Minneapolis: Augsburg Fortress.

Harris, Murray J. 1991. *Colossians and Philemon*. Grand Rapids: Eerdmans.

Harvey, John D. 1998. *Listening to the Text: Oral Patterning in Paul's Letters*. Grand Rapids: Baker.

Hasluck, F. W. 1907. "Inscriptions from the Cyzicus District, 1906." *Journal of Hellenic Studies* 27:61–67.

Hawthorne, Gerald F. 2004. *Philippians*. Rev. ed. Word Biblical Commentary. Nashville: Nelson.

Hecking, Detlef. 2009. "Elitesoldaten und Sklavinnen, der 'Staatsgott' Augustus und der Messias Jesus: Zur Erstrezeption des Christuslobes (Phil. 2,5–11)." *Bibel und Kirche* 64:23–32.

Hellerman, Joseph. 2005. *Reconstructing Honor in Roman Philippi: Carmen Christi as Cursus Pudorum*. Society for New Testament Study Monograph Series 132. Cambridge: Cambridge University Press.

———. 2009. "*Morphē Theou* as a Signifier of Social Status in Philippians 2:6." *Journal of the Evangelical Theological Society* 52:779–97.

Holloway, Paul. 2001. *Consolation in Philippians: Philosophical Sources and Rhetorical Strategy*. Society for New Testament Studies Monograph Series 112. Cambridge: Cambridge University Press.

———. 2006. "Thanks for the Memories: On the Translation of Phil. 1.3." *New Testament Studies* 52:457–69.

———. 2008. "*Alius Paulus*: Paul's Promise to Send Timothy at Philippians 2.19–24." *New Testament Studies* 54:542–66.

Hooker, Morna D. 2002. "Phantom Opponents and the Real Source of Conflict in Philippians." Pages 377–95 in *Fair Play: Diversity and Conflicts in Early Christianity; Essays in Honor of Heikki Räisänen*. Edited by Ismo Dunderberg, Christopher Tuckett, and Kari Syreeni. Supplements to Novum Testamentum 103. Leiden: Brill.

Hoover, R. W. 1971. "The *Harpagmos* Enigma: A Philological Solution." *Harvard Theological Review* 64:95–119.

Huttunen, Niko. 2009. *Paul and Epictetus on Law: A Comparison*. New York: T&T Clark.

Jeremias, Joachim. 1963. "Zu Phil. ii,7: ΕΑΥΤΩΝ ΕΚΕΝΩΣΕΝ." *Novum Testamentum* 6:182–88.

Jewett, Robert. 1970. "The Epistolary Thanksgiving and the Integrity of Philippians." *Novum Testamentum* 12:40–53.

Kampling, Rainer. 2009. "Das Lied vom Weg Jesu, des Herrn: Eine Annäherung an Phil. 2,6–11)." *Bibel und Kirche* 64:18–22.

Käsemann, Ernst. 1968. "A Critical Analysis of Philippians 2:5–11." *Journal of Theology and Church* 5:45–88.

———. 2010. *On Being a Disciple of the Crucified Nazarene: Unpublished Lectures and Sermons*. Grand Rapids: Eerdmans.

Kierkegaard, Søren. 1944. *Attack on Christendom*. Boston: Beacon.

Knox, John. 1960. *Philemon among the Letters of Paul*. London: Collins.

Koch, Dietrich-Alex. 2006. "Die Städte des Paulus." Pages 142–62 in *Paulus: Leben-Umwelt-Werk-Briefe*. Edited by Oda Wischmeyer. 2nd ed. Tübingen: A. Francke.

Koester, Helmut. 1961–62. "The Purpose of the Polemic of a Pauline Fragment (Philippians III)." *New Testament Studies* 8 (4): 317–32.

Koukouli-Chrysantaki, Chaido. 1998. "Colonia Julia Augusta Philippensis." Pages 5–35 in *Philippi at the Time of Paul and after His Death*. Edited by Charalambos Bakirtzis and Helmut Koester. Harrisburg, PA: Trinity.

Kraftchick, Steven J. 2008. "Self-Presentation and Community Construction in Philippians." Pages 239–62 in *Scripture and Traditions: Essays on Early Judaism and Christianity in Honor of Carl R. Holladay*. Edited by Patrick Gray and Gail O'Day. Supplements to Novum Testamentum 129. Leiden: Brill.

Krentz, Edgar M. 1993. "Military Language and Metaphors in Philippians." Pages 105–27 in *Origins and Method: Towards a New Understanding of Judaism and Christianity; Essays in Honour of John C. Hurd*. Edited by Bradley H. McLean. Journal for the Study of the New Testament Supplement Series 86. Sheffield: Sheffield Academic Press.

Lampe, Peter. 1985. "Keine 'Sklavenflucht' des Onesimus." *Zeitschrift für die neutestamentliche Wissenschaft* 76:135–37.

Landmesser, Christof. 1997. "Der paulinische Imperativ als christologisches Performativ: Eine begründete These zur Einheit von Glaube und Leben im Anschluss an Phil. 1,27–2,18." Pages 543–77 in *Jesus Christus als die Mitte der Schrift: Studien zur Hermeneutik des Evangelium*. Edited by Christof Landmesser, Hans-Joachim Eckstein, and Herman Lichtenberger. Beihefte zur Zeitschrift für die neutestamentliche Wissenschaft und die Kunde der älteren Kirche 86. Berlin: de Gruyter.

Lausberg, Heinrich. 1998. *Handbook of Literary Rhetoric: A Foundation for Literary Study*. Leiden: Brill.

Lightfoot, J. D. 1888. *St. Paul's Letter to the Philippians: A Revised Text with Introduction, Notes, and Dissertations*. London: Macmillan.

Lively, Nina E. 2010. "Paul, the Philonic Jew (Philippians 3,5–21)." *Annali di storia dell'esegesi* 27:35–44.

Lohfink, Gerhard. 1984. *Jesus and Community: The Social Dimension of Christian Faith*. Philadelphia: Fortress.

Lohmeyer, Ernst. 1953. *Der Brief an die Philipper*. Kritisch-exegetischer Kommentar über das Neue Testament. Göttingen: Vandenhoeck & Ruprecht. First pub. 1929.

———. 1961. *Kyrios Jesus: Eine Untersuchung zu Phil. 2.5–11*. Darmstadt: Wissenschaftliche Buchgesellschaft. First pub. 1927/28.

Lyons, George. 1985. *Pauline Autobiography: Toward a New Understanding*. Society of Biblical Literature Dissertation Series 73. Atlanta: Scholars Press.

MacMullen, Ramsay. 1980. "Women in Public in the Roman Empire." *Historia* 29:208–18.

Malherbe, Abraham J. 1988. *Ancient Epistolary Theorists*. Atlanta: Scholars Press.

———. 1996. "Paul's Self-Sufficiency (Philippians 4:11)." Pages 125–39 in *Friendship, Flattery, and Frankness of Speech: Studies on Friendship in the New Testament World*. Edited by John T. Fitzgerald. Leiden: Brill.

Marshall, I. Howard. 1993. *The Theology of the Shorter Pauline Letters*. Cambridge: Cambridge University Press.

Marshall, Peter. 1987. *Enmity at Corinth: Social Conventions in Paul's Relations with the Corinthians*. Wissenschaftliche Untersuchungen zum Neuen Testament 2/23. Tübingen: Mohr.

Martin, Clarice J. 1991. "The Rhetorical Function of Commercial Language in Paul's Letter to Philemon (Verse 18)." Pages 321–37 in *Persuasive Artistry: Studies in New Testament Rhetoric in Honor of George A. Kennedy*. Edited by Duane F. Watson. Sheffield: Sheffield Academic Press.

Martin, Dale B. 1990. *Slavery as Salvation: The Metaphor of Slavery in Pauline Christianity*. New Haven: Yale University Press.

Martin, Ralph P. 1997. *A Hymn of Christ: Philippians 2:5–11 in Recent Interpretation and in the Setting of Early Christianity*. Downers Grove, IL: InterVarsity.

Martin, Ralph P., and Brian J. Dodd, eds. 1998. *Where Christology Began: Essays on Philippians 2*. Louisville: Westminster John Knox.

Matthews, Shelly. 2001. *First Converts: Rich Pagan Women and the Rhetoric of Mission in Early Judaism and Christianity*. Stanford: Stanford University Press.

Michel, Otto. 1971. "*Spendomai*." Pages 528–36 in vol. 7 of *Theological Dictionary of the New Testament*. Edited by Gerhard Friedrich. Grand Rapids: Eerdmans.

Migliore, Daniel L. 2014. *Philippians and Philemon*. Belief. Louisville: Westminster John Knox.

Miller, James C. 2010. "Community Identity in Philippians." *Annali di storia dell'esegesi* 27 (2): 11–23.

Nanos, Mark D. 2009. "Paul's Reversal of Jews Calling Gentiles 'Dogs' (Philippians 3:2): 1600 Years of an Ideological Tale Wagging an Exegetical Dog?" *Biblical Interpretation* 17:448–72.

Niebuhr, H. Richard. 1951. *Christ and Culture*. New York: Harper & Row.

Noel, James A., and Demetrius K. Williams. 2012. *Onesimus Our Brother: Reading Religion, Race, and Culture in Philemon*. Minneapolis: Fortress.

Nordling, John G. 1991. "Onesimus Fugitivus: A Defense of the Runaway Slave Hypothesis in Philemon." *Journal for the Study of the New Testament* 41:97–119.

———. 2004. *Philemon*. St. Louis: Concordia.

Oakes, Peter. 2001. *Philippians: From People to Letter*. Society for New Testament Studies Monograph Series 110. Cambridge: Cambridge University Press.

O'Brien, Peter T. 1991. *The Epistle to the Philippians*. New International Greek Testament Commentary. Grand Rapids: Eerdmans.

Ogereau, Julien M. 2014. "Paul's κοινωνία with the Philippians: Societas as a Missionary Funding Strategy." *New Testament Studies* 60:360–78.

O'Neil, Edward N. 1978. "De cupiditate divitiarum (Moralia 523C–528B)." Pages 289–362 in *Plutarch's Ethical Writings and Early Christian Literature*. Edited by H. D. Betz, G. Delling, and W. C. van Unnik. Studia ad Corpus Hellenisticum Novi Testamenti 4. Leiden: Brill.

Osiek, Carolyn. 2000. *Philippians, Philemon*. Nashville: Abingdon.

Pao, David W. 2010. "Gospel within the Constraints of an Epistolary Form: Pauline Introductory Thanksgivings and Paul's Theology of Thanksgiving." Pages 101–28 in *Paul and the Ancient Letter Form*. Edited by Stanley E. Porter and Sean A. Adams. Leiden: Brill.

Peterlin, Davorin. 1995. *Paul's Letter to the Philippians in the Light of Disunity in the Church*. Supplements to Novum Testamentum 79. Leiden: Brill.

Peterman, G. W. 1997. *Paul's Gift from Philippi: Conventions of Gift Exchange and Christian Giving*. Society for New Testament Studies Monograph Series 92. Cambridge: Cambridge University Press.

Petersen, Norman R. 1985. *Rediscovering Paul: Philemon and the Sociology of Paul's Narrative World*. Philadelphia: Fortress.

Peterson, Brian K. 2008. "Being the Church in Philippi." *Horizons in Biblical Theology* 30:163–78.

Pilhofer, Peter. 1995. *Die erste christliche Gemeinde Europas*. Vol. 1 of *Philippi*. Wissenschaftliche Untersuchungen zum Neuen Testament 87. Tübingen: Mohr Siebeck.

———. 2000. *Katalog der Inschriften von Philippi*. Vol. 2 of *Philippi*. Wissenschaftliche Untersuchungen zum Neuen Testament 119. Tübingen: Mohr Siebeck.

———. 2002. "Zwei römische Kolonien auf der Weg des Paulus nach Spanien." Pages 154–65 in *Die frühen Christen und ihre Welt: Greifswalder Aufsätze 1996–2001*. Edited by Peter Pilhofer. Wissenschaftliche Untersuchungen zum Neuen Testament 1/45. Tübingen: Mohr Siebeck.

———. 2009. "Philippi zur Zeit des Paulus: Eine Ortsbegehung." *Bibel und Kirche* 64:11–17.

Popkes, Wiard. 2004. "Philipper 4,4–7: Aussage und situativer Hintergrund." *New Testament Studies* 50:246–56.

Portefaix, Lilian. 1988. *Sisters Rejoice: Paul's Letter to the Philippians and Luke-Acts as Seen by First-Century Philippian Women*. Coniectanea Biblica: New Testament Series 20. Stockholm: Almqvist & Wiksell.

Rapske, Brian M. 1991. "The Prisoner Paul in the Eyes of Onesimus." *New Testament Studies* 37:187–203.

Reed, Jeffrey T. 1996. "Philippians 3:1 and the Epistolary Hesitation Formulas: The Literary Integrity of Philippians Again." *Journal of Biblical Literature* 115:63–90.

———. 1997. *A Discourse Analysis of Philippians: Method and Rhetoric in the Debate over Literary Integrity*. Journal for the Study of the New Testament Monograph Series 136. Sheffield: Sheffield Academic Press.

Reumann, John. 1996. "Philippians, Especially Chapter 4, as a 'Letter of Friendship': Observations on a Checkered History of Scholarship." Pages 83–106 in *Friendship, Flattery, and Frankness of Speech*. Edited by John T. Fitzgerald. Supplements to Novum Testamentum 82. Leiden: Brill.

———. 2008. *Philippians*. Anchor Bible 33B. New Haven: Yale University Press.

Rich, Audrey N. M. 1956. "The Cynic Conception of Autarkeia." *Mnemosyne* 9:23–29.

Riesenfeld, Harald. 1982. "Faith and Love Promoting Hope: An Interpretation of Philemon v. 6." Pages 251–57 in *Paul and Paulinism: Essays in Honour of C. K. Barrett*. Edited by M. D. Hooker and S. G. Wilson. London: SPCK.

Robinson, James M. 1964. "Die Hodajot-formen in Gebet und Hymnus des Frühchristentums." Pages 194–235 in *Apophoreta: Festschrift für Ernst Haenchen zu seinem 70. Geburtstag*. Edited by W. Eltester and F. H. Kettler. Berlin: Töpelmann.

Ryan, Judith M. 2005. "Philemon." Pages 167–261 in *Philippians and Philemon*. By Bonnie Thurston and Judith M. Ryan. Collegeville: Liturgical Press.

Ryan, Scott C. 2012. "The Reversal of Rhetoric in Philippians 3:1–11." *Perspectives in Religious Studies* 39:67–77.

Sandnes, Karl Olav. 1994. *A New Family: Conversion and Ecclesiology in the Early Church with Cross-Cultural Comparisons*. Studies in the Intercultural History of Christianity 91. New York: Peter Lang.

Schapdick, Stefan. 2009. "Irritierende Vielfalt: Szenarien der Heilsvollendung im Philipperbrief." *Bibel und Kirche* 64:33–38.

Schenk, Wolfgang. 1984. *Die Philipperbriefe des Paulus*. Stuttgart: Kohlhammer.

———. 1987. "Der Brief des Paulus an Philemon in der neueren Forschung (1945–87)." Pages 3439–95 in vol. 4 of *Aufstieg und Niedergang der römischen Welt: Geschichte und Kultur Roms im Spiegel der neueren Forschung* 2.25.

Schinkel, Dirk. 2007. *Die himmlische Bürgerschaft: Untersuchungen zu einem urchristlichen Sprachmotiv im Spannungsfeld von religiöser Integration und Abgrenzung im 1. und 2. Jahrhundert*. Forschungen zur Religion und Literatur des Alten und Neuen Testaments 220. Göttingen: Vandenhoeck & Ruprecht.

Schmithals, Walter. 1957. "Die Irrlehrer des Philipperbriefes." *Zeitschrift für Theologie und Kirche* 54:297–341.

Schnelle, Udo. 1998. *The History and Theology of the New Testament Writings*. Translated by M. Eugene Boring. Minneapolis: Fortress.

Schubert, Paul. 1939. *Form and Function of the Pauline Thanksgivings*. Beihefte zur Zeitschrift für die neutestamentliche Wissenschaft 20. Berlin: Töpelmann.

Scott, S. P. 1932. *The Civil Law: Including The Twelve Tables, The Institutes of Gaius, The Rules of Ulpian, The Opinions of Paulus, The Enactments of Justinian, and The Constitutions of Leo; Translated from the Original Latin, Edited, and Compared with All Accessible Systems of Jurisprudence Ancient and Modern*. 17 vols. Cincinnati: Central Trust Company.

Selby, Andrew M. 2012. "Bishops, Elders, and Deacons in the Philippian Church: Evidence of Plurality from Paul and Polycarp." *Perspectives in Religious Studies* 39:79–94.

Smit, Peter-Ben. 2014. "Paul, Plutarch and the Problematic Practice of Self-Praise (περιαυτολογία): The Case of Phil. 3.2–21." *New Testament Studies* 60:341–59.

Snyman, A. H. 2007. "Philippians 4:10–23 from a Rhetorical Perspective." *Acta Theologica* 27:168–85.

Standhartinger, Angela. 2006a. "'Join in Imitating Me' (Philippians 3:17): Towards an Interpretation of Philippians 3." *New Testament Studies* 54:417–37.

———. 2006b. "Die paulinische Theologie im Spannungsfeld römisch-imperialer Machtpolitik: Eine neue Perspektive auf Paulus, kritisch geprüft anhand des Philipperbriefs." Pages 364–82 in *Religion, Politik und Gewalt: Kongressband des XII. Europäischen Kongresses für Theologie, 18.–22. September 2005 in Berlin*. Edited by Friedrich Schweitzer. Veröffentlichungen der Wissenschaftlichen Gesellschaft für Theologie 29. Gütersloh: Gütersloher Verlagshaus.

———. 2013. "Aus der Welt eines Gefangenen: Die kommunikationsstruktur des Philipperbriefs im Spiegel seiner Abfassungssituation." *Novum Testamentum* 55:140–67.

Steely Dan. 2000. "Cousin Dupree." On *Two against Nature*. Warner Bros. Records.

Still, Todd D. 2012. "More than Friends? The Literary Composition of Philippians Revisited." *Perspectives in Religious Studies* 39:53–66.

Stowers, Stanley. 1991. "Friends and Enemies in the Politics of Heaven: Reading Theology in Philippians." Pages 105–21 in *Thessalonians, Philippians, Galatians, Philemon*. Edited by Jouette M Bassler. Vol. 1 of *Pauline Theology*. Edited by Jouette M Bassler, David M. Hay, and E. Elizabeth Johnson. Minneapolis: Fortress.

Sumney, Jerry L. 2007. *Philippians: A Greek Student's Intermediate Reader*. Peabody, MA: Hendrickson.

Tellbe, Mikael. 1994. "The Sociological Factors behind Philippians 3:1–11 and the Conflict at Philippi." *Journal for the Study of the New Testament* 55:97–121.

———. 2001. *Paul between Synagogue and State: Christians, Jews, and Civic Authorities in 1 Thessalonians, Romans, and Philippians*. Coniectanea Biblica: New Testament Series 34. Stockholm: Almqvist & Wiksell.

Thompson, James W. 2006. *Pastoral Ministry according to Paul*. Grand Rapids: Baker Academic.

———. 2007. "Preaching to Philippians." *Interpretation* 61:298–309.

———. 2011. *Moral Formation according to Paul*. Grand Rapids: Baker Academic.

———. 2014. *The Church according to Paul*. Grand Rapids: Baker Academic.

Tite, Philip L. 2010. "How to Begin and Why? Diverse Functions of the Pauline Prescript within a Graeco-Roman Context." Pages 57–91 in *Paul and the Ancient Letter Form*. Edited by Stanley E. Porter and Sean A. Adams. Leiden: Brill.

Tobin, Thomas H. 2006. "The World of Thought in the Philippians Hymn (Philippians 2:6–11)." Pages 88–101 in *The New Testament and Early Christian Literature in the Greco-Roman Context: Studies in Honor of David E. Aune*. Edited by John Fotopoulos. Supplements to Novum Testamentum 122. Leiden: Brill.

Trainor, Michael. 2008. *Epaphras: Paul's Educator at Colossae*. Collegeville: Liturgical Press.

Tucker, J. Brian. 2011. *"Remain in Your Calling": Paul and the Continuation of Social Identities in 1 Corinthians*. Eugene, OR: Wipf & Stock.

Vollenweider, Samuel. 1994. "Die Waagschalen vom Leben und Tod: Zum antiken Hintergrund von Phil 1,21–26." *Zeitschrift für die neutestamentliche Wissenschaft* 85:93–115.

———. 2002a. "Die Metamorphose des Gottessohns: Zum epiphanialen Motivfeld in Phil. 2,6–8." Pages 285–306 in *Horizonte neutestamentlicher Christologie: Studien zu Paulus und zur frühchristlichen Theologie*. By Samuel Vollenweider. Wissenschaftliche Untersuchungen zum Neuen Testament 145. Tübingen: Mohr Siebeck.

———. 2002b. "Der 'Raub' der Gottgleichheit: Ein religionsgeschichtlicher Vorschlag zu Phil. 2,6(–11)." Pages 263–84 in *Horizonte neutestamentlicher Christologie: Studien zu Paulus und zur frühchristlichen Theologie*. By Samuel Vollenweider. Wissenschaftliche Untersuchungen zum Neuen Testament 145. Tübingen: Mohr Siebeck.

———. 2006. "Politische Theologie im Philipperbrief?" Pages 457–69 in *Paulus und Johannes: Exegetische Studien zur paulinischen und johanneischen Theologie und*

Literatur. Edited by Jürgen Becker, Dieter Sänger, and Ulrich Mell. Wissenschaftliche Untersuchungen zum Neuen Testament 198. Tübingen: Mohr Siebeck.

Vos, Johan S. 2005. "Philippians 1:12–26 and the Rhetoric of Success." Pages 274–83 in *Rhetoric, Ethic, and Moral Persuasion in Biblical Discourse*. Edited by Thomas H. Olbricht and Anders Eriksson. London: T&T Clark.

Wansink, Craig S. 1996. *Chained in Christ: The Experience and Rhetoric of Paul's Imprisonments*. Journal for the Study of the New Testament Supplement Series 130. Sheffield: Sheffield Academic Press.

Ware, James P. 2011. *Paul and the Mission of the Church: Philippians in Ancient Jewish Context*. Grand Rapids: Baker Academic.

Watson, Duane F. 1988. "Rhetorical Analysis of Philippians and Its Implications for the Unity Question." *Novum Testamentum* 30:57–88.

———. 2003. "A Reexamination of the Epistolary Analysis Underpinning the Argument for the Composite Nature of Philippians." Pages 157–77 in *Early Christianity and Classical Culture: Comparative Studies in Honor of Abraham J. Malherbe*. Edited by John T. Fitzgerald, Thomas H. Olbricht, and L. Michael White. Supplements to Novum Testamentum 110. Leiden: Brill.

Weima, Jeffrey A. D. 2010. "Sincerely Paul: The Significance of the Pauline Letter Closings." Pages 307–46 in *Paul and the Ancient Letter Form*. Edited by Stanley E. Porter and Sean A. Adams. Leiden: Brill.

Welborn, Lawrence L. 1997. *Politics and Rhetoric in the Corinthian Epistles*. Macon, GA: Mercer University Press.

Wendland, Ernst. 2010. "'You Will Do Even More than I Say': On the Rhetorical Function of Stylistic Form in the Letter to Philemon." Pages 79–110 in *Philemon in Perspective: Interpreting a Pauline Letter*. Edited by D. F. Tolmie. Berlin: de Gruyter.

Wessels, G. Francois. 2010. "The Letter to Philemon in the Context of Slavery in Early Christianity." Pages 143–68 in *Philemon in Perspective: Interpreting a Pauline Letter*. Edited by D. F. Tolmie. Berlin: de Gruyter.

White, L. Michael. 1990. "Morality between Two Worlds: A Paradigm of Friendship in Philippians." Pages 201–15 in *Greeks, Romans, and Christians: Essays in Honor of Abraham J. Malherbe*. Edited by David L. Balch, Everett Ferguson, and Wayne A. Meeks. Minneapolis: Fortress.

Wick, Peter. 1994. *Der Philipperbrief: Der formale Aufbau des Briefs als Schlüssel zum Verständnis seines Inhalts*. Beiträge zur Wissenschaft vom Alten und Neuen Testament. Stuttgart: Kohlhammer.

Williams, Demetrius K. 2002. *Enemies of the Cross of Christ: The Terminology of the Cross and Conflict in Philippians*. Journal for the Study of the New Testament Supplement Series 223. Sheffield: Sheffield Academic Press.

Willis, Wendell L. 2007. "Seeing the Faith as Paul Sees It." Pages 181–92 in *Renewing Tradition: Studies in Texts and Contexts in Honor of James W. Thompson*. Edited by Mark H. Hamilton, Thomas H. Olbricht, and Jeffrey Peterson. Princeton Theological Monograph Series. Eugene, OR: Pickwick.

———. 2012. "The Shaping of Character: Virtue in Philippians. 4:8–9." *Restoration Quarterly* 54:65–76.

Winter, Sara B. C. 1987. "Paul's Letter to Philemon." *New Testament Studies* 33:1–15.

Witherington, Ben, III. 1994. *Friendship and Finances: The Letter of Paul to the Philippians*. New Testament in Context. Valley Forge, PA: Trinity.

———. 2011. *Paul's Letter to the Philippians: A Socio-Rhetorical Commentary*. Grand Rapids: Eerdmans.

Wojtkowiak, Heiko. 2012. *Christologie und Ethik im Philipperbrief: Studien zur Handlungsorientierung einer frühchristlichen Gemeinde in paganer Umwelt*. Forschungen zur Religion und Literatur des Alten und Neuen Testaments. Göttingen: Vandenhoeck & Ruprecht.

Wolter, Michael. 2009. "Der Apostel und seine Gemeinden als Teilhaber am Leidensgeschick Jesu Christi: Beobachtungen zur paulinischen Leidenstheologie." Pages 219–40 in *Theologie und Ethos im frühen Christentum: Studien zu Jesus, Paulus und Lukas*. Wissenschaftliche Untersuchungen zum Neuen Testament 236. Tübingen: Mohr Siebeck.

———. 2010. "The Letter to Philemon as Ethical Counterpart of Paul's Doctrine of Justification." Pages 169–80 in *Philemon in Perspective: Interpreting a Pauline Letter*. Edited by D. F. Tolmie. Berlin: de Gruyter.

Wood, Susan. 1997. "Is Philippians 2:5–11 Incompatible with Feminist Concerns?" *Pro Ecclesia* 6:172–83.

Wright, N. T. 1988. *The Epistles of Paul to the Colossians and to Philemon*. Grand Rapids: Eerdmans.

———. 1991. "Jesus Christ Is Lord: Philippians 2:5–11." Pages 56–98 in *The Climax of the Covenant: Christ and the Law in Pauline Theology*. Minneapolis: Fortress.

———. 2011. *The New Testament for Everyone*. London: SPCK.

———. 2013. *Paul and the Faithfulness of God*. London: SPCK.

Index of Subjects

Index of Modern Authors

Index of Scripture and Ancient Sources